Power and Opposition in Post-revolutionary Societies

*Translated from the French by Patrick Camiller
and the Italian by Jon Rothschild*

**INK
LINKS**

First published as Potere e opposizione nelle societá post-
rivoluzionare
Edizione curato da Alfani editore, Roma 1978
© Quaderni del Manifesto, 1978

This edition first published 1979
© world English language, Ink Links, 1979

Ink Links Ltd.,
271 Kentish Town Road,
London NW5 2JS

ISBN 0 906133 181 cloth 0 906133 19X paper

Typeset by Red Lion Setters, Holborn, London and printed by
Whitstable Litho, Millstrood Rd. Whitstable, Kent

Contents

Appendices: Three Written Contributions

Opening Session

Power and Opposition in Post-revolutionary Societies

Rossana Rossanda

Rossana Rossanda, 53, joined the Italian Communist Party during the resistance. She was later a PCI deputy and was elected to the Central Committee in 1959. In 1969 she was expelled from the PCI along with the other founders of the newspaper il manifesto. *Since then she has been part of the leadership of that newspaper and of the political movement organized around it.*

Comrades and friends, it is with a certain feeling of emotion that I open the deliberations of this gathering. For the first time, the entire Italian left, from the historical to the new, has agreed, despite its long-standing and recent divisions, to open a discussion on one of the most burning issues in its history, that concerning so-called existing socialism.

And, another first, we are doing so not only with French, Spanish, and West German comrades, but also with those comrades of the East European countries, whether emigrés or members of groups operating there, who consider themselves Marxists and socialists. The majority of East Europeans who are here today have been compelled to leave their countries, often after years of persecution and terms in prison or psychiatric hospitals. Very few of the comrades from Eastern Europe who have been able to participate in this meeting or to send written contributions to it (like Hegedus and Michnik) are still in a position to return to their countries. In Poland and Hungary there has been a relative easing of the barriers to dialogue with the European left. We had hoped that yet another barrier would tumble on this occasion, but some passports were confiscated and the term of validity of others was shortened. We therefore lack the physical presence of some participants, who are, however, with us politically. We send them our greetings and solidarity.

But we have not gathered here merely to express solidarity with the comrades of Eastern Europe. Partly for that, of course. Solidarity with these comrades is a moral duty on which the European left has defaulted all too often. This default has sometimes taken the form of silence and sometimes of purely verbal support. But most often it has been even more serious: refusal to clarify one's real, as opposed to diplomatic or formal, position on the 'existing socialisms' that have been established since 1917. This is why the European left's approach to the thorny questions of conflict, power, and opposition in the existing revolutions has been marked by embarrassment, and even a certain intellectual and moral poverty. The left would prefer not to take notice of those socialists who have found it impossible to live and breathe politically, or have even suffered brutal repression, in countries that call themselves socialist. The condition of these comrades who stand in opposition in the East European countries — whether as a class, like in Poland, or in groups, or as individuals — or who are forced to emigrate is perhaps the most tragic aspect of the political struggle of our century. Indeed, those who face the oppression of fascism or of authoritarian bourgeois regimes at least enjoy the warm solidarity of the left, despite the trials of the internal struggle and emigration. They feel themselves part of a great common front. This is not the case for those struggling in the so-called socialist countries. They are not part of any international front; the left offers them only uncertain or fleeting support. Only the enemy welcomes them willingly, content to view their misfortune as proof that socialism is impossible or unnatural. The masses of workers, the vanguard political formations in the West, perceive them as a source of torment, contradiction, and guilt. They relegate them to the status of secondary contradiction and try to forget them if possible.

There is a historic reason for this, which it would be superficial to underestimate. We must begin with this history in order to explain, if only to ourselves, how it is that we are able to hold a conference like this today, for it would have been unthinkable only ten years ago. The western left, the workers' and revolutionary organizations (or at least their leaderships) realized quite early on that the sort of socialism that had been established, above all in the Soviet Union, did not correspond to the main features of emancipation as delineated by Marx in the *Communist Manifesto* in 1848 or even to the more recent experiences of the October Revolution. The left has known that it is not true, to paraphrase the last line of *The Battleship Potemkin*, that the insurgent cruiser had irrevocably hoisted the 'red flag of freedom'. It was realized rather rapidly that these societies were economically ossified and politically repressive.

And yet, the left and the revolutionary organizations have continued to side with them. Why? Because they saw these societies as the main line of trenches in the war of position against the bourgeois bloc, the only secure front after the defeats of the twenties in Europe. As a result, the West, which had not made its revolution, came to console itself with the revolutions that had occurred elsewhere, while these revolutions bore, in their own lack of freedom and impasse, the consequences of the failure of revolution in the West.

However imperfect and reprehensible the socialist countries appeared, against them stood imperialism, colonialism, and, eventually, Nazism. That was how the world was divided in the minds of millions of people before 1945. The same sort of division persisted with the cold war, and even after, albeit less sharply, every time a link in the imperialist chain was broken: China, Cuba, Vietnam, Indochina — the wars of colonial liberation. In 1952 a man like Jean-Paul Sartre, to whom any party discipline or tendency-dictated reticence is alien, sided with the Soviet Union, even though he was not unaware of what was going on in the forced labour camps, and had even denounced it. In doing so he broke not only with his enemies, but even with his friends, Camus and Merleau-Ponty. Deciding to stand with the Soviet Union did not necessarily mean swearing that the USSR was a proletarian state. It was sufficient to note that it stood in objective contradiction with the bourgeois system and that new movements of peoples or classes, struggles against and breaks with capitalism, were arising and growing out of it. We were all inclined to view existing socialism the way one of our theorists viewed Marxism itself in 1921: 'What does it matter', he wrote, 'that there are theoretical limits to Marxism if it becomes an emancipating force, restores speech to enormous masses of the exploited and oppressed, and becomes identity, hope, and consciousness to masses who have been subjugated for centuries?'

In this grandiose and terrible history, born in the wrong place, as Marx would have said, against all predictions and rules (the revolution against Marx's *Capital*, Gramsci was to write), the real relations of production, and therefore the real social classes, in the countries in which the revolution occurred ceased to be transparent or visible.

Their political dialectic was first stunted and then repressed, isolated in dissent. The democratic world, or at least part of it, viewed the Soviet trials of the thirties with distress, but virtually failed to notice the repression against the peasants. The largest workers' movement in the West, in Italy, has begun to view the workers of Gdansk as their class brothers only during the past few years. Dissent is hastily reduced to a creation and concern of intellectuals, and liberty to the mere right of self-expression, essential as it is. But it was not noticed that entire masses of people remained subject to a power exercised in their name and that they are not masters of their own fate — and this is indeed their lot, in different ways than is the case for us (although things are not all that different in the factories and fields). No one was able to see this, or no one wanted to see it, so long as the socialist states remained 'the other side' in the world conflict. Even if they did not represent our guideline and model, these states at least remained the backbone of a revolution which was made more possible by their existence, a revolution we could hope would be 'different'.

But is that still how it is? I believe that if we have come together here to discuss, to examine these societies with less inhibited eyes, and to take positions on the nature of the conflicts unfolding within them, it is not so much because we have suddenly grasped the truth about their character as because the long-standing identification, accepted with a guilty conscience, between 'real socialism' and the anti-imperialist, socialist, and anti-capitalist front in the West has collapsed. It had already deteriorated during the sixties, for several reasons: because of the increasingly explicit role as a great power played by the USSR in world affairs; because of the rifts among Communist parties and states (especially between the USSR and China), followed by the various shifts in China's international orientation, from isolation to the decision to maintain relations only with third-world countries, to the most unscrupulous diplomatic state manoeuvres; and finally, because of the further change in the character of the Soviet state marked by the invasion of Czechoslovakia in 1968. Since then, any support the Soviet Union has accorded this or that sector of the movement, especially in third-world countries, has been ever more ambiguously mixed with and conditioned by the interests of the Soviet state on the world chessboard. Anything the so-called socialist camp had to offer finally disappeared around Vietnam. Two different versions of international strategy arose, not only on the significance and timing of the Vietnamese struggle, but also on whether priority should be accorded the extinguishing of this hotbed of war (peace in Vietnam) or the liberation of this people (freedom for Vietnam). The Vietnamese comrades triumphed because the USSR and China existed, but also despite them (although this applies to the two in very different measure).

In sum, the 'existing socialist' countries are no longer models or guarantees (or buttresses) for our future revolutions, which will be different. It is no longer possible to separate their internal limitations from what their international orientations have finally become, and the latter must be related more to their need for internal stability than to the iron necessities of what used to be called the 'class struggle on a world scale'. The lack of freedom, the inequality, the persistence of relations of exploitation, the exigencies of no-longer-private capital and of the development of the productive forces, the internal manoeuvring among classes, the extent of the militarization of the economy and the role of the armed forces — all these factors do not constitute defects marring a positive international role. Rather, they appear as the real roots from which all the international options are derived, from the special relation between the USSR and the United States to the necessity for the discipline of the socialist bloc in Europe.

China also projects its internal balances and upheavals internationally, primarily in its absence, rather than presence, on a world scale. The western workers' movement no longer sees an identity, or even an alibi, in the 'existing socialist' countries, as it sought to do for decades; these societies are not our models or our ideals; they are not our camp.

That is why the silence of the left is now ending, why even the most tenacious links, those of the Communist Parties, are slackening, and why those who advance a non-apologetic analysis of the USSR are no longer disregarded. The isolation of internal dissent has also ended. These societies are beginning to become more transparent; they can and must be examined. Suddenly the western workers' movement again sees its fate as linked to the nature of the societies of Eastern Europe. But not the way it did during the twenties, under the impact of a great and perhaps naive revolutionary spirit, or with the optimism of 1945 or even 1956. What links them today is not hope, but acute awareness that a crisis is ripening both in the socialist countries and in the rest of Europe, East and West. The Soviet camp is at an impasse, the Communist movement stands divided, China is entrenched in the turn that has halted the Maoist wave. The wave of the left in Europe, whether in its revolutionary anti-capitalist or reformist shadings, has also been halted. Two years ago Eurocommunism appeared assured of an impetuous growth of its hegemony in Spain, of the initiation of a process of transition in Italy, of the secure victory of the left in France, and even of a certain shift in the big Social Democratic parties. Today the retreats, lulls, and pressure from the right are evident. The period has changed, and, in the heart of Europe, Germany is again cause for alarm. The crisis has suddenly given gradualist illusions their due: not only is power far off, but even the defence of democracy and of the unity of the social bloc of workers, both employed and unemployed, which has been the strength of the left in Europe during the past decade, is now being challenged. Eurocommunism, that poor man's version of the Gramscian approach to revolution in the West, stands exposed on all fronts. It is taking its distance from a Soviet Union that has become ideologically aggressive again, but it is also missing opportunities with regard to the whole great movement of southern Europe.

This is the context in which our gathering is being held; it differs from the conference on dissent that will open at the Venice Biennale in several days. There has been too much speculation about the reasons for these two initiatives. Ours is explicitly political. We view the question of post-revolutionary society as a current political problem of the Italian left, and not as past history. We view the problem of power and opposition in the post-revolutionary societies in its totality (or at least we try to do so), because we believe that the question of dissent and the dissidents goes beyond a mere problem of political rights. The conflicts inherent in these societies go well beyond their political expression by the groups of dissident intellectuals, and the repression is much more complex than mere violation of the principles of 1789, since, as is the case in any modern state, the most effective instruments of repression against the oppressed are the mechanisms of integration and compensation. The show trials, prisons, and mental asylums constitute only the tip of the iceberg. We view this as our problem, an aspect of our own future revolutions. We believe that the answer to the question, 'Why have all the revolutions thus far come to grief on the key problem of the state and freedom?' must be sought in the same theoretical and political obstacles that have impeded the revolution in the West. We do not believe in two societies, socialism for backward countries and Social Democracy for developed ones; we still hold to a unified theory of world processes.

And we are convinced that it is only by reacquiring consciousness of this unity that the European left will be able to implement genuine solidarity with their class brothers in the so-called socialist societies. Indeed, there will be no change in those societies unless society changes here; Helsinki conferences, defence of human rights, and simple appeals are not enough. There will be no change unless Western Europe overturns its own capitalist structures, initiates the transformation of the capitalist mode of production, breathes life into the words of Lenin, 'And now let us construct the socialist order', and refashions a state in which the words socialism and freedom recover their true significance in the experience of the masses. In sum, these societies will not change until we hear the salvos of our own *Aurora* in Rome, Paris, or Madrid; it matters little how widely they reverberate, so long as they mark the maturation of a social, and not merely political, revolution, a revolution that is not less but more radical, not Jacobin and therefore non-authoritarian.

It would not be fair for me to take this opportunity to outline the conception of socialist structure for Italy upheld by my political group, for we would certainly be divided on this. But I do want to say this: if the societies of Eastern Europe will not change without revolution in the West, there will be no revolution in the West without a thorough critical examination of the experience of the societies of the East. To ignore them, to draw back, not to get involved, would mean to refuse to understand what kind of society we want and will be able to construct here. It would even mean to renounce political theory itself. We must not forget that in the long and eventful evolution of the 'real socialist' countries — sixty years since October, more than thirty since the birth of the people's democracies, nearly thirty since the liberation of China, nearly twenty since Castro spoke of 'socialist Cuba' — more than a mere hope has been shattered. The very idea of socialism, not as a generic aspiration but as a *theory of society*, a *different* mode of organization of human existence, is fading from view. And here we come to the most difficult point of this discussion in the left: we must ask ourselves not whether these societies are unfree, but whether they are unfree *because* they are socialist or *because they are not socialist*. And if they are not socialist, what are they? There are those who deny that the question itself is legitimate. The rigid models of the past (still maintained by the groups calling themselves Marxist-Leninist, who claim that the construction of socialism in the USSR had been achieved and was simply betrayed by the Khrushchev group) are now giving way to a thoroughly empiricist temptation: there is no such thing as 'socialism'; what exists are 'established socialist systems', for good or ill. These, we are told, are the only reality, the only object of history. They cannot be measured against any particular yardstick, for to do so would be to fall into pure abstraction. Indeed, the very existence of Marxism today is threatened by two evils: the poverty of the 'vulgate' of the Soviet press, and its counterpart, the refusal to formulate any theory of society not merely as history but also as science, which is the real implication of the views of many of the Communist and Socialist parties in the West. I say rejection deliberately, because when this foundation is lost, an entire culture, the language of the movement that had directed these revolutions, the Third Internationalist ideal of the Communists, is shattered.

Neither the Socialist, nor Trotskyist, nor libertarian, nor Marxist-Leninist currents have succeeded in assuming this heritage positively. They cling to old paths, or move reluctantly into new ones, or simply give up. The crisis of ideals is reflected in the uncertainty evinced by European leftist parties when they stand on the threshold of governmental power. Unable to explain the history of revolutions elsewhere, they lose the thread of our own. One of the reasons why the Eurocommunist and democratic-socialist groups have been unable to constitute alternatives is that they themselves suffer the maladies of the 'real' socialist systems as their own limits. Nor have the new left groups dared to deal with this question, for fear that demobilization would set in if they ceased to cultivate myths, and because of the temptation to believe that it was all the result of a 'mistake' and that everything could be set right through a return to 'correct' principles. This is not the least of the reasons for their failure. The crisis, moreover, goes beyond the purely political domain and invests the realm of theory itself. It is a crisis of Marxism, of which the *nouveaux philosophes* are the caricature, but which is experienced by immense masses as an unacknowledged reality. Marxism — not as a body of theoretical or philosophical thought, but as the great idealistic force that was changing the world — is now groaning under the weight of this history.

The 'real' socialisms thus become the only truth, to be uncritically accepted as the fruit of history, impossible to interpret or evaluate. In short, everyone is a socialist as he or she believes or desires; there is no way to decide to what extent anyone really is a socialist, since there are no non-abstract criteria of judgment. It is obviously desirable, say the cultists of 'many socialisms', that each person should be a socialist in the least distasteful manner; but all variants are accorded legitimacy. Both freedom and its opposite, repression, are then detached from their social roots; they have nothing to do with the fundamental mechanisms of these societies; they do not flow from inequality; they are not inherent in persistent separation of the masses from politics. These, we are told authoritatively, are socialist societies with some unfree features. The question of democracy thus becomes purely formal and juridical, a matter of civil rights, a generic value entrusted to the good will of governments, something that everyone hopes will be restored.

I am afraid that many of our comrades from Eastern Europe also share the idea — which may well become one of the stumbling blocks to our discussion — that what they have experienced is indeed socialism and that socialism necessarily entails the disasters they have suffered. Disparagement of the very idea of Marxism, socialism, and revolution is quite common in the East European societies. It is a result of suffering, of the reduction of Marxism to the philosophy of a state power. In a few days an eminent Polish philosopher, Leszek Kolakowski, will tell the Biennale that there is no Marxism except that of the *History of the Communist Party* (*Bolsheviks*); the proof of the pudding is in the eating; the proof of a political theory is in its actual results. But this is a sophism, for it would imply that the proof of one political theory is in another political theory. With this sort of terrorist reasoning one could maintain that whoever upholds democracy as a universal value must also support the B-52s that bombed Vietnam.

We who would like to remain Marxists, however — which, despite everything, is easier in our societies — we maintain, on the contrary, that whatever the nature of the post-revolutionary societies, they can and must be interpreted and that Marxism offers a reliable instrument for doing this. Marxism tells us that in the last instance the nature of a society, its consciousness of itself, and its political expression are always determined by the social relations of production (although not one-sidedly and without mediation). We believe that the analysis of the relations of production in the USSR, Cuba, and the East European countries is the key that will enable us to penetrate the mechanisms of these societies; it will also enable us to see to what extent one of these societies, namely China, 'differs', or at least (so far as we know) consciously tries to differ, from the others, if for no other reason than that it recognizes this problem as the decisive criterion by which to measure the evolution or regression of its entire system.

It is our thesis — to put it bluntly — that Gulag is the product neither of a philosophy nor of a pure idea of power and politics. Rather, it is the result, later theorized, of the incapacity of the new ruling class to express and mediate the interests of the classes that had constituted the revolutionary alliance in the USSR, which exploded after 1917 under the weight of the social division of labour bequeathed by capitalism, the rise of new needs, and the collapse of production. In other words, in coming to grips with what the Bolshevik regime became in the twenties, Lenin's responses in the soviets to the question of 'how to direct production' during the first few months of the revolution and the subsequent forced collectiviza-tion of the land are of greater importance than *What Is To Be Done?* or the theory of relations between the vanguard and the masses. Politics has no independence in the realm of ideas, just as economics has none in the realm of commodities. The new state and new apparatus of production are based on the manner in which the new emerging classes resolve the questions of reproduction and the revolutionization of social relations. If we look at the events of war communism, we see how and why the rapid centralization and extirpation of the soviets resulted not from an ideological option but from the inability to dominate uncontrollable social and productive mechanisms. We may then understand why politics and the state were immediately separated from the soviets.

To be sure, this is a hard lesson, particularly for those who have shared certain facile ideas of revolution. It shows that when a revolution is essentially political — the 'taking of the winter palace' by a vanguard — and not the result of the maturation (before, during, and after the revolutionary breakthrough) of the masses from exploited to producers and from producers to 'politicians' (in the sense of ability to grasp the political, economic, and social content of events), *the exploited can express no more than an immediate demand, need, and intuition for equality*; all elements not reflected in their direct experience elude them. A 'new socialist order' is not the sum total of the self-managed individual units bequeathed by capitalism. It is the shattering of those units and their recomposition under a different logic, a different system of production, controlled by modified social subjects. Nor is it, except in the allusion made by Marx, the unified, totalizing social factory. Capitalism in its develop-ment destroys social figures and re-creates them anew; this is its very logic of reproduction. Socialism, in turn, must shatter this logic, along with the roots of the inequality capitalism has imposed and interiorized even to the extent of the needs of the oppressed. But who shall lead this process in such a way as to ensure that it is liberating and not simply pedagogic, that it frees and does not subjugate the social subjects who must carry it forward? What sort of state and institutions are capable of assuring the working class and the masses — which is a complex formation — that the revolutionary alliance will be maintained, that the structures inherited from the previous social division of labour will be modified, and that a new rationale of production will be fashioned, if not, surely, a state determined to eradicate the existing imbalances, not under the blind impulse of profit, but through the conscious clash of the oppressed cultures, which express themselves and search for a synthesis in the general revolutionary transformation of society? Relations of production, division of labour, and transitional state thus appear as facets of the same prism; each orients and sets the course of the others.

It appears to us that this occurs in a revolutionary and liberating direction only if the new regime never forgets that relations among men are mediated by things, and that the commodity in turn is identifiable through labour, i.e. an inter-human relation. Here again, the decisive years in the USSR, from the revolution to the dramatic events of the twenties, offer significant lessons.

In examining what became of the Soviet regime it is useful to reconsider the initial attempts to do away with the market and money and the subsequent recognition that it was impossible to do so. This was followed by the reintroduction of both, as mechanisms of mediation between the public and private sectors, and then, as a result of errors in pricing policy, by the forced appropriation by the public sector of the goods produced by the peasants. But this sequence of events not only ruptured the worker-peasant alliance and broke the bonds between the revolution and the peasants, driving them to the right again, it also altered the regime that had opted for this action against one of its own social bases, annihilating it as political subject. Analysis of the measures taken after the 1926-27 harvest sheds more light on the system of deportation than does any denunciation of Stalin's despotism or any lucubration on the Asiatic mode of production.

Viewed from this angle, the societies of Eastern Europe become transparent, as societies in which the old conflict between wage earners and the owners of the means of production (which has become the state, or the commune) continues, although under the formal, juridical guise of the new regime. In addition, however, new conflicts, generated by the deep upheaval of society, arise among the *new social subjects*.

This transparency emerges, however, only on two conditions. First, these underlying conflicts must remain visible; and they are visible only if their nature is grasped essentially through an analysis of the social relations of production, i.e. what happens between wage labour and capital, and later in the technical and social division of labour. When, for example, in his old polemic with Bettelheim, Sweezy defines what he calls capital not so much by the relations of production as by the free play of individual units of capitalist property striving to expand in a war whose logic has supposedly been halted in the East by state planning, then these societies become opaque again. They are then made to appear as new formations in which the old relations of exploitation persist but in which the real field of conflict — the engine that can drive these societies forward or in reverse — is the relationship linking the productive unit, the enterprise, and the plan. It is here that the contest takes place, between capital striving to free itself and the plan hemming it in. The social relations of production fade under this view; they are involved only as a moment in the formation of the cost of labour. Society appears divided by a war, on the basis of which the forces of capital fight to arise again from every direction in the mixed economy, the legal economy, the semi-legal, and the clandestine. Is this capitalism? No, says Sweezy. Is it socialism? Out of the question. They are 'new' and indecipherable societies.

Finally, we may note here the application of one of the theses bequeathed us by the Bolsheviks, one which Communists have come to know as the theory of two phases: first the material bases for socialism are constructed (through the functioning of the old apparatus of production regulated by the state, which oversees classical accumulation: extraction of surplus-value from the workers and of excess production, or even non-excess production, from the peasants). Then, in a later stage, 'socialist relations' are inaugurated. Here again, the decisive word is pronounced in the domain of property, and the revolution appears as the transition from private to state property, from the free play of the market to the plan.

But this implies acceptance of a frozen society, because the political form that acts as the fundamental motor force of the new 'socialist order' according to this idea, namely the state, is indeed the hierarchy of the 'global factory', a centralized and univocal state power. It is monolithic not only because it is directed by a single centre, but also because in this attempt to achieve a general harmony of forces (doomed to failure in any event), any manifestation of conflict among the social subjects is considered first an annoyance, or perhaps a deviation, and later a conspiracy or betrayal. The idea here is of a society wholly devoted to labour, well regulated and operating by consensus; contradiction is seen as a malady to be treated with repression. Here lie the roots of the lack of liberty.

These roots run deep. Indeed, we maintain that they lie in the non-socialist nature of these formations, which rest on perfected forms of state capitalism, on the refusal of the revolutionary ruling group to enact immediate economic measures — or economic-political measures, fully conscious of the political and social consequences they entail — that would orient all the producers towards a gradual reduction of the unequal relations determined by the social division of labour, towards a reduction of parcelization and alienation, a reduction of the division of labour itself as well as the division between labour and knowledge and that between city and countryside.

When the will to take such measures is stunted, the process of transition is frozen; and that is why the state that has been erected by the various revolutions that have occurred so far becomes so authoritarian. In sum, these are societies in which the capitalist mode of production has made its historical appearance via a class which is no longer homogeneous; this mode of production has compelled this class to carry out the bourgeois revolution which the old, backward classes had not accomplished and has thereby stamped it as progressive. It is the working class, Preobrazhensky said, that makes itself both the subject and object of exploitation. And very quickly, we believe, only the object. And of course, the entire system is self-reproducing, so much so that no democratization can occur. The events following the twentieth congress, when the East European societies were supposed to see the flowering of liberty, the material bases of socialism having finally been established, are significant here. Twenty years have passed and the mechanism remains the same; the same forces still hold power, and any attempt to streamline economic relations somewhat is still subject to ruinous failure. The rigidity is so great as to brook no real change. There is no longer any talk of advancing to communism, even formally.

Does this mean that the conflict between capital and labour is the same as it is in our societies? To what extent does the state power restore to the producers what it takes from them in surplus-value? The comrades of the Budapest school say, 'a lot'; indeed, they hold that a peculiar relationship of mutual protection has arisen between the working class and the class that holds power, at the expense of other layers.

Others, like the Bettelheim school, say 'little'; on the whole, the working class remains the source of absolute surplus-value, which is what accounts for events like the revolt of the Polish workers. Granted, when the state took classical anti-inflation measures in Poland in 1970, workers' resistance broke out just as in the West; once the mask of unanimity fell, it turned out that society was not merely divided, but polarized to the point of bloodshed. Indeed, this was the only moment of truth, when the real roles were suddenly revealed. The transcripts of the tempestuous assemblies held in the Szczecin shipyards in 1970-71 [between the striking workers and Gierek, the newly elected party leader, there to flatter, cajole and pressure them back to work, Ed.] reveal where the power lies and to what extent the condition of the workers is substantially identical to that which prevails in the capitalist countries.

There remains the great question of whether these societies, although they are societies of exploitation, are really capitalist. This is not an academic question. It is not only that the response affects the way in which we are Marxists, the way we define capital and the state — whether essentially through the relations of production (deriving the infinite social mediations from this) or essentially through other characteristics of classical capitalism. But most important, it affects our political options.

If these societies are new social formations in which the persistence of capitalist relations is secondary and the conflicts, repression, and social atomization originate essentially in the realm of politics and management, then what is at stake is a struggle among 'power centres' and their systems of compensation. In that case, what is needed is a democratic pruning of the system. The targets of our exhortation for 'more liberty' are those who govern. If, however, we are dealing with capitalist formations of a new type (capitalism without capitalists, said Lenin; state monopoly capital, says Bettelheim, with, we would add, intense ideological overtones which make the system more repressive, since it is capable of annulling real class conflict, of preventing its expression), then it is no longer a matter of demanding democracy and civil rights. Instead the class struggle must again be taken up in these countries. Our interlocutors then become not those who rule, but those social subjects who can act as the bearers of this revolutionary upheaval.

This is the political hurdle that must be cleared, and it is certainly not an easy task for the left. This is partly for political reasons, because of the traditional, as yet unbroken links with the rulers of these societies. But there are also deeper reasons: we must consider the subject of this conflict, which is probably not the same working class as in 1917 or 1948, because of the position it occupies in society, its ideological formation, and the extent to which it is politically involved. And alongside the working class there are new layers which are not easily definable. On the right, there are deep pockets of reaction among the peasantry still under the hegemony of the church. Here the dissidents do not always take advanced positions, as the example of Solzhenitsyn amply demonstrates. There is a rising social atomization in which new social figures — youth, women, marginalized elements — seem to disappear, the very elements which were thrust to the forefront — with their independent, bitter, and often even destructive potential — by the Chinese cultural revolution. What is the new social bloc having socialist interests in these post-revolutionary societies? And what are the conditions for its self-expression? What are the possibilities of uniting it and of bringing pressure to bear? Of turning it into a political, and not merely social, subject?

This whole question, which marks the leap from dissent to opposition and from opposition to political struggle, has yet to be broached by the Italian left.

Today, along with the comrades of Eastern Europe, we must decide whether we want to broach it.

For my part, I have no doubt that this is the way forward. But this also means that the road before us, and before the post-revolutionary societies, is a long one. History, of course, is not linear; crises can erupt more rapidly and problems arise more frequently than expected, and not always from the right direction. This is why I spoke of the moment of crisis in which we are again beginning this discussion and posing common questions.

During these three days *il manifesto* hopes merely to subject these questions to a test: to initiate some elaborative effort which, for the moment, consists mainly in finding out if we are talking about the same things. I hope that we are, and that those who are present here today — all of us, of the Italian, Spanish, French, and German left, along with the comrades of Eastern Europe — will take this research and political commitment from the frail hands of *il manifesto* in order to carry it forward together.

SECOND SESSION

The Oppositions

Weakness and Potentialities of the Dissident Movement

Daniel Singer

Daniel Singer is a British journalist and writer, born in Poland and now working in France. He is the author of Prelude to Revolution *(Hill and Wang, New York 1970), a study of the May 68 events in France, and of* 'Le témoin et le prophète, pour et contre Solzhenitsyn' *in* Revue d'esthétique, *nos.2-3, 1976, UGE 1976. He writes for* il Manifesto. *The following text is part of a work being prepared on the social contradictions and possibilities for change in the Soviet bloc.*

A century ago Tsardom seemed in terror of a handful of rebels. Today, the Soviet rulers give the impression of not being unduly worried by their dissidents, despite the echo their protests arouse around the world. The reason for this declining power of the dissident *intelligentsia* cannot be numerical. Without entering here into a semantic argument about the definition of the *intelligentsia*, it is obvious that the educated strata from which it is recruited have grown fantastically in the meantime. Among the people employed in Russia on the eve of the October revolution barely 190,000 specialists had graduated from university or a technical college. By 1976 their number had grown to 24 million.[1] The superior efficiency of a modern totalitarian state, compared with the clumsy cruelty of tsarist repression, cannot on its own explain the political weakness of this new *intelligentsia*.

The *narodnik* terrorists expressed, in a sense, the discontent of the silent peasant masses and announced the voice of a newcomer — the rising working class. Everybody felt at the time that Tsardom was doomed. The post-Stalinist regime, which we shall try to show is by its very nature transitional, may be equally condemned. Yet the voice of the new dissidence, at least such as it is perceived in the West, is clearly not the voice of its grave-diggers. The protesters do not give the impression of speaking for any significant segment of Soviet society, not even for the rapidly growing professional *intelligentsia*.

It is at once easy and awkward to criticize in this way, from a comfortable seat in a safe western retreat, people who rebel against the mighty police state at the risk of their life. But the courage of the Soviet protesters is not here at issue. Even if the Soviet Union is no longer quite the concentrationary universe of Stalin's time, the fate of a dissenter is still abominable. All those who are best known in the West, with the exception of the academician Andrey Sakharov, have travelled through prison, camp or psychiatric ward to reach this prominent position. And these well known figures, though they are permanently harassed and threatened with physical violence or arrest, are relatively safe, protected as they are by the limelight. Far from Moscow, in the distant provinces, the KGB is less bothered by world opinion. In a country where the state is ultimately the sole employer, where the judiciary in political cases is a branch of the police, to express a dissident opinion publicly is a heroic act. What is involved here, therefore, is not the courage of the dissidents but their strategy.

Here again the criticism must be qualified. The common denominator uniting most Soviet protesters[2] is their struggle for civil rights, a perfectly legitimate strategy in the oppressing climate of the allegedly socialist world. That sixty years after the October revolution Soviet citizens of all nationalities can still be deprived of the elementary freedoms of speech, of assembly and expression would have been just unthinkable to a socialist at the time of its outbreak and this is indeed a major indictment of the Soviet regime. Besides, it is very understandable that intellectuals should be obsessed with the freedom of expression. When an author writes for his drawer, when a scientist cannot communicate with a colleague without police permission, when to live and prosper one must 'live a lie', such a preoccupation with freedom of thought is more than natural.

But I was not suggesting that in putting civil rights on their metaphorical banner the dissidents are asking too much. On the contrary, they are asking too little or, to be more accurate, too much in the abstract. Nowhere is political freedom won in a void. In Western Europe freedoms were conquered by the bourgeoisie as it struggled to establish its political supremacy and to consolidate its economic domination. Once it had won, it was in no hurry to continue this process. The upper classes were forced to concede by pressure from below, including the pressure of a labour movement fighting to defend its interests. However abstract and general the great principles may sound, they always reflect a balance of power between social forces (sometimes a balance that has since been upset) and they have reached the statute book or constitution as the result of a struggle, as the political confirmation of a successful social movement. The Russian dissidents, on the other hand, act as if the virtue of human rights increased with their divorce from social reality, as if the people were magically attracted by this very abstraction. In their programmes and proclamations the social content comes as an afterthought, as an insignificant nuisance. This was true from the very beginning. Thus, the important manifesto of Sakharov, Medvedev and Turchin[3] contained a curiously symptomatic footnote: 'we should also deal with social problems'. But the social programme of the dissident movement is still conspicuous by its absence.

The Russian people have heard enough Orwellian double-talk to be suspicious. They know that *in theory* they are the masters of *their* land, of *their* factories and of their own destiny. They also remember that the splendidly democratic Stalin constitution was proclaimed in 1936 at the very height of Soviet lawlessness. Rightly, they tend to look prospective gift horses in the mouth. Yet nowhere do the dissidents explain to them concretely how all these civil rights will affect the everyday life of the labourer and the kolkhoznik, the technician and the office worker. Will all these freedoms include the right to strike, to bargain collectively and, equally collectively, to determine the organization of work? How will equality before the law affect the hierarchy, the disparity of wages and salaries, the gap between the privileged and the oppressed? And once the party bosses have been pushed aside, what kind of system do the dissenters propose to put in its place?

In the absence of any clear answer to such basic questions why should Soviet citizens join the opposition in substantial numbers, knowing full well what tremendous risks such a venture does involve, what abnegation it implies? The misunderstanding is further complicated by the fact that the gap between 'them' and 'us', between the haves and the have-nots, between the privileged and the masses is still profound in the Soviet Union and deeply resented. A battle over civil rights without social content, seemingly a conflict over the right to write or to paint freely, may well look to the ordinary Russian as 'their' quarrel, a settling of accounts among the privileged.

The setback of the protest movement which, one hopes, is merely temporary has coincided with a relative consolidation of the regime.

During the first years after Stalin's death Soviet society seemed in flux, as if it were searching for a new political equilibrium. Brezhnev has frozen it again, re-establishing the total stranglehold of the party apparatus over society and reassuring by the same token the Soviet establishment.

Naturally, the reign of privilege did not start with Stalin's death or the 20th party congress. If anything, statistics suggest a slight narrowing of the range of wages and salaries during the post-Stalinist period. It may be argued that the *datchas*, exclusive shops or journeys abroad are not perceived by statistics. Admittedly. But this is not the real question. Privileges were exorbitant in Stalin's time, but they were precarious. The *apparatchik* apparently at the height of his power ran the risk of landing in jail and then trekking to Siberia. Periodic purges prevented the men of the apparatus and other beneficiaries of the regime from consolidating their position. On the morrow of the death of their tyrant *and* benefactor, their collective aspiration was for security of tenure, for stability, allowing them at least to enjoy their privileges in peace (and, who knows, passing them on tomorrow to their children ...).

Nikita Khrushchev, half-peasant and half townsman, improvising all sorts of reforms yet unable to carry any of them to their logical conclusion, was still too threatening for them because he acted as if aware that for Soviet society to move forward the whole Stalinist heritage would have to be overhauled. Even this clumsy and impotent reformer was too dangerous and had to be got rid of. Leonid Brezhnev, on the contrary, enjoys the confidence of the privileged in general and of the *apparatchiks* in particular, and this for one very simple reason: the basic premise of his whole policy — within and without — is not to embark on anything likely to shake the structure of power and, hence, the network of privileges. Herein lies the secret of the long reign of Leonid Brezhnev and his ageing team. Let us admit it: thirteen years ago nobody would have imagined that this grey bureaucrat would today be still soldiering on in the Kremlin.

The days of Brezhnev may well be numbered; Brezhnevism, on the other hand, can endure. And yet, despite its persistence, it has all the features of a transitional regime, the plaything of events rather than their master, unable really to solve any of the major issues facing Soviet society. Immobility is the price paid for survival: the regime can do no more than to patch things up. Without economic dynamism, with no ideological illusions left among the population,

Brezhnevism accumulates contradictions as it puts off the necessary reforms. It probably prepares for Russia an explosive future. In any case, it prepares the ground for a deeper and more radical opposition.

The Changing Face of Russia

Fundamentally, the present political system is not essentially different from Stalin's. True, the concentration camps are less packed, the terror is less blind and the population does not live in permanent fear. But the protesters know the price of dissent. Above all, as in the past, all decisions, all initiatives flow from the top and are imposed on the population. The new constitution solemnly confirms the supremacy of the Party; in fact, what we see is the rule of the Party apparatus or, to be more precise, of its top leadership.

But if the political system is frozen again, society is not. It goes on being reshaped by profound changes. I shall confine myself here to three interconnected aspects of this transformation: the decline of the peasantry; the rise of the new working class and professional intelligentsia; and, last but not least, the rising level of education, conceived by the regime as a blessing but which may yet prove to be a curse in disguise for the rulers.

Decline of the Peasantry

On the eve of the October revolution, as everybody knows, Russia was submerged in a peasant sea: over 80 per cent of the population was living in the countryside. At the beginning of the last war town-dwellers still accounted for only a third of the total population. Even at the end of Stalin's reign, six out of ten Soviet citizens were living in the country. Today the proportion is reversed: 62 per cent of the population is urban and 38 per cent rural. Employment statistics are even more striking. On the eve of the First World War three-quarters of the working population was employed in farming; on the eve of the Second World War — one half. Now, this share can be estimated at roughly one quarter.[4]

The social landscape of the countryside has altered as well. State farms, the *sovkhozy* — employing over 10 million Soviet citizens out of about 28 million working on the land — perform a much more important economic function than in the past. The difference has also diminished between these *sovkhozy* and the *kolkhozy* (the once dispersed collective farms today amalgamated into less than 30,000 huge units employing, on an average, 500 people). *Matryona's*

House, while still no exception, is no longer really the rule.

One should not jump to the conclusion, inevitably drawn by Soviet propaganda, that Russia is in the process of solving its agricultural problem. Heavy imports of western wheat are not the only proof to the contrary. The fact that productivity in Soviet farming is roughly one-fifth of its American counterpart shows the enormous road still to be travelled. But the political equation has already changed. Before and immediately after the last war, the nightmare of the Soviet leaders was *Bonapartism*, the potential rise of a military leader backed by peasant masses still hankering after private property. This fear is gradually vanishing: this is no longer the main danger for the regime. True, the weight of backward, rural Russia is still very heavy. A quarter of the total labour force employed in an agricultural sector still unable to fill all the country's needs: this is undoubtedly a heavy burden for the economy to carry. But we should not forget that a similar proportion prevailed in France only twenty years ago and in Italy barely ten. In Russia, too, the part played by the peasantry declines in importance all the time. Those who, following in Solzhenitsyn's footsteps, base their plans for the future on the resurrection of the *muzhik*, on the restoration of a Mother Russia dominated by lesser or bigger landowners, are dabbling in nostalgia rather than dealing with politics.

The New Working Class

The relative decline of the peasantry went hand in hand with a rapid growth of the industrial workforce. According to the official statistics on the population structure, workers (and their families) now account for 61 per cent of the total, compared with a third before the last war. Employees account for 22 per cent now compared with 17 per cent then. These figures are somewhat misleading since they include farm workers if they are employed by state farms, but exclude them if they work in collective farms. The data on employment in the national economy are, therefore, more instructive. Industry, building and transport used to absorb 10 per cent of the total workforce before the revolution and less than 30 per cent on the eve of the last war. Today they account for nearly half the working population.

Yet I would like to draw attention to another aspect of this new working class, linked not with its numerical growth but with its nature and its origins. In the first stage of the Soviet industrial revolution — the phase of breakneck industrialization — industrial workers were really peasants transplanted to town; uprooted, semi-literate, these victims of forced collectivization were full of fear and resentment. Once in town, there was no question for them of fitting into a working class with its own political culture and traditions. They *were* the working class. (For some historians, the Gulag was, among other things, the barbarian instrument designed to break those peasants to the discipline and rhythm of factory life during the period of so-called 'primitive socialist accumulation'.)

Today things are quite different. The urban labour force now expands mainly from within its own ranks. Migration from country to town still counts as a factor but it is becoming marginal. And the new arrivals themselves are no longer quite the same. Soviet papers occasionally complain that the most advanced elements from the countryside — mechanics, tractor-drivers, animal-specialists etc. — are too often attracted by 'city lights'.

It will be objected that even this new working class is uninterested in politics, sounds cynical and has no collective consciousness or tradition. Given the historical context the opposite would be surprising. The fact remains that these workers, themselves the sons of workers, are less traumatised by the Stalinist nightmare, less frightened and, above all, more educated than their elders: they therefore represent a potential political force.

Relatively the level of education is even higher among the 'employees', a heterogeneous group accounting for about 30 per cent of the Soviet workforce outside collective farming. The Soviet Union has not yet reached the stage of the big boom in the services sector. The number of workers and employees, i.e. of blue and white collar workers, has risen in recent years at roughly the same pace. Among the white collar workers the fastest expansion has taken place in the social services, particularly in education and health.

'Employee', incidentally, is a convenient concept for statisticians dealing in global figures. You lump in the same bag, on the one hand, teachers, municipal employees, shop assistants, all of them at the bottom of the wage scale, and on the other, high dignitaries, academicians, all sorts of top servants of the regime, richly rewarded for their devotion. By working out an average you *show* that employees have lower wages than industrial workers. Thus it is *proved* that proletarians are the masters in the 'workers' fatherland' and the propaganda trick is duly performed.

It is claimed that there are now in the Soviet Union more than thirty million graduates from universities and technical colleges.

Deducting from this figure officers in the armed forces, old-age pensioners and housewives, one is left with around twenty-four million working in the national economy. Of that figure university graduates make up nearly ten million. Among them over a third are engineering graduates while teachers account for another third; economists, doctors and agronomists share the bulk of the remainder. Graduates from technical colleges — the NCO's of the army of labour — are roughly 14 million. All sorts of technicians account for nearly half that number; junior staff in medicine, education and planning follow well behind. As we saw, this growing professional intelligentsia is very far from homogeneous. Its members differ greatly with regard to their wages and privileges, their place in the hierarchy or the part they play in production. The dissident movement, when it picks up again, will have to analyze carefully these 'new strata' and work for a division in their ranks, just in the same way as the western labour movement can count on an alliance with only one part of the so-called 'middle classes'. But here I just wanted to emphasize a deep social change: with 20 per cent of the labour force having more than a secondary education and 75 per cent more than an elementary one, Soviet society is very different from the formation which gave birth to Stalinism.

'Woe from Wit'

Let us not read a miracle into these figures: a quarter of the working people — one half in the collective farms — still have only an elementary education; among the rest many have not actually completed their secondary schooling. Let us not credit the Brezhnev regime with the achievement either. If anything, it has slowed down the rate of progress. 'Full secondary education' was planned to be the absolute norm some time ago and it still does not apply throughout the country. Evidently, the current regime is merely reaping the benefits from an option taken on the morrow of the October revolution — the decision to invest heavily in education. The cumulative effects are now being felt and the average level of education rises substantially from year to year.

I cherish no illusions either about the subversive effect of education as such. The part played by education in the reproduction of the existing system needs no demonstration here any more than one needs to point out the conformist ideal of the Soviet educational model, with its selective nature, its hierarchical structure, its specialization and its famous courses in Marxism-Leninism, fit only to disgust entire generations. That said, however, the more educated young people of today may prove more exacting and less compliant than the uprooted peasants of yesterday. The men in the Kremlin did not bother about it until recently because they thought they had found a magic solution in permanent growth.

The Soviet leaders are probably the only ones still to believe in the 'scientific revolution' and the virtue of growth for its own sake. At a stage when the countryside was beginning to dry up as a source of manpower and when the effects of the falling birth rate were about to be felt, the newly educated workers were going to come to the rescue, ensuring a rapid rise in productivity and thus paving the way for the 'Soviet miracle'. The solution was political as well as economic. Gone are the days when the leaders in the Kremlin were offering their citizens and the world at large the prospect of an alternative, different mode of producing and consuming, a different way of life. Their project is the Russian version of the 'American dream'; and it is by American methods that they hoped to integrate the population. Durable consumer goods — the telly, the washing machine, tomorrow the car — were gradually supposed to replace the *knout* and the *Gulag* as the means of social control. Khruschev had even found a name — goulash socialism — to describe this strange hybrid.

Economic Dilemma

But the miracle did not happen. The mechanism through which Stalinism was to be dismantled — reforms-progress, progress-reforms — got stuck and then even began functioning in reverse. The dream may well turn into a nightmare for the regime. The rising generations, yesterday the source of hope, are now a major cause for worry. How are they to be contained and integrated into a system which lacks political drive and cannot even compensate this lack by economic dynamism?

The Slackening Pace

The contrast between the Khrushchevian dream and Soviet reality can be illustrated graphically. In a famous speech at the 22nd Party congress in 1961, Khrushchev set the country's economic targets for 1980. At the last Party congress, Kosygin presented the five-year plan to be completed in the same year. The gap between the two blueprints is enormous. If the curve had followed Khrushchev's forecasts rather than the new version, by 1980 the Soviet economy would be using twice as much electric power and the Russians would be eating twice as much meat. And they would be quadrupling the present annual increase in housing stock.

The irrepressible Nikita, it will be said, had more imagination than his pedestrian successors. Undoubtedly. But his 'communist programme' for 1980 was no flight of fancy. Like a vulgar Doctor Strangelove from some Hudson Institute, he merely projected past curves into the future. The difference between his programme and the new one thus shows a radical change in the tempo of growth, a shift that is actually confirmed by official figures: the annual rate of growth now being planned (4.7%) is not even half what it used to be in the fifties. The decline has been slow but steady; in the long run it is perturbing for a regime which, like its western counterparts, must rely on material progress to contain social pressures. What can it do to spur on the economic engine and give it a new lease of life?

One possibility must be ruled out by definition: the search for a socialist way out. To decentralize by shifting initiative to the rank and file, to attack the hierarchical system and its values — none of this can be confined within the four walls of the factory. The whole system stands together and it would collapse under such a push from below. The rulers in the Kremlin have no death wish and the very idea of a workers' council, of a genuine *soviet* sends shivers down their spine. Hence, one must envisage either closer integration into the capitalist world market — with borrowing of both capital and technology — or internal reforms in the management of the economy (the first solution leading inevitably to the second).

Russia has partly opened its frontiers. In the last ten years foreign trade has expanded twice as fast as the national product and the share of advanced capitalist countries in this trade has increased. This shift is not insignificant; on the other hand to have a major influence on the Soviet economy, the collaboration would have to move beyond the stage of western credits repaid through Russian export of raw materials. Western capitalists would have to invest heavily into Soviet industry and this they would only do for a profit: which bring us back to the managerial reform.

Stalinist planning had become too crude and centralized for the complex economy it had helped to develop. Already back in the fifties it was necessary to provide more flexibility by allowing increased scope for profits as a measure of efficiency.[5] This is not the place nor is there the time to review all the abortive reforms, all the half-measures that have failed since then. It is enough to ask why they have failed. The usual explanation pins the blame on the resistance of the *apparatchiks*. Admittedly even in those versions which left the key decisions to the central planner, the reform would have deprived the party apparatus of its role as overseer at all levels and thus would have loosened its stranglehold over society. But this explanation, though correct within limits, is not sufficient. For there seems to me to be a deeper reason. Pushed to its logical conclusion, the economic reform must lead to a reform in the management of the firm, to wider powers being granted to the factory director, including the power to hire and fire as well as to decide the level of wages. Yet such a reform would mean for the workers an open attack on what is left of their conquests of October — the security of employment with all that it involves. It could thus lead to the revival of an autonomous labour movement. Hence the hesitation waltz of the post-Stalinist regime and the ultra-conservatism of Leonid Brezhnev. And yet, because the alternative road of workers' democracy is blocked, this is the direction the regime is likely to take sooner or later.

From above or from below

Let us look in this context at the old controversy over the nature of possible change in post-Stalinist Russia. Will it come from above or from below, from the apex or from the base, from within or from without the Party? These debates were a kind of western counterpoint to Khrushchev's goulash socialism. In their more sophisticated versions the gradualist, Fabian theses did not simply rely on the goodwill of the reformers. They combined it with social constraints and pressures from below to imagine a Russia travelling in reverse the road which had led from the dictatorship of the proletariat to the tyranny of the General-Secretary. This controversy is now out-dated. Even before Khrushchev's fall, and certainly since the invasion of Czechoslovakia, it has become obvious that the system has its logic, the bureaucracy has an instinct for survival and will not hesitate to strike ruthlessly if its vital interests are at stake.

Does this mean that inner struggles at the top are of no interest to us? Not at all. Naturally, it would be absurd to wait the advent of socialist democracy as a gift from above, as the result of the action of some 'liberal-democratic wing'. All hypotheses of this kind rest on the strange premise of a Soviet Union already enjoying a socialist structure on to which must be added a democratic superstructure.

Let us be serious. We are interested in such inner struggles at the top not for what they can bring by themselves but because of the influence they can exercise on mass movements. Russia will probably have to move further to the Right, if one may use such a term, before it jumps in the opposite direction. The system will continue to consolidate privileges, strengthen the hierarchy and increase the powers of the managers before it sets its grave-diggers into motion.

Here I would like to make what looks like a digression and put at the heart of our debate the question of Poland where, in December 1970, the workers made a sudden and spectacular entry onto the political stage and where, without programme or organization, they have weighed heavily on the course of events ever since. Is Poland the exception to the rule within the Soviet block or is it, as I believe, simply in advance, foreshadowing the social struggles to come? Obviously, every situation is specific. The development of the movement in each country will depend on circumstances, on traditions, on the economic situation, on the cleverness or stupidity of the leadership, and so on. But the same causes should, in the long run, produce the same effects. The Polish workers were driven to action by attempts to put the house in order, to 'modernize'. The whole of Eastern Europe is now entering a period of restructuring and it would not be surprising if the Polish example were infectious.

The part played in Poland by dissident intellectuals is equally instructive. They, too, once preached in the desert. In 1968, the police clubbed rebellious students amid the sinister silence of society at large. In 1977, on the other hand, after the second workers' rising, a few intellectuals seized the occasion to insert themselves into a social movement by founding the KOR, the Committee for the Defence of Workers. Everywhere dissident intellectuals will count as a political force to the extent that they manage to forge links with the working class.

Before concluding I would like to clear up some possible misunderstandings. In such a brief intervention, sketchy by its very nature, I left out of account many possibilities. On purpose. Thus, in the Soviet equation I did not mention at all the national question nor did I envisage the convulsions which may shake a society without apparent outlets. Secondly, I hope that in putting the emphasis on the labour movement, I did not create a lyrical illusion nor give the impression that in Poland, in Russia or elsewhere a proletariat fully armed with political consciousness would take over tomorrow. I know that the making or re-making of a labour movement, the transformation of the working class into a class-for-itself is always a complex process, with dramatic highlights but also with long periods of slow, subterranean growth. This process will be particularly difficult in countries suffering from collective amnesia, where legal organization is impossible and where any action is terribly dangerous. All I wanted to insist on is that our old friend the mole does not stop digging on reaching the border of the Soviet bloc, that there, too, social contradictions can provide the opportunity for revolutionary change. I wanted to suggest one possible way.

If hope there is, it brings obligations in its wake. For our East European comrades the task is immense and tough. Not only because they have to face ruthless police repression. To think and even more to speak as a Marxist in countries where the very term has been usurped for the gospel preached by the rulers, the exploiters, those who wield the club and call in the tanks is not an easy mission. And yet the only chance for the dissidents lies in this direction. If it gets involved in social struggles, if it is backed by the working class and its new potential allies, if it manages to present its interests as 'the superior interests of society as a whole', then and only then will the new dissident movement be able to play a historical role in Eastern Europe.

There is no need to add that it has every right to demand our solidarity. Our struggles are common in more senses than one. The international economic crisis opens a new era, foreshadows upheavals the shape and size of which we can only guess at. A rigid, frozen Soviet bloc would act as a brake on changes in the West. But the reverse is even more true. If a breach were to be opened within the western capitalist bloc, if in France, in Italy or in Spain, the movement were to get down to the real issues — social relations, equality, the hierarchical order, the division of labour, the withering away of the State — if it showed in this way that the workers can really become the masters of their fate, the echo would be tremendous not just in Prague or Warsaw but in Kiev and Moscow too. Hence, oblivious to current Parisian fashions, I shall conclude with a quotation from Marx, speaking to the Chartists on the anniversary of another Polish insurrection: 'So you Chartists must not simply express pious wishes for the liberation of nations. Defeat your own internal enemies and you will then be able to pride yourselves on having defeated the entire old society.'[6]

NOTES

1. Ekonomicheskaya Gazeta no.17, April 1977.
2. It is not our purpose here to analyze the small but extremely varied dissident groups which stretch from reactionary Russian chauvinists to people who consider themselves Marxist socialists.
3. Published back in *Le Monde* 11/12/13 April 1970.
4. Depending on how one calculates the share of the families of the kolkhozniks working on the small private plots, the last remnants of private property in the countryside.
5. These ideas were known in the west as Libermanism, as they were linked with the name of a professor of that name from Lvov.
6. Marx and Engels Collected Works, Lawrence and Wishart, London, Vol.6, p.389.

I CLASS STRUCTURE OF THE POPULATION (%)				
	1913	*1939*	*1959*	*1976*
Workers	14.6	33.5	49.5	61.2
Admin. Tech. & Managerial	2.4	16.7	18.8	22.4
Collective farmers		47.2	31.4	16.4
Peasants	66.7	2.6	0.3	
Bourgeoisie etc.	16.3			
Total	100	100	100	100

II OCCUPATION BREAKDOWN IN THE NATIONAL ECONOMY (BY BRANCH IN %)

	1913	1940	1965	1975
Agriculture	75	54	31	23
Industry & Construction Ind.	9	23	36	38
Transport & Communication	2	5	8	9
Commerce & Distribution	9	5	6	8
Health, Education & Culture	1	6	14	16
Administration		3	2	2
Miscellaneous	4	4	3	4
Total	100	100	100	100

III LEVEL OF EDUCATION OF THE WORKING POPULATION (%)

	1959	1959	1970	1975
Higher education	(15)	3.3	6.5	8.4
Incomplete higher educ.	(13)	1.2	1.3	1.8
Specialised secondary educ.	(12)	5.8	10.5	11.3
General secondary educ.	(10)	7.2	15.9	20.3
Incomplete secondary educ.	(8)	25.8	31.1	33.4
Primary education	(5)	56.7	34.7	24.8
Total		100,0	100,0	100,0

The brackets indicate the average number of years of study in each group.

IV SPECIALISTS IN THE NATIONAL ECONOMY (1000s).

	1941	1965	1975
Higher education of which:	909	4891	9477
Engineers	295	1631	3683
Economists	57	301	775
Doctors	142	501	765
Agronomists	65	303	513
Specialised secondary educ. of which:	1492	7175	13 319
Technicians	324	2887	6093
Medical personnel	393	1454	2277
Teaching "	536	1282	1595
Planning "	31	571	1465

V SOVIET PLANS (OR DREAMS AND REALITY)

		1975 annual production	1980 Brezhnev plan	1980 Khrushchev plan
Electricity	billion kwh	1038	1360	2850
Natural Gas	billion cubic meters	289	418	700
Steel	billion tonnes	141	165	250
Corn	" "	140	218*	302
Meat	" "	15	15.3*	31

*Annual average.

VI ANNUAL AVERAGE GROWTH IN 5 YEAR PERIODS (%)

	1951-1955	1956-1960	1961-1965	1966-1970	1971-1975	1976-1980 (plan)
National production	10.80	9.72	6.45	7.11	5.22	4.73
Industrial production	13.09	10.40	8.59	8.45	7.42	6.50

'Forward together or Down together'

Leonid Plyushch

It is hard for me to speak about theoretical and philosophical questions at a time when Soviet dissidents are in such grave danger. All the oppositional forces, whether of a national, religious or other character, now find themselves under the enemy's fire, having already suffered the heavy blow of the Belgrade Conference. Nevertheless, I shall try to raise a number of general problems for consideration.

I agree with comrade Karol when he says that the dissidents will not represent a real attacking force until they are united around a social movement. But that will not be easy. The fact that there is no workers' movement in the Soviet Union is a fundamental point of contrast with the situation in Poland. Of course, this difference has historical roots: our working class has been oppressed for a longer time and never went through the stage of democratic struggle; it lacks a tradition, since, before the revolution, it could only work underground for political objectives. In short, then, we have to consider the entire structure of the Soviet Union if we are to understand the phenomenon of dissidence and explain its specificity. And that can only be done if we dwell upon certain historical questions, going back to the origins of the Soviet regime in the October Revolution. One still potent virtue of Marxism is its capacity for self-criticism: it is easy to criticize one's opponent, who is by definition in the wrong; but the most important thing is to make a critique of oneself. For example, Marx's critique of his own Hegelian formation was the pre-condition of his theoretical independence. It would therfore be a good idea to begin with a critique of the Russian Revolution, and even of that which preceded it: Marx himself.

Writing in the twenties to Commissar for Education Lunacharsky, the Russian author Korolenko said that although he was in favour of socialism, he did not consider the Russian empire as a whole to be ripe for it. He based his argument on the fact that Russia did not even have a democratic tradition, since it had not passed through the stage of bourgeois revolution and bourgeois democracy. The lack of such experience left all the peoples of Russia with no self-awareness and no sense of right. In the Russian tradition, it was naked force, the fist (*kulak*), which decided everything, including the law. And so, the Tsar's arbitrary power gave place to the Communist Party's equally arbitrary and uncontrolled power, based on the Bolshevik thesis according to which every norm should be replaced by the consciousness of the proletariat, or in other words by the consciousness of those with the guns. In the different conditions of today, the dissident movement still confirms the validity of Korolenko's arguments and preoccupations.

The whole of Russian political thought, as it existed about the time of the revolution, may be ranged under two broad currents, the Menshevik and Bolshevik, each of which embraced several political parties. Now, both these currents tried to tackle the problem I have just mentioned: both were aware that Russia was neither economically nor politically mature for socialism; and that the newly-born Russian bourgeoisie had to travel a long road before it could catch up with western capitalism if only in terms of industrial development. However, lacking the necessary initiative, this cowardly bourgeoisie, with no traditions of its own, was incapable of assuming the direction of the economy. It was prepared to give in to the old order, and had actually sought an alliance with feudalism instead of struggling against it. The Mensheviks concluded that the role of the bourgeoisie should therefore be assumed by the socialist movement, however strange that might seem. They retained from Marxism its conception of economic determination — and, in particular, the necessity of a stage of economic revolution with a bourgeois state; only after the productive forces had been developed through capitalist domination would it be possible to talk of the construction of socialism.

The Bolsheviks also saw the length of the road which Russia had before it, but they concluded that all existing forces must be summoned to race through the historical stages. They kept another element of Marxism: its stress not on necessity but on voluntarism or consciousness. After all, did not Hegel once şay that freedom is itself a form of necessity? For the Boslheviks, then, there could be no question of waiting for capitalism to develop: the situation in Russia was complicated by the fact that the bourgeoisie was incapable of grasping the reins of the country and solving its problems. 'No one stands in our way. We ourselves shall assume the responsibility for a process of accelerated development — a process of racing through stages and taking history by force. Today is too soon? But it will be too late the day after tomorrow. We have to act tomorrow.' As Napoleon put it: *On s'engage et après on voit*. Such was the first step in the subjectivist approach to reality.

There was more than a little Slavophilia in this extraordinary choice, influenced as it was by the old conviction that Russia had a destiny of its own by virtue of which it would not have to follow the road taken by other peoples. Since it was supposedly not obliged to go through all the stages of capitalist development, Russia would therefore be able to move straight into socialism. Lenin was himself marked by this messianic belief in a specific Russian destiny, although he combined it with his characteristically subjectivist need to force reality. But Lenin also seems to have clearly understood that Russia was not yet ripe for socialism, and that the situation would present a historical task of enormous magnitude. It is not for nothing that, shortly before the Russian Revolution, Lenin was laying stress on the German State's capacity, under the given conditions, to reorganize capital by concentrating the power of command. He thought, wrongly in my opinion, that it would be possible to do the same in Russia once the state was in the hands of the proletariat, overlooking the fact that the working class was not then prepared either to manage capital or to assume control of the state.

Greatly oversimplifying matters, we could say that only two paths then seemed open: either the one normally followed by the bourgeoisie, or else that of a capitalism at the service of the working class. And that is where both the Mensheviks and the Bolsheviks made their mistake. Although they were both socialist currents, they would not admit that the role which they were preparing to play did not belong to them by right — the role, that is, of the bourgeoisie and state capitalism respectively. Perhaps Lenin's mistake was the lesser of the two, but it was a mistake none the less. It is this contradiction between what Russia seemed to be and what it really was that explains many of the events which followed, even during the October Revolution itself.

The missing factor was a class that could really sustain socialism. The small working class had only recently left the countryside and undergone its basic training. The Bolsheviks, who succeeded in taking power under quite specific circumstances, went on to make a general law of that abnormal situation, believing themselves able to dispense with social and economic laws. The quickened pace was justified by erecting voluntarism into the law of politics — a course expressed in the formation of the *Cheka* ('Extraordinary Commission for Combating Counter-Revolution') later to become the KGB. If reality was to conform to this project, it was necessary to clear away all enemies: first the Tsar's General Staff, the white officers and the counter-revolution, next the socialists and the Workers Opposition, and then the kulaks. Society was remodelled by terror: for what I call 'Chekism' is but an extreme form of re-education. Although Lenin himself said that you cannot drive someone into paradise with a stick, that is precisely the philosophy according to which the Cheka acted. In its time, the Inquisition called itself by a similar name: the most holy extraordinary commission — only the abbreviation Cheka has 'pan-Russian' instead of 'most holy'. This is no doubt a formal analogy, but the two commissions do perhaps have a common root in voluntarist exaggeration.

When the gulf between state-capitalist reality and socialist phraseology began to be seen, as it did shortly afterwards, along came an ideology whose purpose was to fill the gap. Thus, 'socialist realism' in art and in literature has as its function not to represent reality, but to fabricate a propagandist image of the latter — it is the extension of the Cheka into the realm of culture. Quite simply, a lens-filter is needed to prevent the workers seeing reality as it is. It is interesting to note that, before the Revolution, the founder of socialist realism, Maxim Gorki, was accused of being a disciple of Mach; and, in reality, it was precisely the philosophical current inspired by Mach which became the theoretical basis of socialist realism. Again, if we read Gramsci's notes on the 'realism' of fascist art, we find a number of extraordinary points of similarity between the two phenomena — above all when Gramsci criticizes the voluntarism and subjectivist deformation of reality characteristic of fascist art.

Traces of this voluntarist exaggeration can be found wherever one cares to look. Let us recall the case of biology. When it was discovered that collectivization of the land had been a failure with regard both to the country's overall needs and to the interests of private individuals, then a new lie became necessary. It had to be shown that the political choices had not been wrong, but that backward methods had been employed in implementing them; and so the Soviet genetics of Lysenko and Michurin came to serve as the scientific basis for this operation. It was not a question of a determinist theory, as some have argued, but of a mystical variant of

Lamarckism: a truly magical view of things. Similarly, how can we explain the fact that the use of psychiatric hospitals for political repression first appeared in the Soviet Union, rather than being invented by the fascist regimes? As far as I know, the first political victim to be interned in a psychiatric hospital was Kirov's wife, who knew the secrets of her husband's assassins. Even the psychiatric hospital reflects the mentality of Cheka voluntarism: break people's back in order to re-educate them; drive them into heaven by force; persuade them through socialist realism and matching propaganda that there is already heaven on earth, that Soviet man is of a special stamp ... Just as 'Soviet genetics' was an attempt to solve biological problems in a mystical way, so is psychiatry a tool for 'fixing' the brain and remoulding the psyche. Both are based on the need to hide the true face of reality and persuade people that it is different. By all means necessary. There was psychiatric abuse before Khrushchev, but only with him does it become a widespread phenomenon: for only then did western pharmacology manage to perfect its methods of altering the human mind. It was western capitalist medicine plus Khruschevite voluntarism which made possible mass-scale psychiatric abuse.

However, once again there are historical roots peculiar to Russia. Already in the time of Nicholas I a political opponent was pronounced mad: the ideology of Tsarism claimed that only the Tsar, Russian Orthodoxy and the god-chosen Russian people could be right. If anyone dissented in this the best of nations, guided by the most correct ideas, then he had to be either a madman or an enemy. And if he was an enemy, then he was in league with the devil. Such was the old system — and it was my fate to experience its modern variant when I was examined by Serbski in the institute bearing his name. Now, Serbski is a psychiatrist: he has written that all oppositionists are either Jews or lunatics. This is not just his idea, being actually quite widespread: 'we are the best', 'we are the most correct', 'we have the best regime, the truest ideas to be found anywhere'. This belief, which is peculiar to the Russian tradition, has been taken up and concentrated in Bolshevism. But I fail to see what it has in common with Marxism.

The operation of a double-standard morality provides a key to understanding this tragedy. Once it is agreed with Lenin that everything which serves the revolution is moral, then everything is permitted. To some extent, this a-moralism is derived from Marx, who ignored the moral dimension in his analysis of social processes.

Another question of great importance is the basic economic option in favour of state capitalism. Whereas Lenin studied the experience of Germany, Marx began, towards the end of his life, to examine the Asiatic mode of production, based on slavery and statism, in which the land and productive enterprises belonged not to private individuals but to the state. Leninism and statism combine, in a bizarre manner, elements of the first-world-war German experience with the old tradition of the Asiatic mode of production described by Marxism.

This weight of the past can be found in the two-truths theory to which I alluded. But when I said that, with the October Revolution, a split opened between the level of pronouncement and the level of fact, I did not add that this is a traditional practice in the history of Russia. Everyone is probably familiar with the 'Potemkin villages' invented during the time of Catherine the Great. Before the empress travelled from Petersburg to the Crimea, the route was lined with the facades, and only the facades, of new villages, in order to deceive both her and the foreigners accompanying her. Catherine was in regular correspondence with Voltaire and Diderot: it was important that she should be able to relate that the Russian countryside was prospering under her enlightened leadership. When she stopped in a log-cabin, she found peasants dishing up a chicken; but as soon as she left, that same chicken was whisked off to the next *isba*. Similarly, throughout her trip the trees were moved around so that she might continually see flowers.

The strangest thing is that an almost identical procedure was adopted when Khruschev visited Kirghizia: a special airport and motorway were built; and thatched cottages were hastily erected, decorated with paintings, and supplied with televisions and refrigerators instead of chickens. But Khruschev did not even go inside, and everything was soon taken back from the peasants. Only one was ingenuous enough to think that Khruschev had really made a present of the TV and the fridge; he even threatened to report to Khruschev himself that the authorities intended taking the goods back. He was accordingly permitted to keep them.

These Potemkin villages exist everywhere. One day Fidel Castro arrived in Kiev, at a time when I was still one of his great admirers. (He was the last leader for whom I shouted: 'Hurrah!') Anyway, the students were dressed up in national costume so that Castro could be shown the prosperous situation in the Ukraine. Solzhenitsyn describes a visit made by Mrs Roosevelt to a Soviet prison, where she saw a very beautiful 'Potemkin cell' complete with every comfort and a statue of Buddha. More recently, some Austrian psychiatrists were tricked in the same manner, even though we had warned them in advance. We also told a delegation of old French Resistance fighters that they were going to be shown some 'Potemkin camps'. But the Soviet authorities found out and, in the end, there was no visit to a camp. In short, then, a whole system of lies still exists today.

Once, when my wife was working as a low-grade clerk in the educational administration, she attended a meeting at central level. There she was shown round an exhibition on kolkhoz creches — the only problem being that they were really town creches at which kolkhoz chairmen and village school-teachers had been photographed together with ministry functionaries. Just whom did they hope to deceive? The Central Committee had supplied the idea, the Ministry of Education the money; but both kolkhoz chairmen and school-teachers were well aware of how things really were with creches. So in the end, no one was deceived. The lie was as blatant as could be.

All this has to be known if we are to understand the phenomenon of dissidence. We are now living in the age of technical-scientific revolution: whereas the industrial revolution was characterized in Marx's time by mechanization, and in Lenin's time by electrical energy, the essential thing today is the circulation and control of information. However, Soviet society is built on lack of information and general lying — lies everywhere from factory to kolkhoz, lies distributed both vertically, from top to bottom, and horizontally. They are full-scale, reciprocal lies, perfectly understood as such. Do we have here, then, a society which is structurally incapable of joining a real technical-scientific revolution? Some people fear lest the USSR should follow the western model and exploit its technological successes. But such a course could not be followed through, given that technology requires control techniques of a certain level. Imagine, for example, that national planning were brought under an automated calculation system, as is proposed by the Academy of Sciences, and that the whole national economy really came to depend on computers, as our technocrats and cyberniticians would like to see happen. What these specialists seem to forget is that, on the input side, men would still have to feed information into the machine. And why should they be honest with machines when they are dishonest with bureaucrats? Why should they respect academicians when they do not respect the Party Central Committee? If information is distorted on the input side, it will be so on the output side as well — that is the tragedy of existing Soviet structures.

Ground between a voluntarist, untruthful state and uncontrollable industrial disorganization are to be found the scientific and technical intelligentsia. It is no accident, therefore, if the majority of today's dissidents are scientists and related intellectuals working in the human sciences. We are often accused in the West of being naively humanistic and utopian moralists, and in a sense this is true. But it must be understood that behind the utopian appearance of our movement lies, above all else, a need for information and truth. We need to live without falsehood — or, as the Socialist-Revolutionaries used to say at the beginning of the century: 'We are thirsty for justice.' In their quest for a truthful and just society, the dissidents are putting morality back into politics: they are the ones demanding freedom of speech and information, and fighting for human rights; it is they who ask that the economy become scientifically transparent and that society be organized in a transparent manner. Sometimes people reproach us for raising problems at a political rather than social level. But although this is again partially true, it is so above all because, as I said earlier, our workers movement has been crushed into silence, or because it rebels for emotional rather social reasons. It is, for example, when the police kill a worker that a movement flares up.

Now, what is the significance of the demand for political democracy in a society where there is no private ownership of the means of production? One of our movement's positions is that consistent democratization involves respect for all rights; and for us Marxist socialists, that implies a revolution not only in political rights, but also in social relations. The movement's present failure to take up the question of the right to strike amounts to depriving the working class of its basic weapon and its most essential right. Moreover, the right to strike is a kind of guarantee of all other rights — which is precisely why the Soviet Constitution lists nearly every right except the right to strike. As long as this has not been achieved, all the other rights will remain effectively suspended.

Ours is truly a paradoxical situation. We still have to make our bourgeois-political revolution even though we have already destroyed private property: it is history back to front. The abolition of private property was not enough to improve our society, for exploitation is still with us, chauvinism is continually developing, and police terror is still practised. We have all the basic features of the fascist state, and that is why we are faced with the problem of a revolution to conquer the rights specific to democracy. Yet this is not a revolution that will secrete a *bourgeois* social and political structure, but something quite different and even unprecedented. What name shall we give to it? Since the term socialism has been discredited among our people, some prefer to speak of 'scientific democracy', 'scientific planning', 'a scientific model', 'scientific communism' or 'Christian humanism'. But it does not really matter. However we call it, the opening of a democratic process will carry us closer to socialism as it was understood by Marx. (This is not to say that everything Marx wrote is correct, or that he said the last word on everything. For example, he wrote nothing about the importance of the national question — which, as Lenin grasped shortly before his death, is perhaps the fundamental question in the USSR.)

Karol would have liked me to end on an optimistic note, but I am afraid I have no grounds for optimism. If we suffered a defeat at the Belgrade Conference, it was not only because the western powers decided to respect the status quo in the Warsaw Pact countries, out of fear that a revolutionary upheaval in the East might produce a similar upheaval in the West (where there is a much worse crisis than in the USSR). That is indeed the reason why the policy of détente has become a new Munich. But in a way, we have also been betrayed by the forces of the western Left. They did not want to struggle resolutely for the principles of Helsinki, for détente as it is understood by someone like Sakharov; well before Helsinki, in fact, Sakharov had formulated the idea of a common struggle for peace and technological progress, against hunger, and for a solution to the problems of humanity as a whole. I have no reason to be optimistic about the fate of my dissident comrades when the western Left also has a certain responsibility for what is happening. Nor are there grounds for optimism concerning the more distant future. Nevertheless, I am personally hostile to pessimism, since it can only disarm us. Even if there were only one slight chance of overcoming the crisis, we would still have to fight; and those pessimists who say we have already lost are in effect disarming us before the struggle has been waged to a conclusion. From my standpoint of 'optimistic pessimism', I see only two alternatives before us: either thermo-nuclear war and complete destruction of our planet — and my country does seem to be taking this road towards death, demoralization and the final impasse; or else a more humane society issuing out of the cul-de-sac in which our entire civilization is now entrapped. Even if the West may suffer less, since classical capitalism is better than the state capitalism which resembles fascism in many respects, the deadly tendency to destruction exists here as well as over there. I am optimistic simply because we shall either perish or find the way out. And one thing is certain: either we go forward together or we go down together.

Function and Political Importance of the Churches in Eastern Europe

Giorgio Girardet

Giorgio Girardet, a pastor of the Waldensian church, was formerly editor of the magazines Presenza cristiana *and* Nuovi Tempi. *From 1961 to 1966 he was director of the ecumenical centre Agape. He is now a member of the editorial board of the leftist Catholic-Protestant weekly* Com-Nuovi Tempi.

The political function of the church and of Christians in contemporary society is rarely the object of study. This observation applies especially to the East European countries. A few historical facts are generally registered, the persecutions and harassment, for example. It is noted that the Christian groupings resisted and survived. But with the exception of the ecclesiastical organizations themselves, which are obviously attentive to this situation, it is rare that questions are raised about the social role and political function in the East European countries of the vast sectors of the population who profess Christianity. (There are, of course, many studies of the policy of the Vatican, but this is only one aspect of the problem, important as it may be). It is therefore difficult to know where to begin. This contribution, even more than the others at this conference, will be provisional. It proposes simply to offer a few guidelines for investigation.

If we are to understand the political importance of Christians and the churches in the post-revolutionary societies, we must begin with two preliminary considerations, both of them rather obvious. The first is that the roots of the present situation lie deep in the history of the various countries and in the relations, which differ from country to country, that have been established between the people and the religious institutions over the centuries. Of all the aspects of life in Eastern Europe, religion has undergone the fewest changes during the past several decades. In fact, apart from the numerical erosion and the change in the nature of relations between church and state, there has scarcely been any change at all. Culturally, religious life constitutes a window on the past. It is consequently impossible to understand the present religious situation in these countries without taking account of this heritage of the past. Furthermore, and this is the second of my preliminary remarks, there are immense economic, social, historical, and cultural differences among what we refer to as 'the East European countries'. To begin with, the boundaries of 'Eastern Europe' in the sense in which we are using the term were drawn by the advance of the Soviet army at the end of the Second World War. In reality, however, this 'East' contains two regions: a section of 'Mitteleuropa' (East Germany, Czechoslovakia, and Hungary), from which a semi-colonial expansion towards the East went on for centuries, and a more properly oriental area composed of peoples who have struggled for a national identity of their own, first against Asian and later western pressure. This region includes Poland, the Baltic countries, Russia, Romania, Bulgaria, and, to some extent, Yugoslavia.

These two premises compel us to dwell a moment on the diversity of the religious situations in these various countries.

The situation in the central European sector may be defined as western in type. There are many different sects and a long lay and secular tradition. The religious wars, which continued up to the seventeenth century, and the industrialization of the nineteenth century produced a high degree of secularization. Here, as in other western countries, the churches developed concurrently with capitalist society, fulfilling a variety of functions of mediation between past and present, between aristocratic classes in crisis and transformation and emerging entrepreneurial classes. The churches developed the cultural agility and capacity for adaptation that have characterized them, to varying degrees, for the past two centuries. There have been such divergent trends as Pietism, the various forms of modernism, social Christianism, and the *aggiornamento* of the Vatican Council. It is thus understandable that in these countries the churches have evinced a relatively greater capacity to adapt and respond to the challenge of 'real socialism'.

The situation in the more properly oriental area is quite different. Here again, there are variations from country to country, Poland and Yugoslavia representing two transitional cases, although for different reasons. In the countries in which the Orthodox tradition holds sway the course of development has been very different from that in the West. In these countries the October Revolution and the Soviet advance caught the masses (apart from very narrow elite circles open to western influence) in the midst of a feudal-agrarian epoch; in other words, under a social system in which religious tradition played a significant role of social mediation and cultural expression and was not necessarily antagonistic to the interests, even the material interests, of the subject classes. It is true, for example, that the Russian Orthodox hierarchy was wholly dominated by the Tsar and defended his interests, a fact which must be emphasized if we are to understand the development of the anti-religious struggle in the years following the October Revolution. But it is equally true that during previous centuries the close relations between the church and the people had constituted an element of real or potential opposition which the Tsars had been concerned to control. Indeed, it must be borne in mind that the Orthodox church, unlike the western, was able to maintain close ties to the popular masses through a number of its intellectual personnel: monks, hermits, married secular clergy. These strong popular links, combined with the church's lack of interest in political and social commitment in the strict sense of the word, lent Orthodox spirituality great internal cohesion. At crucial moments this was transformed into de facto political strength. Orthodox theologians thus followed a path different from that of their western colleagues, whether Catholic or Protestant. Whereas the latter, over the centuries, were often concerned primarily with mediating between philosophical thought and religious tradition, reinterpreting the latter according to the exigencies of the epoch, Orthodox theologians have sought primarily to lend dignity and, to some extent, universality, to the religious traditions and sentiments of the people.

To this must be added the several centuries long tradition of passive resistance by the Orthodox communities to Turkish and Tatar domination. This led on the one hand to the fortification of the church's links with the oppressed population and on the other to the development of the more unusual, almost esoteric, characteristics of the cultural and liturgical tradition. These characteristics reflect a defensive posture rooted in the historic consciousness of these churches, which created the pre-conditions for survival in a hostile environment.

It was with this historic background that the churches and the Christians confronted the challenge of the October Revolution and, a generation later, the revolutions carried out from above by the Soviet occupation. Obviously, they faced this confrontation not purely as Christians but also and more importantly as citizens of their countries called upon to construct a new society and, for this very reason, drawn into a radical process of economic and social change. There is no doubt that emerging sectors of the popular masses, above all the working class, experienced the October Revolution primarily as a liberation, just as there is no doubt that the new people's democracies after 1945 favoured the workers at the expense of the bourgeoisie. At the same time, the play of social forces unleashed by the revolution and by the policy of the leaders set in motion a profound process of social transformation which inevitably influenced traditions and the way the masses interpreted reality. It is here that some of the problems arise which are generally not dealt with by students of the history of the church in Eastern Europe. For example, it must be asked whether (and if so to what extent) there was a cleavage along religious lines between supporters of the new society and those who remained tied to the old regime economically or psychologically. The upper echelons of the Russian hierarchy were undoubtedly linked to the Tsarist system; but does this mean that the peasants' attachment to religious traditions necessarily expressed an attachment to the Tsar? Or was the converse perhaps the case, that religious attachment was reflected politically in some form of nostalgia for the old regime? We may also suppose that the process of rapid modernization and industrialization, with the consequent social mobility, acted as a powerful factor for secularization, as in the western countries. For the first few decades after the revolution, that is. But later — and this is a second problem — when society settled into new patterns and found itself smothered by rising bureaucratism, there was a reversal of the trend: the pre-revolutionary past acquired a new importance, and so did national identity and religious attachment. Can these two phenomena be linked?

An overall assessment of the situation of the churches and the Christians in Eastern Europe would require a detailed examination of the policies of the various governments towards the churches and religion itself, an analysis of the response of the ecclesiastical hierarchy, the attitude of the religious masses (not always identical to that of the hierarchy), and the international dimension of the problem too. But this would require a much more extensive presentation than is possible here. Hence I shall limit myself to a few observations.

1. Until the Second World War, the policy of the USSR towards religion, officially inspired by Lenin, consisted essentially in repression and persecution. This was followed by a period of strictly supervised liberty marked by continued persecution and tight control of the hierarchy but greater tolerance for cultural-religious manifestations among the people, even on a mass scale (pilgrimages, for example). This was combined with bureaucratic attempts to control the organizational apparatus and internal communications systems of the churches, a policy which inevitably drove the church into opposition. Paradoxically — or perhaps not all that paradoxically — the government favoured the most traditional expressions of religious piety and was hostile to attempts at cultural or theological modernization. In a recent pamphlet 35,000 copies of which are being distributed by the Leningrad section of the 'Council for the Propagation of Scientific Atheism' one N S Gordienko takes a firm position against what he calls the 'modernistic tendencies' of the Russian church. (This document was reproduced in full in *Idoc International*, number 5, July 1975.)

2. The USSR suggested (or perhaps insisted) that its political analysis of religious affairs be applied in the other Comecon countries. Indeed, periodic gatherings of the officials charged with religious matters by the various governments are held in order to define common policies. Nevertheless, there are often differences in approach, either because of the experience of the USSR, which cannot be considered positive even from the Soviet standpoint, or because of the more or less active role of the churches (or some sectors of them) in the anti-fascist struggle during the war. In some countries repressive measures, including nationalization of church property, were taken after the seizure of power. Real clashes occurred only as a response to the tough anti-communist policy of the

Catholic Church under Pope Pious XII. Here one may mention the cases of Berán in Czechoslovakia, Mindszenty in Hungary, and Stepinac in Yugoslavia. This is where the international dimension of the problem comes in, as well as the response to the anti-communist policy of the West, in which the Catholic church played a major role, utilizing its hierarchical supremacy over the churches of these countries.

3. The responses of the church organizations varied greatly from country to country and also changed with the passage of time. We have seen variations ranging from more or less forced collaboration to semi-underground opposition. There are cases of loyalism based on a position of strength, like the Orthodox church in Romania; of latent opposition, also from positions of strength, as in Poland; of prudence tainted with conformism, as in Russia itself. Among Protestant circles in central Europe an attitude of critical collaboration developed, after two decades of crisis, re-examination, and even passive resistance; the work of the Czech theologian Josef Hromadka, who died in 1970, was of particular importance here.

4. In the East, as in the West, the attitudes and religious sentiments of the Christian masses depend very little on the immediate actions of their respective church organizations or theologies. Reliable information and even mere statistics are difficult to come by; it is often the case that neither the state nor the church has any interest in divulging such facts, or even in compiling them accurately. It does appear, however, that the religious presence is numerically and culturally significant, although it affects only a minority of the population. Apart from Romania, which reports a religious affiliation of 95-97 per cent, and Poland, 95 per cent, the percentages in the other countries range from 68 (East Germany) to about 33. As may be seen, these are significant figures, probably not substantially different from those of the western countries. Thus, it does not appear that religion tends automatically to disappear with progress towards communism. It must be acknowledged that thirty or even sixty years of propaganda, anti-religious teachings in the schools, and repressive measures have not had catastrophic effects on religious affiliation. There has, of course, been some erosion, but no landslide. May we therefore affirm that the anti-religious policy of the USSR must be counted a failure?

5. On the other hand, one may reasonably ask whether the phenomenon of secularization does not develop in parallel manner East and West, in accordance with a similar social dynamic. The

countries of Eastern Europe have undergone a process of profound social transformation and, naturally, industrialization. Moreover, the working class in these countries probably occupied a predominant position, or even one of hegemony, during the initial years after the seizure of power, and the working class, even well before the October Revolution, was never especially religious. Do these factors, along with the pressure of the bureaucracy, suffice to explain the decline in religious affiliation in these countries?

6. During the past decade there has been talk of a revival of religious interest and a rise (or greater openness) of religious dissidence in Russia. There seem to be similar developments in other countries. Relevant government statistics in Bulgaria have reported that whereas 33 per cent of the population declared themselves 'religious' in the broad sense in 1968, the figure had risen to 48 per cent in 1972. It may be supposed that one of the reasons for this revival is the conformist and monotonous character of official culture, the absence of discussion and lack of imagination. The traditional religious world, closely linked to the current reassessment of the national past, thus manages to exert some attractive power.

7. A special case is presented by the evangelical Baptists, the number of whose churches and members has soared precisely during these sixty years of repression. And it is precisely through the vehicle of the Baptist Union that the only organization of dissent commanding a structure and mass base of its own has arisen, although this obviously involves a small minority of the population, perhaps half a million or so. During the early sixties a formation called the Initiative Group was founded; it accused the leadership of the Baptist Union of yielding to government pressure and abandoning its evangelical mission. This group then fostered organized dissent, through a network of clandestine communities. Even though entire Christian communities have been driven underground, and despite the repression, this movement continues to exist as an organized reality defending those of its members who have been tried and sentenced. It has even moved to the counter-offensive, smuggling appeals for respect for human rights to the West. This is far and away the most significant manifestation of organized dissent, and it assumes some objective political importance, even though the Baptist (and Pentecostal) dissidents reject any explicit political discourse and ask only for freedom of religious profession and the right to religious education for their children.

In conclusion, we may ask what the political significance of the church and the Christians may be in the countries of 'real' socialism.

From the standpoint of the ruling forces and official ideology, the churches and religious sentiments represent a dangerous source of conflict. It is probable that the functionaries charged with public order are seriously concerned about the existence of these institutional structures, which have their own mass base, strong internal cohesion, and widespread organization. Indeed, they are the only organizations the rulers cannot control directly. Moreover, these churches communicate and come to agreements among themselves through a code-like language based on biblical or liturgical references. In some countries, East Germany for example, the churches also command some economic power. Here the facility of their contacts with the West and the impressive influx of material goods they receive from West Germany objectively make them a not inconsequential political force, despite the caution and loyalism of their leaders. This is also the case in Poland, where the power and mass base of the Catholic church constitute a political problem of prime importance. It is difficult to govern Poland today without some consensus with the Catholic church. Thus, under a highly centralized system which has managed to monopolize all means of mediation and now controls the entire apparatus of communications, in countries in which neither trade unions nor any kind of associations are able to act with the slightest independence, these churches, with their great cultural prestige, mass base, organizational structures, independent economic resources, and international ties, still remain. There is only one phenomenon comparable to religion, and that is the national question, the other great unresolved superstructural political problem.

Moreover, the religious organizations are part of a sort of International *sui generis* whose power bases and ideological roots lie in the West. This means that the repression of church members is immediately known in the West and generates greater emotion. It also means that the opinions of ecclesiastical leaders have greater credibility and influence than those of the politicians themselves. Then there is the policy of the Vatican, which defends the cause and rights of the Christians to some extent, although, in accordance with its traditions, it tends to concern itself primarily with the hierarchy.

Finally, the churches can become (even against the will of their leaders) a natural place of refuge for potential opposition, a sort of reservoir and *impluvium* for all those who are discontented or seeking alternatives.

It may be that the scions of the new intelligentsia and the peasantry will someday see the church as the place where a new class alliance against the present power structures can be forged.

These are some of the reasons why communist militants in the West should be concerned with this question. There is no doubt that the churches in the East European countries, more than in the West, represent a force of tradition turned towards the past and objectively conservative, with the possible exception of the Russian Baptists and some tiny minorities of 'progressive' Christians. The churches constitute a conservative reality in the heart of societies which are essentially conservative inasmuch as they are ossified. What if these two conservatisms ultimately converge? If, sometime in the future, the fragility of the economic situation, a great international crisis, or the emergence of a strong opposition induces the present rulers to seek allies in their efforts to maintain the status quo, where could they turn with greater success than to the churches? Indeed, this is just what Stalin did in 1941 and what Gierek has been doing since 1970. And it would be strange indeed if the Vatican's policy in the East were determined by a strategy opposite to that which it applies in the West.

Hence the political necessity, even in the West, of not underestimating the utopian dimension of the Christian message, which has succeeded, in every century since its origin, in stimulating contradictions within the ecclesiastical establishment. This utopian ferment is not at all absent in the East and central European countries, although it is difficult for it to find expression because of the repression, often the joint repression, by the state and the ecclesiastical authorities. It is sufficient to recall the work of Hromadka or the achievements of the early days of the Christian Peace Conference, which was under the leadership of progressive theologians for several years. It was for this reason, and not purely because of the Prague 'normalization', that the conference was brought to heel. But there is ferment in the air, and this is one of the reasons why it is important for Christians that socialists in the western countries seek to establish links with those churches and religious groups which are moving, or would like to move, in the same direction in the East European countries.

In a political conference like this, of course, the Christian comrades do not ask for support in their work of testimony for Jesus Christ. But they do ask for recognition of the importance, in the current political situation, of a Christianity experienced in its utopian dimension, as a possible method of breaking the front of nostalgia and conformism now prevalent among broad sectors of the churches in Eastern Europe. Here again, as is unexpectedly happening in the West, the Christians and the churches can contribute to the construction of a new and more human society.

'The Churches: That is not the Whole Story'

Leonid Plyushch

I am all in favour of dialogue between Marxists and Christians, so long as it is honest. In the Soviet Union, such dialogue is like that between a man wielding a newspaper and another wielding a stick. The Christians may be able to speak, but the communists' big stick is nevertheless waved at them. Not only Christians but also we Marxists fear that those who are proposing dialogue have only put their stick aside for a brief time. Although I have no wish to criticize the Christians, I am afraid that I shall have to do so in this contribution. I should like to make clear a few important points concerning the Church in the Soviet Union.

Unlike the Catholic Church in the West, Russian Orthodoxy has been tied to the state ever since the time of Peter the Great, and perhaps even beyond. There was absolutely no separation between lay and ecclesiastical power; and the fact that the Church has always been subordinated to the existing power has given rise to quite a few ambiguities. The current Patriarch has adopted positions which could almost be described as 'lay atheism': the positions of the KGB. The dialogue between the Pope and the Patriarch is something very peculiar indeed, rather like detente between the devil and Jesus Christ. Let me give you a few examples. The Ukrainian Church was completely annihilated before the war, despite the fact that the Bolsheviks initially supported it in order to divide the Russian

Orthodox Church. Ukrainian Catholicism was destroyed in turn after the war. In Lithuania, the KGB tried to separate the Catholic Church from the Vatican, but it did not succeeed. It then turned to the Vatican and asked for its help. Now that this has been granted, the Vatican ratifies bishops nominated by the KGB. The question arises as to why the Vatican acts in this way. I do not agree with Girardet when he says that the Vatican thereby gives assistance to believers. It does in Poland and some other countries, but in the Soviet Union it is sacrificing Catholics — not to mention the situation of Protestants and followers of Orthodoxy.

The plight of Protestants and of the Georgian Church is truly appalling; and frightful persecutions are organized against Pentecostalists and Baptists.

There are two kinds of believers: those who do and those who do not bow down before the existing power; or in other words, the opportunists or collaborators, and those who do not collaborate, the true Christians. Pastor Vins is among such true Christians, and that is why he is in prison: all honest believers are persecuted. At the same time, the Communist Party regards the Orthodox Church as the lesser evil and therefore prefers believers to belong to it. That is a factor of considerable significance.

Baptists are being killed and persecuted in the most cynical manner: I think it extremely important to solidarize with them. Only when they show solidarity with, and support for believers in the Soviet Union will Italian Communists have shown that they are seeking a real dialogue.

I do not think it is correct to say that religious feelings are on the wane in the Soviet Union; on the contrary, since 1956 they have grown within both the literary and the scientific intelligentsia. Speaking as a Marxist and atheist, I regard the present situation as positive. For despite the utter moral devastation that gradually set in after 1956, the quest for a human ideal remains alive, whether it takes the form of a return to Christ or of a return to the roots of Marxism.

I would like to contrast the role of the Polish Church with that of the official Church in the Soviet Union. As far as I am aware, the Catholic Church acts in Poland as it does in Chile — that is, in a very Christian manner. However, the same cannot be said of the Russian Orthodox Patriarch, nor unfortunately of the Vatican.

I also wanted to mention the conflict between the tradition of Church submission to the state and the situation that has arisen in recent years. Like every official religion, the Russian Church goes so far as to spread falsehoods: I have myself seen the contempt shown for Baptists, Jews and the Ukrainian Catholic Church, as well as the way in which religious feelings are trampled underfoot even within the Russian Orthodox Church itself. But on the other hand, there are individuals like Yakunin and Reghelson who are honest priests of the Orthodox Church. That is all I wanted to add to Pastor Girardet's account.

Intellectuals and the Contradictions of Existing Socialism

Franz Marek

Franz Marek joined the Austrian CP in 1934. An exile in France, where he took part in the Resistance, he was captured by the Nazis and condemned to death. He was expelled from the Austrian CP in 1969 for having opposed the Soviet invasion of Czechoslovakia. Between 1946 and 1969 he was principal editor of the review Weg und Ziel. *Now he edits the monthly review,* Tagebuch. *He is the author of* Philosophy of the Revolution *as well as numerous articles on Stalinism.*

I would like to speak concretely about the role of organic intellectuals in the eastern oppositions. Emphasis has correctly been laid on the specific nature of the lessons we can learn from the Polish workers' revolts of 1970 and 1976. We should hold in great esteem the Polish KOR's courageous attempt to bridge the gulf that has separated workers and intellectuals since the events of 1968 and 1970. But unfortunately, we have no assurance that their attempt will succeed.

From what we know, even some workers whose defence has been taken up by the committee still have certain reservations about intellectuals. I have the impression that things are much better in Czechoslovakia: Pelikan will talk about this shortly. There, Charter 77 has also been signed by some workers, and apparently it has had a great resonance in the factories. Events have shown that Karel Košik, the Czechoslovak philosopher, was right when he said that intellectual freedoms are not just freedoms for intellectuals. It really is the case that the most elementary, left-wing and revolutionary demand in Eastern Europe is the demand for freedom of opinion and expression.

That is what Charter 77 and Rudolf Bahro have taken up. Unfortunately, Bahro's book has not yet been translated into Italian or French, but it contains the most profound analysis of the eastern systems to have come out of those countries.[1] To be sure, it is marked by its national origin, and we should be wary of generalizations when talking about any aspect of the countries in the East. For example, one can still find people in the German Democratic Republic who consider themselves and who may rightly be considered as Marxists. That is much more difficult in Warsaw, and almost impossible in Moscow. Bahro has come from that milieu, marked by Marxism as it is taught in his country: he knows nothing of Gramsci, and his interpretation of Marxism is determinist in character. Still, his work is a huge step forward in the context of the existing deep crisis; it is of great importance for this gathering. The author goes beyond all previous critiques, developing the problematic inherent in the relationship between intellectual and manual labour, as well as in egalitarianism. This is the first time that someone in the East has attempted an analysis starting out from such values and criteria. That is why I sometimes ask myself: 'Every week the papers inform us about a new statement by Sakharov, who lives in conditions of partial freedom — and, of course, I wish him to be as free as possible. But how can we explain the near-total silence about Bahro? He is still behind bars, yet no one talks about him.' Perhaps this gathering ought to launch an international campaign to demand the immediate release of this courageous communist and true Marxist.

I would like to mention a serious fact, which worries me a great deal. These last years, there has been much talk about the brain-drain — about the intellectuals, scientists and doctors who have left Africa, Asia or Latin America for the United States. There are now more Latin American doctors in the USA than in Latin America. Well, we now have what could be called an East-West brain-drain. First, there are those who are forced to leave their country: the intellectuals, poets and technicians who have left the GDR in such number that some people have even spoken of a haemorrhage of German poetry. Everyone knows of the Budapest School, but there will be very few of them left after Agnes Heller goes. Apart from this phenomenon, which narrows the field of action of the opposition and organic intellectuals, we have been witnessing another very disturbing and perhaps crucial phenomenon: namely, the whole mass of brilliant intellectuals, musicians, composers and mathematicians who silently leave their country. 'We don't need geniuses, we need loyal citizens,' the Russian police once said to a world-famous mathematician.

This emigration is taking on quite disturbing proportions. Until recently there was a Budapest school of structural linguistics (the Hungarians are born linguists, given that no one can understand their language): none of its members is there any longer. Thus, although Hungary is thought of as the brightest spot in the socialist camp, it too is experiencing a brain-drain. The Czechoslovak poet, František Halaš, has written that there are moments when speech becomes tomorrow's betrothed: so it is worrying to see those who anticipate the future in words leaving their countries, the countries of Eastern Europe.

One last remark about a problem which has already been raised: the national problem. In my view, the dominant ideology in Eastern Europe is nationalism. First, the Russian chauvinism in which both Brezhnev and Solzhenitsyn meet up — we have very bitter discussions with some of our Russian friends, who show how far anti-Chinese instruction has touched even our friends. Then there is the anti-Russian nationalism to be found at sports events, for example; that is just one point in a problematic concerning the Russian empire as a whole. Sometimes people talk about the Crimea, because Stalin robbed the Tatars of their lands and their native country. But more generally, it is through the Russian empire that nations endowed with a long and eventful history have become what Engels called 'unhistoric nations'. The Ukraine has as many inhabitants as Italy, yet what is its identity? Our Russian friends tell us that there are some magnificent poets in Estonia. We cannot say; all we know is that these are 'unhistoric nations'. This is a very serious problem, which may have highly dangerous consequences. The fact that these

60

societies will thereby undergo major crises sometimes arouses great optimism in us. But national contradictions are always fraught with grave dangers.

NOTE

1. Rudolf Bahro, *The Alternative in Eastern Europe*, London 1978.

No More Mistakes Like Dubcek's

Jiri Pelikan

Jiri Pelikan became a member of the Czechoslovak CP in 1939, joined the Resistance and was arrested by the Gestapo in 1940. Formerly the director of Czechoslovak television and a member of parliament, he took an active part in the Prague Spring and was elected to the CP Central Committee at the Fourteenth Party Congress, held in secret just after the invasion. Deprived of his job, excluded from the Party, stripped of his position as a member of parliament and of his citizenship, he was granted political asylum in Italy in 1968. He is active in the Czechoslovak socialist opposition and edits the revue Listy. *In addition he has written an autobiography,* If They Kill Me *and a second book,* Socialist Opposition in Eastern Europe: The Czechoslovak Example, *London 1976.*

First of all, I would like to thank the *Manifesto* comrades for their initiative in calling this conference, which has enabled us to meet comrades from the Italian and western Left, as well as other comrades from Eastern Europe. To tell the truth, I as a Czechoslovak Communist at first thought that the initiative should have come from the PCI or other communist parties, given that the 1968 'new course' brought us very close to these parties. However, I do not want to start blaming anyone; the important thing is to open the discussion. At this early stage there may well be a clash of opinions: the distance between those coming from the East and from the western Left is too great for the problems to be immediately understood in the same way. Nor is this just a question of political information. The main problem arises from the weight of personal experience on comrades who have lived through thirty years of 'real' or 'existing' socialism — experience which is not shared by those for whom socialism is still only an objective.

During recent years, each of us has followed his own course. In Czechoslovakia, we have concentrated on the internal opposition struggle, convinced that socialist change can come about in the East only through such opposition. We do not think we can be liberated by western governments or by any other external force. For its part, the western Left has continued to stress that revolution in the West would be the most powerful factor in changing the status quo. Now, both these positions are correct. We ourselves learnt from the bitter experience of 1968 that it is impossible to go beyond Stalinism or build a genuinely socialist society within the confines of a single country. Such changes must take place in several countries at once, both in the West and in Eastern Europe.

Why then has the western Left shown so much hesitation with regard to oppositional forces in Eastern Europe and to exiles coming from those countries?

Rossana Rossanda has already spoken of our situation as disturbing allies who cannot find decisive support from any quarter. The very fact that we are socialists and Marxists forces us *both* to raise a number of problems and doubts stemming from our experience *and* to be concerned that the western Left should not repeat the mistakes which we made during the construction of socialism and a new society in the East.

I can well appreciate that the western Left cannot understand why exiles from the Soviet Union are not like the first political exile, Leon Trotsky, who arrived ten years after the October Revolution still subscribing to his old ideas. Those who leave today belong to a generation which has known socialism only in its Stalinist form, and they subscribe to the so-called bourgeois freedoms characteristic of liberal ideology. We must all understand the grave danger that many such exiles and internal oppositionists, encountering incomprehension on the part of the Left, will be driven into becoming a tool of the Right.

Now, unlike the Soviet Union and other countries, Czechoslovakia did experience a mass movement: the Prague Spring. The western Left does not seem to me to have yet fully grasped the scope of this experience. I see it as a kind of Paris Commune, in the sense that, for the first time, socialist transformations took place in a developed country with the same economic structure and political traditions as those of western countries. No doubt our own errors were among the reasons for our isolation, and there will be other occasions on which these can be discussed. But it is precisely because the masses went through this eight-month experience that the regime of 'normalization' is today unable to convince people that the Prague Spring was a counter-revolution.

We posed to the western Left a problem which neither Marx nor Lenin could foresee: how to initiate socialist changes when the first socialist revolution took place in the weakest country of the imperialist chain (Russia), which has nevertheless become an economic and military super-power? That country might defend the revolutions in certain other countries, but there is a risk that, in defending them, it will contaminate them with the deformations arising from its own experience. I am convinced that, just as the Soviet authorities could not tolerate the socialist and popular movement of the new course [in Czechoslovakia — Ed.], so they will not be able to tolerate a future experience of the same type — whether it be in Italy, France, Spain, Portugal or elsewhere in the West. Among the obvious reasons for this is the fact that such a development would have major consequences inside the East European countries themselves. Here lies the great weakness of that section of the Left which speaks the language of diplomacy: 'The Soviet comrades will understand in the end ...' Dubcek, too, continually said in 1968 that the Soviet comrades would eventually understand that our actions were in the interests of socialism. But that was a serious mistake on his part: right from the beginning, he should rather have prepared for the inevitable, even if temporary, clash with the Soviet bureaucracy. Such a clash cannot be avoided if you want to build a really different kind of socialism — like that to which we aspired in Czechoslovakia or which is projected in Italy, France, Spain and elsewhere.

I would now like to answer the question posed by Rossanda. Which social bloc, she asked, is today capable of converting the dissident movement into a political force in the East? For us, this is indeed the key question. There can be no doubt that the great majority of citizens are discontented, and that what is called dissidence really does exist. But it is dissidence in a very general sense of the term, affecting above all artistic and scientific layers. And only very recently, in Czechoslovakia and Poland, have people tried very cautiously to bridge the gap between dissidence, on the one hand, and protests and political opposition, on the other. There are also, so to speak, heretical truths: for example, when comrades have to ask themselves whether it is necessary to create an illegal communist party or a revolutionary party. We cannot wait for a new Khrushchev bearing new concessions that will allow progress to be made. In Czechoslovakia and Poland, the Left has come to the conclusion that liberalization cannot be expected from above — from the political establishment. Although that may once have been possible, it is no longer so after the great purges. (In Czechoslovakia, for example, 500,000 Communists were expelled from the Party.) The only victories we shall see are those which are won through rank-and-file pressure and oppositional struggle. Where then are the forces necessary to this end?

Leonid Plyushch said that the difference between the Soviet Union and Poland lies in the lower degree of working-class activity in the Soviet Union. In Czechoslovakia, too, as Franz Marek pointed out, the main force to have appeared is represented by progressive intellectuals. However, I would like to stress that this is not an elite of intellectuals dissatisfied with their personal predicament. In every newly-emerging situation — for example, the resistance to fascism — intellectuals have the capacity and skills to express certain problems specific to the popular masses. It is because the latter recognize themselves in dissident plays or songs that cultural dissidence is an important element in laying the ground for political opposition. In Eastern Europe, I can see only one way to create a truly political force which would oblige the ruling group to make concessions: namely, unity of the working class, intellectuals and the youth.

The youth is today a completely unknown yet very important social force. In Czechoslovakia, for example, young people who did not experience the Prague Spring but who have suffered the effects of normalization are now making their opposition known to the regime in a number of ways: through demonstrations or protests at pop concerts, and through a variety of non-conformist attitudes. They do not yet have an ideology: they are disillusioned with the CP, saying that the communists capitulated to Soviet aggression. In any case, they do not have a right-wing ideology, but seek to base themselves on something completely new which they have not yet found. There is also a Christian component. As comrade Girardet rightly pointed out, more than one current exists among the Catholics and Protestants: there are those who are prepared to collaborate with the regime and those who are opposed to collaboration; right-wing elements and progressives.

We shall be able to get results only if we unite all progressive forces around a programme — a programme whose main content, as Marek said, is the demand for the national sovereignty and independence to which the masses are so deeply attached. Everything also hinges on international solidarity. Comrade Kavin, who has only recently left Czechoslovakia, will give you his account in a moment. But I can also mention a number of messages from comrades inside Czechoslovakia: they show that, during January and February, the Eurocommunist parties won much support through their protests against the repression which befell the Charter 77 signatories; but that their popularity has been declining since the Madrid summit — from which the opposition may have expected too much — while that of President Carter is clearly growing. We should have the courage to admit the truth: Carter's popularity has risen not only among petty-bourgeois and middle layers but even among the popular masses; and this growth is due to the fact that he has been saying things against Brezhnev which the Kremlin find unacceptable.

Why are European communists not doing as much? It seems to me that whatever happens, the Left must not remain indifferent. I know that things have changed a lot, and that a great deal of attention is being given to these problems. But it seems to be much easier to mobilize the Left for a mass demonstration against West Germany than it would be if the GDR were involved. There is much more hesitation in the latter case.

In his contribution, Karol asked us to be more optimistic. Well, I don't know if he is here at the moment, but I am certainly optimistic. I am convinced that very serious conflicts are brewing in Eastern Europe. The problem is to know how change can come about: through gradual reform or through popular explosions. One possibility is that there will then be a Left capable of elaborating a programme acceptable to the majority of citizens and of keeping things within certain limits. But if that does not happen, highly negative consequences will result. At any event, we have to prepare for that moment. I feel that, despite the tanks and the considerable weight of the establishment, discontent will continue to grow and soon break into the open. We must not allow ourselves to be caught unawares.

I agree with many points in Plyushch's contribution, but not with his argument that we were betrayed by the West and the western Left on the occasion of the Belgrade Conference. In my opinion, the fact that the Helsinki Conference managed to work out a text on the defence of civil rights was itself of positive significance. But we should have no illusions that the event was anything other than a conference of governments, a diplomatic encounter. If my memory serves me right, Solzhenitsyn stated after Helsinki: 'That was the funeral of Eastern Europe.' And we have seen that results can be achieved only if there is a force within these countries capable of using such (rather ambiguous) agreements as the pretext for a struggle over civil rights. Thus, Charter 77 and the Polish Committee were the offspring of, among other things, the Helsinki Conference. Thus we should be more realistic and not expect too much from events of this kind while above all, asking ourselves how we can use them as points of departure.

Charter 77: The Prelude to a Mass Movement

Ludvik Kavin

The Czechoslovak dissident Ludvik Kavin was a leader of the CP during the Prague Spring and was formerly a regional secretary of the Party. After he signed Charter 77 he was forced to leave the country.

In 1960, Novotny proclaimed Czechoslovakia a socialist republic. At the same time, he announced that the social basis of communism would be laid by 1965 and that we would be living in communist society by 1980 at the latest. The regime also declared that solving the problems of accommodation and social services was among its key objectives.

By 1961-62, we realized that these targets had been purely mythical. During the Sixties, we strived as communists to bring about new conditions utilizing the forces existing in the Party. Togliatti's Yalta Memorandum and the publication for the first time in Czechoslovakia of some of Gramsci's studies did a lot to carry us in this direction.

One of the major questions debated at the time was whether the Communist Party should hold a political monopoly in a socialist society. There was a still fairly strict division between those defining themselves as progressives and those who came forward as conservatives. The former, stressing the need for mass consensus, thought that the Party should play a leading role only through the force of its ideas; while the latter argued for leadership based on very firm authority, thereby backing the Party bureaucrats' desire to see everything decided within the Party.

Things stayed like that until 1968, when the progressive wing, supported by the population as a whole, won an overwhelming majority in the Party. Then we were sent the tanks, followed by the very harsh period of so-called normalization. Out of one-and-a-half million communists, 600,000 were expelled from the Party — including, of course, the best and most active members. Many of these were convinced that it would only be possible to fight normalization once the occupation forces had left. Time has proved those comrades right. We cannot speak of socialism in a country occupied by 500,000 Soviet soldiers (now down to 160,000), who enjoy extra-territorial rights on Czechoslovak soil. Nor can we speak of socialism where an ideologically sterile Communist Party is a mere transmission belt for the Soviet leadership; or where the Plan is a god whose priests do all in their power not to respect it.

Society must naturally be able to satisfy its material needs. But we cannot speak of socialism when, instead of genuine information, there is nothing but lies about the domestic situation and the international arena. During these last three years, awareness of the need to defend civil rights has spread more and more; and so we have come to Charter 77. The Charter is not a political organization in the real sense of the term, since any political organization would have been immediately liquidated by the police. But nor is it a group of intellectuals. Fifty per cent of its supporters are workers — especially young workers who were almost children at the time of the Prague Spring, and who, following the Soviet invasion, were deprived of all political expression. Only now, through Charter 77, can they begin

to formulate their demands. In my opinion, the Charter's importance lies precisely in its having introduced the younger generation to
political life. Also important is the fact that it evinces a vital interest
in civil rights. Charter 77 is a living movement, even though the
number of signatories (800) may give the impression of a limited
movement. Among its merits should also be mentioned its success in
re-animating the ideological life of our country.

Czechoslovakia is today living under repression: it needs international solidarity from all democratic forces, but above all from
those of the Left. In Czechoslovakia itself, the forms of resistance are
more and more numerous, the search for a solution to the crisis more
and more energetic. But the terror is growing all the more.

In this connection, I would like to describe the situation of the last
few months, basing myself on my personal experiences. This may
strike you as a kind of intellectual or family strip-tease, but it may be
useful in helping the Left to understand what everyday life is like in
the countries of 'actually existing socialism'. Well before the police
found out that I had signed Charter 77, my wife and I were
summoned, taken to the police station and subjected to a long
interrogation: even at that time, the police would continually summon
and interrogate all potential signatories. This was really preventive
questioning, the aim of which was to dissuade people from eventually
signing the Charter. In the course of interrogation, the police
discovered that I had celebrated the New Year in a country-house
together with some of my friends. They then brought along my
brother-in-law and other members of my family, and asked them
why they had lent us their country-house. They also asked them how
I had managed to become a factory-worker, when everyone knew
that I had been expelled from the Party and was not able to work.

Now, my brother-in-law is in the Party, and under the pressure of
nightly police visits, he asked us to clear out. Otherwise, he would
very quickly have lost his own job. But even though he is a Party
member, he shouted: 'You've no idea what a bunch of swine these
communists are! If you don't go away, we'll all be in danger!' In the
end we could no longer resist all this pressure, and so we decided to
quit the factory and the house and go to another village.

The secret police had so much time on their hands that they often
went to the kindergarten where we took our son. There they tried to
persuade the child-minders to boot him out, saying that he was the
son of a traitor. They also went to see the management of the theatre
where my wife worked, and they succeeded in getting her sacked.

I am telling you all this because it happens to virtually every Charter signatory. Of course, the fate of those under arrest has been the worst of all.

The Charter was made public on 1 January 1977, although it has never been officially published in Czechoslovakia. On 10 January, I spoke about it with the workers at my factory and gave them a copy of the text. Eighty per cent of the workers said they agreed with the document and that they were prepared to sign it. But at that time, we had not yet decided whether the text should be signed by the masses or only by a limited number of people.

Perhaps it was a mistake not to have immediately asked the workers to sign *en masse*. Anyway, a full-scale campaign soon began against the signatories, radically changing the atmosphere. From then on, everyone was afraid of losing his job or some minor privilege. It has to be recognized that although the regime is afraid, the workers are also afraid, since they have a lot of things to lose. Thus, each worker is dependent on his foreman or on a manager who, being a member of the local Party committee, also gives orders to the trade union. If a worker wants to go on holiday in Bulgaria, Hungary, Romania or another socialist country, he has to have a stamp from the trade-union organization. And that stamp is also required in order to buy clothes, a cupboard or a house, as well as to register the kids at school. The trade union has to give its approval, and the trade union can do nothing unless the factory manager agrees. I could give thousands of similar examples, but what really counts is that, in spite of everything, many workers are beginning to mobilize.

They mobilize around social and other problems. We should not overestimate this movement for civil rights, but it is beyond doubt that something is now moving. One of the Charter documents contains an analysis of the social situation in Czechoslovakia, criticising among other things the semblance of 'women's emancipation'. As a matter of fact, the authorities never let slip an opportunity to reassert that all women are emancipated in Czechoslovakia, because nearly every one is out at work. However, their average wage is less than a third of the man's, and one reason why they all work is because no worker is in a position to support the whole family on his wage alone. People also discuss ecological problems such as the building of nuclear power-stations; the intensive exploitation of uranium mines almost exclusively for export to the Soviet Union; the living conditions in villages where the mineral is extracted; and so on.

One new initiative, the founding of Jan Patocka University, is of particular importance. As far as I am aware, *Il Manifesto* is the only paper to have mentioned police aggression against this university. It was created for students who are prevented from continuing their studies as a measure of political persecution. People are now talking, for the same reasons, about forming independent trade unions. Unfortunately, we also know from the most recent interrogations that the police are already looking into this initiative. Violent clashes have occurred between young people and the police — most notably in Bescigne and Gdynie, where many were injured and some actually killed.

What would have seemed political fantasy a few months ago has now become a reality. And the situation is evolving in such a way that a Marxist, Christian and democratic opposition will soon be able to develop.

Finally, I would like to stress that, in my opinion, all hope and all possibilities of success for the opposition depend upon their links with the western Left. Like many comrades inside Czechoslovakia, I believe that the present movement is but the prelude to a *mass movement* that will develop the experiences gained in the struggle against fascism.

China: The Dialectic of Revolutionary Upsurges and Counter-revolutionary Waves

Edoarda Masi

Edoarda Masi, born in Rome in 1927, is a librarian and has been a student of Chinese language and history since 1953. She has taught modern Chinese literature at the Oriental Institute in Naples and spent ten months in China in 1957-58 and fourteen months there in 1976-77. From 1945 to 1958 she was a member of the Italian

Communist Party. Later, as a far-left militant, she served on the editorial boards of Quaderni Rossi *and* Quaderni Piacentini.

It is almost impossible to schematize the complex world of China according to criteria and parameters external to it. If I make the attempt anyway, it is only because I am aware of the importance of the process being initiated here. And it would be absurd not to take account of such a rich experience as China has had over the past twenty years, and especially over the past twelve years. To this day, despite many positive achievements, neither peaceful compromises nor frontal assaults have succeeded in halting the rise of an extremely powerful bureaucratic corps which now controls all society in practice.

China is a predominantly agricultural country. The bourgeois-democratic experience is completely alien to it. Nevertheless, the fundamental political and social problems posed in this country, ever more explicitly since the cultural revolution, are similar to the political and social problems of the other societies of our time, whether socialist, non-socialist, or semi-socialist. They are even similar, to a large extent, to those of the industrialized societies. In this talk I will concentrate on one central point: the close relationship between the growth of the authoritarian state and the conflict of interests of the various components and classes of society once private property in land and capital has disappeared. I will focus in particular on the great specific weight of the educated middle classes and the use that has been made of these classes in bolstering the authoritarian state. In illustrating these points, I will briefly mention some of the contradictions which have yet to be resolved and have contributed to causing the recent counter-revolutionary turn.

1. The contradiction between a system of leadership and management based on the transmission of decisions from a coordinating centre at the top to the various base units at the bottom and the demand by these base units for decision-making power and for a system of management based on direct and independent contact between the base units. The present top-down leadership has a three-fold root: the pyramid of power in the old China; Soviet-type centralism and state planning; the exigencies of up-to-date economic management of large-scale units and conglomerations with a view toward productive efficiency aimed at maximizing profit. The demand for autonomy of the base units, however, can be interpreted

in various ways. It may be seen as a demand reflecting narrow concern with the parochial clan or unit, complemented by the view that only direct inter-human relations are important and that these are more authentic the smaller the unit. It may be seen as analogous to the demand made by the individual bourgeois entrepreneur for autonomy and freedom of the enterprise. Finally, it may be seen as a demand for workers' self-management, with or without workerist or anarchistic overtones.

2. In the educational system, the contradiction between the need to train highly specialized elite personnel able to fill posts in the top-down planning and management system and the demand for culture and the elimination of hierarchy on the part of the masses.

This contradiction, which could be considered peculiar to a technologically and culturally backward country, is actually central in contemporary industrialized society, where the masses — who receive a basic general culture (secondary school) in addition to whatever technical-professional instruction may be required for production — are demanding unlimited access to higher education and rejecting functional education tailored to a particular mode of production, which imposes hierarchical and meritocratic discrimination.

3. The contradiction between the demand that all individuals enjoy unlimited exercise of all those liberties permitted by and necessary to the degree of culture and power they possess and the demand of those who are less educated, poorer, and have less or no power for the exercise of control over this power. Here again, this contradiction, although it arises in a society with a mandarin-type hierarchy, coincides in certain respects with a phenomenon now tormenting the industrialized countries as well.

I will limit myself to these three examples. It should be added, however, that political options in favour of one or the other pole of each of these contradictions are not decisive in and of themselves in determining whether the process set in motion as a consequence of those options will be liberating or oppressive. For example, the demand by the 'powerless and un-learned' for control over the 'powerful and learned' can turn into a suffocation of intellectual activity by rude and ignorant cadres actually detached from the rank and file they claim to represent. On the other hand, the demand by the learned and privileged for freedom and autonomy can turn into the more or less elitist or technocratic oppression of the uncultivated, through an alliance of mandarins and bureaucrats.

It would be difficult to ascribe the causes of these and other similar features of Chinese society purely to the absence of a bourgeois-democratic phase in Chinese history. The forms of power in all countries are linked to the past one way or another (Tsarist in Russia, Confucian in China, ragamuffin bourgeois in Italy, etc.). The substance, however, must be sought not in this specificity but in a more general political framework. It would seem to me equally erroneous to regard these contradictions as characteristic of non-socialist, or fake-socialist, society. In reality, they are characteristic of all societies of our epoch, socialist and non-socialist alike. Nevertheless, they are sharper and more central in Chinese society than in capitalist society. The hierarchical system, for example, is rigid, as is control over single individuals; but rebellion, when it does manage to rise to the surface, is radical, either in the form of the demand for individual autonomy or in the apparently opposite demand for egalitarianism against the hierarchy of bureaucrats.

I believe that in considering particular forms of society, one must first of all examine the social relations on which these forms arise. A complex of objective and subjective circumstances since the beginning of the cultural revolution and especially since the turn of the past year makes it quite clear that the bureaucratic regime in China is founded on the conflict of interest between various components and layers of society. The interests of the workers conflict with those of the peasants; even among the mass of peasants, there is no lack of cause for conflict, since their economic and cultural conditions are anything but homogeneous, especially from region to region. There have been virtually frontal clashes for about ten years now between workers and peasants on the one hand and the growing masses of learned (or at least somewhat educated) urban middle classes, the highly cultured minorities, and the scientists on the other.

The conflict between the elderly and the youth is also quite sharp. And the repression women have suffered lays the basis for a revolt which is inevitable, although it has not yet broken out. Unfortunately, there is not enough time to go into detail and I must limit myself to merely mentioning some of the problems. I shall cite only the passive resistance of a great number of teachers (except for the very youngest) and their sabotage of the innovations wrought by the cultural revolution. Many of them saw the entry of workers and peasants into the universities as a personal affront and a diminution of their own status, and they refused to seek out new methods of teaching adapted to these less cultivated youth. It is also true that the workers' propaganda squads in the schools often turned into cliques of indolent and annoying little bureaucrats.

The contradictions of Chinese society to which I have alluded are merely so many manifestations of these conflicts of economic, cultural, and power interests. The elimination of the landlords and private capitalists raised to prime importance the conflicts among other strata and components of society, which also exist under capitalism but appear secondary compared to the central confrontation between capital and the proletariat. The bureaucracy deforms these conflicts into the interplay of political factions. This or that individual or grouping falls from time to time, but the complex bureaucratic corps lives on, imitating the behaviour of an old and extremely clever ruling class. But this is only on the surface. All appearances to the contrary, the underlying reality is neither the interplay of bureaucratic ruling groups nor the internal dynamic within the political domain alone, but the interlacing and conflict of interests of the various social groups.

Can socialism discover forms that would enable such contradictions and even conflicts among the various components of society to be worked out within a system of guarantees, somehow analogous to the system the bourgeoisie established for certain social layers in its capital cities, but extended to the entire population? Back in the mid-fifties, Mao Tse-tung, in conflict with himself, set out to seek an answer to this question, but did not succeed. His approach was marked by a deep distrust of juridical-institutional guarantees (which are, however, included in the constitution and laws of the People's Republic of China, including the right to strike), unless they were accompanied by an incessant struggle by the weakest layers to make them effective. In reality, the guarantor of the institutions has always been the bureaucratic corps — which to a large extent is precisely the enemy that has to be fought. But no other vehicles by which to mediate the real conflicts of society have arisen. The cultural revolution, directed against the bureaucratic regime, uncovered these conflicts more dramatically than may have been anticipated by those who had supported and favoured it. Instead of a more or less united population in struggle against the bureaucrats, conflicts among the various components of the population erupted as soon as bureaucratic control was temporarily removed. This ultimately rendered the country completely ungovernable and led to the defeat of the revolution itself, as the bureaucrats were called upon to set things in order again.

The great wave of the cultural revolution, liberating though chaotic, was followed by a restoration of order, which has been taking root ever since 1972. The instances of violence, bloody clashes, and killings during the years of the cultural revolution were the work of groups organized against others in society; they were not the work of the state, which intervened only as mediator and peace-maker. During his lifetime, Mao used all the prestige he enjoyed to prevent any one section of the population from seizing the state apparatus in order to repress the people. And he sought to guarantee a certain room for manoeuvre for workers, communes and vanguard agricultural brigades, students, mass organizations of youth and women, and trade unions, which clung firmly to some of the conquests of the cultural revolution (the 'new socialist things') and struggled to reappropriate them when they seemed to be lost.

A certain equilibrium — with the left in a subordinate position, except in a few cities — was maintained through the coexistence of several factions within the party, factions representing the interests of the various components of society, albeit in a deformed manner. But it was a paralyzing equilibrium: the faction of order, the expression of the mass of the middle class supported by backward sectors of peasants and leaders, did not succeed in monopolizing absolute power, but it was strong enough to deprive the opposing faction, which expressed the forces and tendencies that had emerged from the cultural revolution, especially workers and youth, of any freedom of action. What is worse, the dominant faction imposed its own methods: the search for positions of power through control of sectors of the apparatus and the camouflaging of any living thought behind the meaningless jargon of doctrinaire discourse.

The tension, which lasted for years, created an intolerable atmos-phere, especially in the cities in which the struggle was sharpest, like Shanghai. The equilibrium was artificial and untenable, both for the social base and for the political factions, and was based largely on the personal prestige of a few old leaders (above all the duo Mao and Chou En-lai). The death of Mao marked a complete reversal of the political course. This was much more serious than the victory of one faction of the bureaucracy over another. It involved two important phenomena: first, an alliance between a patchwork of factions within the bureaucracy and some components of society designed to control the other components; and second, the transformation of the state into the representative of the interests of certain classes against the interests of the others.

This reversal of the political course has marked the end of control by workers and peasants (and youth) over the educated middle classes, the researchers, scientists, and technocrats who direct the Academy of Sciences, and a certain number of the old intellectuals; it is now these latter categories who control the workers and peasants. This operation is an ongoing and highly difficult one; it is impossible to say how it will end. The majority of people over forty years old in the urban middle classes sincerely feel that the present situation represents a thaw. And they have not shied away from paying for what they regard as their liberation by handing down death sentences against young workers who 'rejected discipline', 'sowed discord and indolence', and demanded access to culture, thus threatening their own privileges (privileges of culture and power, not economic ones, at least not as yet). They have not hesitated to pay the price by once again evoking continuity with the old China, expressing all their own resentment through nationalism (thereby exorcising the class struggle), and repressing any inclination towards criticism among the youth. (The watchword in the schools these days is: the students must obey their teachers and the teachers must love their students. And the latter, many of them men and women of twenty-five years of age, tremble — quite literally — before the reinstituted examinations.)

The peasants have been thrust back into their traditional passive obedience; their cultural backwardness and prejudices (including sexist and patriarchal ones) are being hailed as national and popular values. Recent directives condemn the tendency of the peasants to waste time in recreational and cultural activity. At the same time, there have been attempts to block any process of socialization of the land at the level of mutual aid teams, which teams too often reproduce the old clans. The educated classes have not hesitated to pay for the reconquest of their elitist positions in the schools by going back to selection and by expelling from university students of peasant background and members of the workers' teams. Professionalism and order have also been bolstered in the factories, at the cost of disbanding the revolutionary committees — leadership organs made up of representatives elected by all the personnel. For months now it has been virtually impossible to speak to workers when visiting factories. Where the repression has been sharpest one is sometimes received by a single bureaucrat, something inconceivable only a little more than a year ago. In compensation, the workers, unlike the peasants, have obtained some wage increases.

I will stop there, because it is impossible to go into a detailed description here. But I want to repeat that a great portion of the adult educated middle class views all this as genuine liberation from abuses of power and oppression. There is little doubt that this class has acquired some shreds of power in recent months. Nevertheless, it has never been so far from any real freedom since the fall of the Kuomintang. It must be added, however, that the least politicized section of the population would not view a return to the clashes of the period of the cultural revolution with enthusiasm.

If we want to draw general conclusions from the Chinese events, we may ask ourselves why the contradictions between the interests of those who make up society have been so acute as to render that society ungovernable without recourse to repression — which has entailed the automatic growth of the police-like and bureaucratic character of the organs of government and power. Viewed from the vantage point of capitalist society, it seems inexplicable that there could be contradictions even less tractable than the contradiction between capitalists and wage workers. I believe that we must abandon this vantage point, along with any and all theorizations of socialism fashioned *a priori* within bourgeois society. The first prejudice which we must divest ourselves of is the idea that the relationship between private capitalist and wage worker is the ultimate and perfect form of class rule, the elimination of which supposedly opens the road to communism, socialism being a more or less peaceful phase of transition. The truth is just the reverse. Objective difficulties and subjective interests opposed to communism are clearly manifested, even with extreme violence, in socialist society.

I will mention just one instance of this, already visible in Italian society, where some elements of socialist consciousness exist. The need for strict control over the mass of producers (with the corollaries of centralization, discipline, obedience, and the ethic of sacrifice and unity) runs up against the refusal by the producers to put up with people who put obstacles in the way of an immediately free and happy life (with the corollaries of rejection of hierarchy, delegation of responsibilities, and division of labour, sometimes to the extreme point of the rejection of work itself when it appears as a burden imposed on one section of the community). Both these aspirations, be it noted, must be qualified as socialist. The enormous objective difficulty becomes explosive when the opposing poles of such a contradiction are defended by particular social groupings, each of which sees the counterposed set of demands as a challenge to their liberty and even their very reason for being. It seems that the closer we come to communism the further away we get. There are many who, seeing no way forward, turn backwards in despair. One point, however, seems incontestable to me: subjective choices have greater and greater weight in a situation in which the relation of subordination is limited less and less to economic exploitation in the strict sense, in which no search for liberty can be separated from the search for non-delegated power on the part of all citizens. In other words, this search for liberty must be translated into a renunciation of the use of culture as an instrument of power on the part of the minorities that command this extreme privilege. This also means that any neo-Leninist or post-Leninist attempt by any political force to use intellectuals as a corps operating in its own service must be firmly rejected, for such attempts inevitably transform the intellectuals into mandarins bolstering arbitrariness disguised as rationality.

Our Strike in Szczecin

Edmund Baluka

Edmund Baluka used to be a worker at the Warski shipyards in Szozecin, Poland. He was elected president of the strike committee at the time of the momentous strike from December 1970 to January 1971. It was in this capacity that he chaired the now celebrated encounter between the workers and the leaders of the Polish United Workers Party, the proceedings of which were secretly recorded and smuggled out to Western Europe (they appeared in English in New Left Review 72, *March/April 1972). Like all the other strike leaders, he was sacked afterwards and had to leave the country. For a time he lived in Manchester, England, before moving to Paris.*

It gave me great pleasure to accept the invitation of the Italian left and the *Manifesto* editors to take part in this conference on Eastern

Europe or what is called 'the Soviet bloc'. The little time allocated for each contribution does not allow me even partially to analyze the Polish people's struggle of the last thirty-two years against the bureaucratic regime in their country. Nor shall I be able to discuss the key role played by Stalin's heirs, Khrushchev and Brezhnev, in continuing his work of what I would define as bureaucratic imperialism. Please allow me, therefore, to leave on one side the post-war period and the countless valiant deeds of the Polish resistance, as well as the 1956 workers' struggles in Poznan, the 1968 student revolt, and the many individual rebellions against the Polish United Workers Party (PUWP).

What I shall talk about is the four days in January 1971, described by numerous journalists and politicians as exceptionally different from the grey, ordinary days which make up the 'survival-life' of our enslaved people. December 1970 marked a turning-point — a 'wrong' turn, a turn which meant that 'we lost contact with the working class'. The factions struggling for power within the Party laid the blame on their predecessors, only to take the same path and commit the same mistakes once the situation had been brought under control.

The price rises of 1 December 1970, which averaged twenty per cent, were the result of the contribution paid by People's Poland, within the framework of Comecon, to further Soviet world expansion. They were at once a necessity and a provocation on the part of the Moczar and Gierek factions struggling for the post of First Secretary of the PUWP Central Committee.

On 14 December, the workers of the *Lenin* shipyard in Gdansk became the first to down tools and take to the streets. The buildings of the PUWP Regional Committee, the trade unions and the local oligarchies were soon in flames, and the same day, the neighbouring towns of Gdynia, Elblag and Slupsk were also in revolt. Thanks to road-blocks and the silence of the press, radio and television, it took three days for the revolt to break out in Szczecin. According to later estimates, over 3,000 people — many of them children, women and old people — were massacred in the towns of the Baltic Coast. On 19 December, Edward Gierek took over power from Gomulka: but the whole of Poland came out in favour of an Italian-style general strike. The new ruling faction came together at the Eighth Plenum of the Central Committee in order to appoint new Central Committee secretaries and set the jammed productive machine in motion again. However, the new First Secretary of the Szczecin Regional Committee made a mistake: he interrupted the Eighth Plenum and obliged Gierek, Jaroszewicz, Szlachcic and Jaruzelski to go to the *Adolf Warski* shipyard in Szczecin. It was the noisy press, radio and television campaign promoting the 'good intentions' in the field of production which sparked off the mobilizations against the new PUWP ruling group: the Gierek faction.

On 22 January 1971, the day after this campaign began, about 6,000 workers from the *Adolf Warski* shipyard decided to leave work and burn down the radio and television stations that were broadcasting false reports about the (good) intentions of raising production. I was head of the Szczecin strike committee in January 1971; I saw women, children and workers slaughtered in the streets. I very soon realized that there was no point in dealing with the local authorities, since they did not have the power to grant our demands. That is why I called on the shipyard workers not to leave their workplace, but to deepen the occupation and insist that Gierek and Jaroszewicz come and explain whether they intended governing the country like Gomulka.

The workers agreed to my proposal: they occupied the radio-station which was located in the management buildings; they shut the entrance-gates, and then threw a security ring around the shipyard. Within a few hours, however, the yard was completely encircled by the militia and security police (about 6,000 men in all) — equipped with tanks, landing-stages and dozens of helicopters flying in formation. The authorities cut off the electricity and water, and for three days refused to allow our relatives to give us food.

At the same time, the strike spread to all the industrial plants in Szczecin, as well as to the railways, the postal services, commerce and urban transport.

Workshop delegates then elected a 40-person strike committee empowered to take decisions and represent the workers' demand through delegates permanently in contact with the committee. The strike committee was divided into five commissions with the following functions:
1) Protection of plant and defence of the workers against militia and security police provocations.
2) Relations with other enterprises.
3) Propaganda activity, drawing on a radio transmitter and a printing-press able to produce leaflets and posters for the inhabitants of Szczecin.
4) Provision of food for the workers.

5) Preparations for combat. This commission was charged with finding bottles for Molotov cocktails, and with creating anti-tank barricades in the case of a militia attack — an eventuality that was considered by the PUWP Central Committee in Warsaw.

After three days of occupation, we were still cut off by the repressive forces, starved, threatened with an attack by the militia with whom we had already had a few skirmishes. Then we saw that behind the ring of militiamen and security agents there was an enormous crowd of some 100,000 people which was growing all the time: these were the inhabitants of Szczecin who threw us food and cigarettes over the iron gates. At that moment it became clear that our leaflets and posters had mobilised the populace of Szczecin to actively support the shipyard workers.

Gierek too was informed of this active and general solidarity with the Szczecin workers. And so, at six o'clock on the evening of 24 January 1971, he stood in front of the closed shipyard gate and pronounced those historic words: 'I am Edward Gierek. I am First Secretary of the PUWP. Please would you open the gate for me.' We opened up, because the letter that had been sent to Gierek asked him to come to the shipyard.

The First Secretary was accompanied by Prime Minister Jaroszewicz, the Minister of Defence, General Jaruzelski, the Minister of the Interior. Franciszek Szlachcic, and a few more dignitaries of the new ruling faction. The discussion between Gierek and the strike committee, which went on for nine hours, was relayed live throughout the shipyard by means of loudspeakers. The 'speeches' of Gierek and Jaroszewicz, as well as the interventions of delegates from the 36 shipyard sections, were thus also heard by the inhabitants of Szczecin standing just behind the militia cordon.

I should here stress an important point: Gierek did not want this nine-hour discussion to be heard outside the shipyard, but the strike committee absolutely refused to give way ...

Out of the twelve points we had drawn up, Gierek accepted eleven, including the demand for democratic elections in the Party, the trade unions and the youth organizations. However, the call for a reduction in prices was not satisfied. Gierek shed real tears when he came to discuss the economic problems of the country, yet he went on to promise that the twelfth demand would be met in the near future. The shipyard workers gave him their trust, although not without stating that they would rise up against the Party if it were to commit fresh mistakes.

One of our points called for the strike committee to remain in place as a 'workers' commission', whose task would be to ensure that satisfaction was given to all the demands of the shipyard and other workers in Szczecin. Gierek went back on his promises in less than a year: the most active worker militants encountered a thousand difficulties, including sackings and unjust court sentences; and a few comrades who had shown exceptional ardour during the struggle were even found dead in obscure circumstances.

These sacrifices were not wasted. The revolt of the coastal towns was the main factor in the change of government and Party leaderships; and Gierek's trip to the Szczecin shipyard made the Polish working class aware of the fact that determined and united opposition to the bureaucracy can force it to give ground.

The June 1976 events have shown that it is possible, even in a system of totalitarian power, to organize a general strike within twenty-four hours and compel the regime to go back on its decisions. The opposition now fighting in our country has effectively blocked the authorities' decision to lower the Poles' standard of living; and it is also active in demanding greater democratic freedoms. The solidarity of Polish intellectuals and students with the workers marks another defeat for the PUWP renegades.

Thirty thousand Romanian miners have forced their dictator, Ceausescu, to set out on the same pilgrimage as the one Edward Gierek had to make under the pressure of the working class of the Polish coast. I do not think that these miners were inspired by the example of the Polish shipyard workers. They made their own discovery that there is no use discussing with 'small fry' — that the fish starts to rot from the head down! And to cut off the head is to halt the process of decomposition eating away at the societies of the Soviet bloc.

There is no need for me to add, I trust, that the same kind of gangrene is in the process of destroying the capitalist societies. The only difference between the two is in their names, in their outward appearances and in their modes of exploiting the labour force. The sharks of the Kremlin, Peking, Washington and Latin America, the racists of South Africa and all the Idi Amins of this world have no other aim than to exploit the labour force out of love of authority.

The Italian working class, too, is fighting against all that.

Once again, dear comrades, I would like to thank you for your invitation and ask you to excuse the hurried and unmethodical character of this contribution.

The Structures of Society in 'Existing Socialism'

The Nature of Soviet Society

Charles Bettelheim

Taken as a whole, the preceding contributions have clearly brought out the depth and diversity of social and political contradictions in the so-called 'socialist' countries. They have shown concretely how the development of such contradictions gives rise to various forms of repression on the part of the state apparatuses. Of course, all of us here already knew this in general terms. But the speakers have done us the great service of concretizing this reality and showing that acts of repression are neither 'accidents' nor 'mistakes' committed by individual leaders. Rather these acts are bound up with objective contradictions and with the objective position of the state power in the totality of economic and social relations.

This raises the question of the nature of the dominant economic and social relations in these countries. The question is posed all the more sharply in that an entire tradition laying claim to Marxism asserts that there can no longer be relations of exploitation once juridical private ownership of the means of production has disappeared. In such a case, it is argued, the classes (or even the 'social groups') remaining in existence are related to one another by ties of fraternity and exhibit fewer and fewer points of divergence.

The most typical expression of this view is to be found in Stalin's speech of 23 November 1936 presenting the new draft constitution. Stalin here describes how private ownership of the means of production has disappeared in the Soviet Union, and goes on to identify this process with the disappearance of capitalism. He then draws the conclusion that there is no longer an exploiting class, but only two friendly classes: the workers and peasants, and the social group of 'intellectuals'. And the latter cannot but serve the workers and peasants, since they no longer have other classes to serve.

Reality itself was to give the lie to this falsely optimistic vision. Since 1936, other analyses have provided us with a more dialectical conception. This is the case with Mao Tse-tung's writings of 1950 and after dealing with the continuation of class struggle under the dictatorship of the proletariat — particularly his analysis of contradictions among the people, and above all, his interventions in the course of the Cultural Revolution. Emerging from these interventions can be seen the crucial theses on the existence of a bourgeoisie within the Party, and on the danger — now actually realized in the Soviet Union — that the ruling communist party will change into its opposite: a fascist party.

Such important analyses are evidently in contradiction with a series of simplistic formulations now very widespread in both Eastern and Western Europe.

I would next like to say a few words about the theoretical conceptions that claim to provide a basis for these simplistic formulations. In reality, the latter rest on a postulate and a deduction. The postulate is that the *economic base* of the social formation of the 'socialist' countries (and I shall now refer essentially to the Soviet Union) is a socialist economic base. The deduction is that, given this base, there is no longer any place for antagonistic classes; and that the state's role therefore consists above all in organizing social production and defending the country against external and internal enemies. These internal enemies do not compose a hostile class, being nothing more than counter-revolutionary 'individuals' or 'elements' weighed down by the force of the past or acting as foreign agents. Once this conception is adopted, it becomes easier and easier to regard anyone who voices disagreement with Party and state policy as being 'in the pay of imperialism'.

Thus, denial that very real contradictions exist leads those concerned to 'legitimize' harsh repression in the name of 'defending the country' or 'defending the revolution'.

We must now examine, above all, the postulate that the economic base of the Soviet Union is a socialist base, or that it has been so since 1935 or 1936.

First, this postulate identifies the juridical relation of state ownership — which belongs to the *superstructure* — with a relation of production rooted in the economic *base*.

Second, it implicitly confuses state property (or co-operative or kolkhoz property) with what is termed 'socialist property'. The postulate sets out *state property* as a form of *social appropriation* by virtue of which the proletariat has disappeared as such. This is precisely the point made by Stalin in his speech of 23 November 1936: the Soviet working class is no longer a proletariat but an entirely new class, since 'it owns the means of production in common with the whole people'.

It is thus abstractly asserted that state property 'resolves' the contradiction between the social character of the productive forces and the private property of a class. We are faced with an ideological system which, although operating in a very uncomplicated manner, is completely alien to historical materialism. It suggests:

1) that state property = social property = socialist property; and 2) that property is the *foundation* of the relations of production. From the moment that 'socialist state property' exists, the relations of production are also supposed to be socialist; and hence, the wage relation is but an 'empty' form or appearance concealing 'entirely new' social relations. (See, for example, the *Manual of Political Economy* published by the USSR Academy of Sciences in 1954 — a book which summarizes Stalin's 1952 declarations on the same problems.)

Such formulations spring from an idealist conception characteristic of bourgeois juridical ideology; they do not derive from historical materialism. This is clear from the way in which the *key role* is given to the juridical form of state property. In effect, the attribution of a key role to legal ownership corresponds to a process of 'back-sliding' into Proudhonism and Lassallism. As long ago as 1846, Marx showed in a letter to Annenkov the inconsistencies of such a view of things: 'Finally, the last category in Mr. Proudhon's system is *property*. In the real world, on the other hand, division of labour and all Mr. Proudhon's other categories are social relations forming in their entirety what is today known as *property*; outside these relations bourgeois property is nothing but a metaphysical or legal illusion ... By presenting property as an independent relation, Mr. Proudhon commits more than a mistake in method: he clearly shows that he has not grasped the bond which holds together all forms of *bourgeois* production.'[1]

This passage very clearly states that *property*, in the deepest sense of the word, is not a merely juridical category but the product of social relations as a whole, and especially of the division of labour. Now, the point is that the social relations which characterize the Soviet Union are fundamentally the same as those which characterize the capitalist mode of production.

The notion of 'socialist property' conceived as a juridical notion abstracts from the real process of appropriation into which producers and non-producers are inserted; it abstracts from the social relations which are forged within, and on the basis of that process. Far from being 'deducible' from the legal property form, these relations can only be grasped through concrete analysis.

As Marx stressed in *Capital*, the capitalist mode of production will be maintained as long as the means of production still confront 'all individuals really active in production as alien property'.[2]

The fact that capitalist relations of production are maintained on the basis of state property appears clearly in the reproduction of the wage-relation. The existence of this relation signifies that the economic base of the Soviet social formation is still constituted by capitalist relations of production. As Marx said: 'The wage presupposes wage-labour, and profit — capital ... Capitalist distribution differs from those forms of distribution which arise from other modes of production, and every form of distribution disappears with the specific form of production from which it is descended and to which it corresponds.'[3]

Already in the *Grundrisse*, Marx had shown that the existence of the value form at the level of distribution (and therefore the existence of the wage form) proves that 'production is not [yet] *directly* social'; that it is 'not the "offspring of association", which distributes labour internally'; and hence, that 'social production is not subsumed under individuals, manageable by them as their common wealth'.[4]

Thus, both the form of the production process and that of the distribution process testify to the reproduction of capitalist relations of production in Soviet enterprises.

If the Soviet Union can be said to have once had a socialist character, this is not by virtue of the transformation of the economic base. It is rather the result of the October Revolution — of a political power that asserted its will to struggle for the transformation of social relations and rally the workers for that end. When this struggle was abandoned, and especially when it was falsely claimed that the transformation of social relations had been 'realized', the Soviet social formation lost its socialist character. The abandonment of the struggle demonstrated that the class relationship of forces had been reversed, thereby allowing capitalist relations of production to be securely reproduced.

This conclusion is brushed aside by the ideology that has invented a 'socialist mode of production' — an imaginary mode with no status in theory. For socialism is not a mode of production; it is the transition between capitalism and communism.

The ideology of a 'socialist mode of production', which has

contaminated a large part of the world workers movement, plays a quite blatantly apologetic role. In the Soviet Union, it functions as a justification of the existing state of affairs — as a theoretical 'foundation' for the strengthening of *repression and the state*. By denying that there is a proletariat in the USSR, such an ideology denies the existence of proletarian class struggle and thus gives priority to the struggle of those who dispose of the state power and the means of production. In other words, it favours the struggle of a state bourgeoisie to maintain its power and brand as 'counter-revolutionary' all those who oppose this reactionary power.

State capitalism such as it functions in the USSR is a profoundly contradictory reality. On the one hand, it ensures reproduction of the antagonism between bourgeoisie and proletariat. On the other, it maintains a permanent crisis. It leads to superexploitation of the masses and arouses the discontent of all who perceive the contradiction between the discourse and the reality of power. That is why such power is *necessarily repressive* in character. Only the struggle to destroy this state and abolish the capitalist division of labour is compatible with the development of democracy for the masses.

Notes

1. Marx-Engels, *Selected Correspondence*, Moscow 1975, pp.33-4.
2. Marx, *Capital Volume One*, Harmondsworth 1976, p.1003.
3. *Capital*, Vol.3, Moscow 1971, p.883.
4. Marx, *Grundrisse*, Harmondsworth 1973, p.158.

Marx and Lenin read in the Camps

Boris Weil

Boris Weil has been described by Plyushch as 'a veteran of the Marxist opposition'. A Soviet school teacher, he was sacked for his political activity, imprisoned many times and sentenced to forced labour. He has had many types of work, occupying himself for a time in a puppet theatre. Since his departure from the USSR in October 1977 he has been living in Denmark with his wife, Ludmila, who has shared his political itinerary with him.

This is the first time I have spoken in public in the West, and more generally, the first time I have ever taken the floor in front of such a large audience. It is true that it would have been impossible in the Soviet Union to speak about the things we are discussing here. I was able to do so in the prisons and camps among a very restricted group of comrades — that is, at certain hours when a few of us were allowed to get together and talk. But never anywhere else.

When I came into the hall, I was extremely surprised to see a portrait of Lenin. I leave the Soviet Union and what do I see here? A table covered in red. In my country, that means official ceremony — an insufferably boring period which people go through only because they have to, and which they cannot stomach. I too always shared that attitude, but I can see today that it really is possible to sit around such a table and speak one's mind. That is something extremely precious for me.

In the Soviet Union, the party in power has no contact with us; it is content simply to throw us in jail. However, even within our ruling party, there are people who materially assist the so-called dissidents; of course they are anxious to remain anonymous, since if their deeds were to become known, they would suffer serious penalties such as expulsion from the Party. And in the Soviet Union, that is tantamount to a judicial procedure, with all the consequences that follow. I am happy that comrades from the PCI and PCE — which may tomorrow come to power — are taking part in our proceedings, and that we are able to engage in a dialogue with them such as would be out of the question in the case of Soviet Party leaders.

In fact, I am grateful to everyone here for concerning himself with problems in the East, with our problems. When I arrived in Vienna a month ago, I was told that people in the West had had enough of dissidents; that they were tired of hearing the same things over and over again; and that, after all, they have their own problems to face in the West. That is doubtless true as far as the average man in the street is concerned. But do we or do we not want to get to the bottom of things? After all, the world is *one*, and its fate is today decided in Moscow, Washington or Peking. Everything that happens in the Soviet Union has repercussions on the whole of humanity.

Yesterday, we heard Leonid Plyushch speak. As you know, he was declared insane in the Soviet Union — not only because he is a dissident, but also because he is a Marxist. We should have no illusions on this score: if Marx himself were to appear in the Soviet Union today, he would probably also be declared insane. And as for Lenin, everyone knows that he spent the last two years of his life virtually under arrest in his isolated government apartment.

I would just like to say a few words about the fate of Marxism in the USSR. Do you remember Lenin's observation that 'Russia *vystradala* Marxism', or groped towards it through suffering? Well, that process is still not over. It is easy to understand why no philosophy is more unpopular than Marxism in the Soviet Union today. For monstrous deeds have been perpetrated under cover of a Marxist terminology that no longer excites anything but indifference, or even disgust, among the majority of the population. Who indeed would not feel utterly disgusted by something imposed on him by violence? Even the most beautiful of things arouses nothing but aversion if imposed by force.

What I have just said applies to the broad masses of the Russian people. Those in power do still refer, of course, to Marx and Lenin, but in reality they are profoundly indifferent to Marxism. It has come to resemble a game of patience in which each card bears a different quotation: for each situation you ever come across in daily life there is always a corresponding quote. You just shuffle the pack however you like, and place one card here, another there ... A quotation game — that is what Marxism has become in the USSR. From a living theory it has degenerated into a quote-machine, one of whose little phrases can justify any action whatsoever.

It is true that, working at the Institute of Marxism-Leninism and other brain-washing centres, are scientists who call themselves Marxists. Such people turn Marxism into a business and draw their dividends from *Capital!* One can indeed be a Marxist and, at the same time, live a fine bourgeois existence on the proceeds. This post-Stalin generation of Soviet ideologues did their studying together with my friends and myself. And they have certainly made it by now. These ex-classmates of ours have their own house and country *dacha*, whereas we are deported or, like Plyushch, thrown into a lunatic asylum.

Not the slightest trace remains of the original essence of Marxism: critical, dialectical thinking. That is why the workers have such a horror of ideology. The authorities may pay verbal homage to Marxism, but they snuff out any flicker of Marxist thought. It is hardly surprising, therefore, if a large number of dissidents — or, if you prefer, oppositionists — have no sympathy for Marxism.

I should tell you that many dissidents regard Plyushch and myself as dinosaurs — as members of a doomed prehistoric species who have inexplicably managed to survive. However, more clear-sighted people go beyond such analyses. Sakharov, for example, in his polemic with Solzhenitsyn, correctly pointed out that the authorities use Marxism as a mere screen behind which to take shelter.

It may be accepted in theory that there could be another ideology in the USSR. But, it is asked, what is the point of changing? Things have developed historically in a particular way, and people have grown used to the situation. And yet, we have to recognize that this is not a very practical attitude. Anyone wanting to study Marxism is, in effect, seeking to think dialectically; and dialectics is incompatible with the Soviet regime. Sad to say, people like Plyushch and myself appear as lunatics in the eyes of broad sections of society. It seems sheer madness to read official documents which are printed by the million and lie forever, unread and unbought, on the shelves of libraries and bookshops.

When I left the Soviet Union, I brought with me the third edition of Lenin's *Collected Works* — the one edited by Bukharin. My friends were at a loss to understand why I was taking the books. Just as perplexed were those customs officers who asked: 'What for? What

good will they do you?' What I was doing was completely incompre-
hensible to the average individual.

When I was in prison or a camp, I had the right to read Marx.
Religious literature, by contrast, was officially prohibited: believer or
no, if you were caught reading the Gospel by the head-warder or an
assistant, he would confiscate the book and throw you in the 'cooler'.
You could read Marx to your heart's content, but the warders still
scratched their heads: 'What are you reading Marx and Lenin for?'
The camp authorities would look askance, regarding us with much
greater suspicion than the religious believers. For it was understandable that they should read the Gospel. But why did we persist in
reading Karl Marx?

All the things we have been debating yesterday and today I used to
discuss in the camps with those who shared my views. And I repeat, I
had a strange feeling when I found myself among you: on the one
hand, seeing the picture of Lenin on the wall and the table draped in
red, I had the impression that I was back in the USSR in an official
meeting-hall; but on the other hand, I felt as if I were again in a
prison camp, since only there was I able to discuss these problems. In
the USSR, those in power are afraid of the least analysis: they have
no use whatsoever for it. The only thing they like to hear is endless
repetitions of a single speech. Danger looms as soon as someone
begins to analyze something.

Yesterday, we talked about socialism, state capitalism, relations of
production, the class struggle. And I noticed that, here in Venice,
the walls of certain buildings — especially of the one we are in now —
are covered with all manner of slogans and graffiti. In the Soviet
Union you cannot do that with impunity. Last year in Leningrad, a
group of artists wrote some slogans on a number of public buildings,
including the Peter-Paul Fortress which, once a Tsarist prison, is now
a museum. On the fortress walls they wrote: 'You are crushing
freedom, but its spirit is everlasting', or something like that. They
were arrested and brought before the city court — not, as you might
think, for anti-Soviet propaganda, but for defacing a historical
monument. Now I would really like to meet someone who writes on
public buildings and gives a thought to the fact that he is defacing
historical monuments. Anyway, these 'defilers' got off with a 'light'
sentence: only three or four years in a camp, plus a huge fine of
about 20,000 roubles. The paper *Evening Leningrad* wrote: 'Our
beautiful city has such splendid historical monuments, and yet there
are vandals who come and spoil them ... ' However, the paper did not

say a word about what they had written: it spoke only of hooligans defacing public buildings ...

I would like to take up some more general problems. Your conference is of a theoretical character, and it is extremely important that it began with a discussion of the nature of our state and our society. You should know that, in the Soviet Union, even many dissidents regard the discussion about socialism and state capitalism as purely scholastic; it is only too easy to say that ours is a totalitarian system and leave it at that. However, scientific analysis calls for a different kind of approach: we must trace the phenomenon to its origins and grasp what it really represents. I hope that this initiative of the *Manifesto* leaders will be followed by other conferences, less impressive in terms of the numbers participating and perhaps stretching over a longer time.

The invitation I received bore the words: 'actually existing socialism'. The inverted commas were obviously not there by chance. If those who wrote the invitation felt obliged to place these categories between quotation marks, they must have felt that they had not found the precise term. After countless heated discussions, I and my co-thinkers in the USSR have for a long time been in no doubt about the correctness of the term *state capitalism*. No doubt this is a complicated problem to which many studies and theoretical meetings should be devoted. But we have to clarify the concepts we use. We cannot live with inverted-comma concepts, or with definitions that rely on the word 'not' or other negations. I would therefore like to make a few cursory observations on this notion of state capitalism.

1) In the Soviet Union, the means of production are owned by the state. But as Bettelheim said, they are not public property: they do not belong to society.

2) The workers' labour-power has remained a commodity. This point is very important, since many other factors stem from it. In 1956, Soviet economists themselves recognized that labour-power is a commodity. But it is forbidden to say so in the Soviet Union today. If you go up to an official economist and ask: 'Is labour-power a commodity in the Soviet Union, yes or no?' he will do his best not to answer. He will avoid giving an answer, because he cannot give one.

3) Added value and the means of production are used by those who control the state without the producers having the slightest say or control over their disposal.

4) The state serves the interests of the ruling class. But here, of

course, there may be disagreement about the relationship between ruling class and state.

The subject is too vast to be tackled in a few words. The last speaker very rightly said that it is above all the workers who do not feel the masters of production; but he added that the leaders do not feel so either. The manager only manages: everyone carries out a will coming from on high — from a 'super-manager'. So who gives the orders? To whom does the enterprise or factory belong? Who purchases the commodity labour-power? In *Anti-Dühring*, Engels wrote a quite brilliant passage on the 'general' capitalist. Reading it today, one has the impression that Engels himself visited the Soviet Union. Taken separately, each representative of the ruling class of the Soviet Union may feel that he is not master. For he exercises domination only as part of a whole, only when he is with others. It is together that they dominate, own the commodity labour-power, and dispose of added value.

There is, of course, a certain class mobility in our country — although it is less significant than in the twenties and thirties, since the state is today more stable. Nevertheless, in order to mount the social ladder, one has to belong to the ruling class, the ruling party. This brings us to a very important category. What is the Party in the Soviet Union?

The Party of a single-party state (Uganda as much as the Soviet Union) is not the same entity as even the ruling party within a multi-party system. Moreover, the CPSU has constituted itself as a party of a new type — a point which must be borne in mind when talking about the Party. It is not a party in the normal sense of the word, in what I shall call the bourgeois sense. In his book *Lectures on Fascism*, which has recently been translated into Russian and enjoys great popularity among dissidents, Togliatti talks of a party of a new type when dealing with the genesis of the fascist party. We should also remind ourselves of Stalin's definition: 'The Party is the army.' That is the new-type party: *an army-party*. The parties 'of old' are just unions of like-minded people. The Communist Party of the Soviet Union is not one of those: it is an army. This structural element already existed before the Revolution. In the extremely difficult conditions of underground work, the Bolshevik Party had to operate in secrecy, assuming a structure that was not altogether democratic. But when they left clandestinity and came to power, the Bolsheviks retained and even strengthened this element. Although there was a possibility of opposition until 1927, this was no longer the case after that year: what followed stemmed from all that had preceded it. In order to understand the Bolshevik Party, we need to remember Engels' famous statement: 'The key to the ape's anatomy lies in the anatomy of man.' In order to understand a process of development, it is enough to consider its most accomplished forms. Or think of Christ's words: 'By their fruits ye shall know them.' That too, it seems to me, is a dialectical approach. The fate of our Soviet Russia was therefore largely determined by the structures of the Bolshevik Party. Still, we should not forget that it was originally a union of like-minded people. It is clearly no longer such a union — except in the sense that people are grouped around a big cake and that all the others who want a share are driven away.

The present state of relations between the intelligentsia and the popular and working masses is a very painful subject to discuss. In Russia, the intelligentsia is very isolated from the people; as one of our writers put it, there is an invisible wall between the two. When I say intelligentsia, I am referring above all to those who reflect in a critical manner, for the task of intellectuals is, by very definition, to think critically. Those who engage in apologetics and draw a salary from the regime for so doing do not deserve to be called intellectuals at all.

Anyway, the best among the intellectuals are isolated from the masses. That is our misfortune. The workers and peasants are neither interested nor concerned about the problems of civil rights and political prisoners in Russia. What does matter for them is their economic situation, their living standards, their ability to buy the goods they need; and at this level, the crisis is uninterrupted. Although the problem of clothing supply has now been resolved, things are in a sorry state as far as meat and other food products are concerned. This is what people think about in the Soviet Union today. Not having had their fill, they think about free speech less than about anything else. To be sure, there are a good many conscious workers, yet they are still only a small and divided minority. There are, of course, no trade unions in the traditional sense of the word. The Party, as we have seen, is no longer a party but something else; the unions are certainly not unions, however they may call themselves; the soviets or councils are neither soviets nor councils as these used to be understood; and elections are not elections but something purely formal. People put a slip in the ballot-box without even bothering to read what is written on it; for they know that there is only one candidate for each seat and that everything has been settled in advance.

But I think you already know all that. As a result, we members of the USSR intelligentsia find ourselves in a position rather similar to that of the 19th-century Russian populists. They went among the people, giving out political literature; but the people did not want to read it and handed it over to the police. However, although our own 'alienation' recalls that of the past, we find that ordinary men and women do begin to see things in a different light once we get to explain the situation to them. After all, we are telling the truth; and people always understand what is true and what is false. The plague of official lies ends up affecting everybody: if the population is now apolitical, this is because it has been fed to overflowing with official lies. People show sympathy for the dissidents whenever they understand what is at stake. It should be said, however, that the masses in the Soviet Union have forgotten how to rise above their immediate concerns: they always weigh things up on a profit-and-loss basis. So when they see a dissident, they say to one another: 'What's he after then? What's he getting out of it?' Only when we are in jail is it clear that we get absolutely nothing out of it!

I think my friend Plyushch made a mistake yesterday, when he said that protest actions by the Russian working class are purely emotional in character. In fact, they are of an *economic* rather than emotional character. Thus, in 1961 in Novocherkassk, there was a workers' demonstration against price rises. It was drowned in blood. Many were killed. The streets were later washed by council water-sprinklers in order to remove the traces of blood. This incident is very little known in the Soviet Union, and even less so in the West. (The Soviet mass media have never mentioned it, designed as they are for a quite specific purpose.) At various times there have been similar demonstrations in other towns: I myself witnessed a small-scale economic strike in Siberia. However, such small strikes are not planned, breaking out spontaneously and assuming a purely economic character.

It seems to me that we should support Marek's proposal to intervene on behalf of Rudolf Bahro. We should also speak in public about the arrests in the Soviet Union of members of the Helsinki Monitoring Groups there.

I would like to add a word or two in reply to the question: 'Why is our dissident movement so non-socialist — so unrepresentative of the working class and so purely intellectual?' Obviously, each of us dissidents has gone through a *particular* experience. But now we have found a form of political existence that we had been seeking for many years. We have discovered a form with no organization, no programme and no statutes — yet which manages to stay alive. The authorities are not able to destroy the movement, although, if I may say so, it is undoubtedly destroying itself through the emigration of 'members'. Still, there is a living chain of mutual relations. The authorities may break a few links, but a replacement immediately springs up within the living organism. The whole movement for the defence of human rights is of a general democratic character.

I do not want to go over my time. So let me just ask each one of you how it is that human rights are defended not by Marxists, but by physicists, scientists and so on. Why do the Marxists seem to have lagged behind in the struggle? There is certainly food for thought here. Personally, I am convinced that because Marx lived in a society, England, where legality had some real existence, the problem of human rights was not posed for him as sharply as it is for us. For whether we are Marxists, Christians or positivists, our first goal and duty in a country with no foundation in law is to struggle for human rights. In the present state of things in the USSR, the struggle for freedom of expression and information (our century being marked by a growing need for information) is itself a stage in the struggle for socialism. And we should not stand aside from this struggle for socialism.

Of course, it is both correct and vitally necessary for us to discuss the class struggle, surplus value, and so on. But I find it painful to hear my socialist co-thinkers talk about such matters without remembering Marx's statement that one real step forward is more important than a dozen programmes. When people in the West — even non-Marxists, even those not on the Left — give various kinds of aid to Soviet political prisoners, they are coming to the help of mankind as a whole. Such strictly practical human aid may prove to be more useful than a dozen programmes. And when a single political prisoner regains his freedom in the Soviet Union, I am filled with rejoicing. For the tree of life is still standing firm, and there is no theory which does not have to be transfused into human veins. We know that theory is not something inert; that it cannot fail to share in men's fate, in the fate of people threatened with prison or the lunatic asylum. And we also know that the appeals of Soviet dissidents should not make us forget the problems of Chile and many, many other countries. We are drinking wine while somewhere in the world people are held in jail or tortured. Does that mean we should stop drinking? No, we will go on drinking, but without forgetting those other people.

Terrified Contemplation of Contradiction Is Not Enough

Franco Fortini

Franco Fortini, poet, author, critic, and translator, participated in the major magazines that sparked the cultural life of the Italian left after the Second World War: Politecnico, Ragionamenti, Officina, Quaderni piacentini, *among others. In 1972, after a long period as a Socialist militant, he stood as a candidate in the legislative elections on the Manifesto slate. He has collaborated with the newspaper* il manifesto *since then. A professor at the University of Siena, Fortini has published many volumes of poetry and criticism. Among his collections of essays are* Dieci inverni *(1958),* Verifica dei poteri *(1965), and* Questioni di frontiera *(1977).*

There seem to be two contradictory elements to this conference. One is the political significance of opposition in the countries we have called post-revolutionary; the other is its non-political, or meta-political, significance. Rossanda and the other comrades want a social and historical interpretation of what has happened and is happening in these post-revolutionary countries. They are quite concerned about those of us who have a tendency to consider what the comrades from Eastern Europe have told us as not political, but literary, sentimental, moralistic, or ideological.

I have the impression that these Italian comrades are asking the Russian, Polish, Czech, and Hungarian comrades not to deprive them of their dear red flags, their illusions that a good socialism is possible, their conviction that although things have gone badly in the past, they will necessarily *have to* get better in the future. But the testimony we are hearing from the East is not couched in this sort of language; it does not leave our illusions intact. The East European comrades here are speaking to us in the name of a historic defeat of enormous dimensions. We, in our country, have not fully suffered a defeat of such scope. We do not want to drain the glass of that defeat. And we are prepared to react a bit hastily, to console ourselves with the tragedies of others — tragedies which are also our own, of course, but which we feel less directly. Somewhat in the manner of Madame Dubarry facing the guillotine, we entreat the historic executioner, 'Just a moment, Mr Executioner, please'. The Czech, Hungarian, or Polish comrades, however, are telling us quite clearly that the regimes under which they are living are regimes of oppression, unqualified enemies of the people.

At this point we hesitate. Why? Why do we continue or, in any case, why do we want to continue to draw distinctions between the East and what, *here in the West*, has been getting more and more like Eastern Europe. Why do we refuse to consider the nihilistic and desperate reversal that has occurred among entire sectors of those layers of youth who had courageously proclaimed the identity of the private and the public.

If I look at how things were fifteen years ago, I note that we used to speak of the identity of political activity and private life, of the public and the private, as a tendential identity. This is what was written, and is written, in writings of Marxist persuasion. But during the past ten years, throughout the West, we have seen the forceful assertion that there must be an *immediate* identity of the public and the private. Demanding this sort of immediacy is like demanding that the circle be squared; in other words, it is absurd. But a great many youth, a great many of those who have profoundly altered the spirit of the left formations in Western Europe over the past ten years, have lived and are living *in* and *by* this absurdity.

Now, exactly because we are unable to renounce the dream of immediate unity, and also because we do not want to abandon our certainty that the masses are demanding immediate fulfilment and happiness, we find it necessary, in order to survive, to believe in a sort of world revolutionary potentiality that will compensate for the historic setbacks.

We have been told, for example, that the Chinese experience may demonstrate that the closer we come to communism, the further away we get. I would regard this phrase as a tragic, more than dialectical, assertion. It speaks of a fatal laceration, or collision. True, there is a moment in the life of every individual when personal biography and the life of the human race intersect and simultaneously diverge forever. But that is the moment of death. And I wonder whether this quest for communism could be this quest for death. Naturally, I do not think so.

This terrifying recognition of the absolute contrariety of the historic road that is supposed to lead humanity out of its millenia of misery is certainly heroic, even sublime; but it is ghastly.

In face of this prospect, the so-called *nouveaux philosophes*, who evoke a self-satisfied smile from all of us, myself included, acquire a semblance of justification. But, as I have written elsewhere, I would be cautious in dismissing them too rapidly as merely bad philosophers. No offence, comrades philistines, but what does it matter to us whether the *nouveaux philosophes* are bad philosophers? Since when has one idea really been able to acquire its strength from the weakness of another?

A bad philosopher is often a sign of the times, and (to leave the French *nouveaux philosophes*) it may be that behind the words we have heard from our East European comrades lurks the shadow of another personage we have learned to disdain or to regard as of no interest to us — namely Captain Solzhenitsyn.

Personally, of course, I share neither the positions of Solzhenitsyn nor those of Sakharov and the other dissidents. Nevertheless, I must consider all of them as expressions-limits whose shadow falls over our arguments and compels us to caution. They propose extreme theoretical and moral remedies for extreme evils. Even though we cannot follow them politically, their radical quality is precious to us.

The point is not to take summary positions, as would inevitably be the case if they were related to this or that formulation. I believe that Comrade Masi is correct when she affirms that the differences between China and the West are smaller than we think and that our conflicts, all our conflicts, constitute an internal phase of socialism. But when she asserts, for example, that both the demand for strict control by the mass of producers and the rejection of that control (which can go as far as the rejection of work itself) are both socialist options, I cannot help but wonder whether we are not dealing with yet another tragic-heroic transposition, a terrible, enchanting — but immobilizing — rhexis. The mistrust with which I regard such heroism is all the greater in that it ends up as a vision of mounting conflict.

There is a risk in all this. I would call it a risk of aestheticization. Seen in this light, the moments of contemporary history pass before us with the tension of a great historic drama, a great historic tragedy — Shakespearean or Brechtian, if you will. Like some sort of enormous spectacle in which we are enticed to participate. It will be our own decapitation instead of Mary Stuart's, but this does not substantially alter what we may call the sublime-theatrical aspect of it. And this is just what frightens me.

Rossanda and the majority of us are here to draw political lessons, and it is clearly necessary — as more than one comrade has said — to stick closely to the immediately political domain, even though, as I have pointed out, this may sometimes give the impression that we are too firmly wedded to our dear banners and, in part, to our dear illusions.

The comrades of Eastern Europe seem to present demands which we should call, to use a term of approximation, ethical. The distance between the language of the East European comrades and our own is still very great, and the third position that has been expressed here is, as I have said, the terrified contemplation of contradiction.

It is clear that it is our duty to seek the point at which the category of mediation can be applied, particularly against what I have called the temptation of heroism and heroicism. We are still under the shock of the testimony from the East, and we deeply and increasingly feel the magnitude of the historic catastrophe of the post-revolutionary societies. This could lead us to cynicism or to the love of nihilistic agonies. We must instead wrench the terrifying and alluring tragic mask from the history we have lived and are living, and from the history that awaits us. We must — at the price of the temporary loss of that unity of the 'personal' and 'political', which has been a conquest more verbal than real — absorb the tragic element of the lesson of the history of the past twenty years wholly into the lives of our *individual* existences; at the same time, we must expunge it from our political action. In a word: pessimism about our own lives, optimism about the lives of others.

The Nature of the State in 'Existing Socialism'

Political Power and Dissent in Post-revolutionary Societies

István Mészáros

István Mészáros, who at present teaches at Sussex University, England, was a pupil of Lukács until forced to leave Hungary in 1956. He is the author of several books on philosophy including Marx's Theory of Alienation, *Merlin Books, London 1975, which won the Isaac Deutscher Memorial Prize. The article which follows is an extended version of his actual speech at the Venice conference and first appeared in English in* New Left Review 108, *March-April 1978.*

The question of political power in post-revolutionary societies is and remains one of the most neglected areas of Marxist theory. Marx formulated the principle of the abolition of 'political power properly so-called' in no uncertain terms: 'The organization of revolutionary elements as a class supposes the existence of all the productive forces which could be engendered in the bosom of the old society. Does this mean that after the fall of the old society there will be a new class domination culminating in a *new political power*? No. The condition for the emancipation of the working class is the abolition of every class, just as the condition for the liberation of the Third Estate, of the bourgeois order, was the abolition of all estates and all orders. The working class, in the course of its development, will substitute for the old civil society an association which will exclude classes and their antagonisms, and *there will be no more political power properly so-called*, since political power is precisely the official expression of antagonism in civil society.'[1] And he was categorical in asserting that 'When the proletariat is victorious, it by no means becomes the absolute side of society, for it is *victorious only by abolishing itself and its opposite*. Then *the proletariat disappears* as well as the opposite which determines it, private property.'[2] But what happens to political power in post-revolutionary societies when the proletariat does not disappear? What becomes of private property or capital when private ownership of the means of production is abolished while the proletariat continues to exist and rules the whole of society — including itself — under the new political power called 'the dictatorship of the proletariat'? For according to Marx's principle, the two sides of the opposition stand or fall together, and the proletariat cannot be truly victorious without abolishing itself. Nor can it fully abolish its opposite without at the same time abolishing itself as a class which needs the new political form of the dictatorship of the proletariat in order to secure and maintain itself in power.

It would be mere sophistry to try and get out of these difficulties by suggesting that the new political power is not 'political power properly so-called', in other words that it is not the manifestation of deep-seated objective antagonisms. For the existence of such antagonisms is painfully in evidence everywhere, and the severity of measures devised to prevent their eruption — by no means with guaranteed success — provides an eloquent refutation of all evasive sophistry. Nor is it possible to take seriously for a moment the self-justifying suggestion that the political power of the post-revolutionary state is maintained — indeed intensified — in function of a purely *international* determination, in that political repression is explained as the necessary consequence of 'encirclement' and as the only feasible form of defending the achievements of the revolution against external aggression and its complementary: internal subversion. As recent history loudly testifies, 'the enemy within and without' as the explanation of the nature of political power in post-revolutionary societies is a dangerous doctrine, which substitutes the part for the whole in order to transform a partial determination into wholesale *a priori* justification of the unjustifiable: the institutionalized violation of elementary socialist rights and values.

The task is, clearly, an investigation — without apologetic preconceptions — of the specific political antagonisms which come to the fore in post-revolutionary societies, together with their material bases indirectly identified by Marx's principle concerning the simultaneous abolition of *both sides* of the old socio-economic antagonism as the necessary condition of proletarian victory. This does not mean, in the least, that we have to commit ourselves in advance to some theory of a 'new class'. For postulating a 'new class' is only another type of preconception which does not explain anything — which, on the contrary, badly needs explanation itself. Nor does the magic umbrella term 'bureaucratism' — which covers almost everything, including the assessment of qualitatively different social systems approached from opposite standpoints, from Max Weber to some of Trotsky's followers — provide a meaningful explanation of the nature of political power in post-revolutionary societies, in that it merely points to some obvious appearances while begging the question as to their causes: i.e. it presents the *effect* of far-reaching causal determinations as itself a *causal explanation*. Similarly, the hypothesis of 'state capitalism' will not do. Not only because it confounds the issues with some present-day tendencies of development in the most advanced capitalist societies (tendencies very briefly touched upon already by Marx himself), but also because it has to omit from its analysis some highly significant objective characteristics of post-revolutionary societies in order to make the application of this problematic label look plausible. Labels, no matter how tempting, do not solve complex theoretical issues, only bypass them while giving the illusion of a solution.

By the same token, it would be somewhat naive to imagine that we can leave these problems behind by declaring that the dictatorship of the proletariat as a political form belongs to the past, whereas the present and future are to be envisaged according to the principle of political pluralism — which, in turn, necessarily implies a conception of shared power as a 'historical compromise'. For even if we accept the pragmatic viability and relative historical validity of this conception, the question of how to constitute and exercise political power which actively contributes to a socialist transformation of society, instead of postponing indefinitely its realization, remains just as unanswered as before. There are some worrying dilemmas which must be answered. In the framework of the newly envisaged pluralism, is it possible to escape the well-known historical fate of Social Democracy, which resigned itself to the illusion of 'sharing power' with the bourgeoisie while in fact helping to perpetuate the rule of capital over society? If it is not possible — if, that is, the political form of pluralism itself is by its very nature a submission to the prevailing form of class domination, as some would argue — in that case why should committed socialists be interested in it in the slightest? But if, on the other hand, the idea of pluralism is advocated in the perspective of a genuine socialist transformation, it must be explained how it is possible to proceed from *shared power* to *socialist power*, without relapsing into the selfsame contradictions of political power in post-revolutionary societies whose manifestations we have witnessed on so many occasions. This is what gives a burning topicality to this whole discussion. The question of political power in post-revolutionary societies is no longer an academic matter. Nor can it be left anchored to the interests of conservative political propaganda and dismissed by the Left as such. Quite unlike 1956 — when these contradictions erupted in such a clamorous and tragic form — it is no longer possible for any section of the Left to turn its back on it. To confront the issues involved has become an essential condition of advance for the entire working-class movement, under conditions when in some countries it may be called upon to assume the responsibilities of sharing power, in the midst of an ever-deepening structural crisis of capital.

The Ideal and the 'Force of Circumstance'

If there has ever been a need to go back to the original sources and principles in order to examine the conditions of their formulation, together with all the necessary implications for present-day conditions and circumstances, it is precisely on these issues. But as soon as we admit this and try to act accordingly, we are immediately presented with some great difficulties. For Marx's original definition of political power as the necessary manifestation of class antagonism contrasts the realities of class society with fully realized socialism in which there can be no room for separate organs of political power, since 'the social life-processes ... becomes production by *freely* associated men, and stands under their conscious and planned control'.[3] But try and replace the plan consciously arrived at by the totality of individual producers by a plan imposed upon them from above, then the concept of '*freely* associated men' must also be thrown out and replaced by that of a *forced* association, inevitably envisaging the exercise of political power as separate from and opposed to the society of producers, who must be compelled to accept and implement aims and objectives which do not issue from their conscious deliberations but, on the contrary, negate the very idea of free association and conscious deliberation. Or, vice versa, try and obliterate the concept of '*freely* associated individuals' — worse still, arbitrarily declare, in the spirit of whatever form of Stalinism, that such concepts are purely 'ideological' remnants of a 'moralizing bourgeois individualism', even if this means that from now on, however surreptitiously, a significant portion of Marx's own work too has to be obliterated with the same label — and there will be no way of conceiving and envisaging (let alone practising) the elaboration and implementation of social planning except as a forced imposition from above.

Thus we witness the complete transformation of Marx's ideal into a reality which replaces the self-determining life-activity of freely associated social individuals by the forced association of men ruled by an alien political force. Simultaneously, Marx's concept of a conscious *social* plan (which is supposed to regulate, through the full involvement of the freely associated individuals, the totality of the life-processes of society) suffers the gravest reduction, becoming a one-sided, technocratically preconceived and often unfulfilled mere *economic* plan, and thus superimposing upon society in a new form the selfsame economic determinations whose supersession constituted the framework of orientation of scientific socialism from the moment of its inception.

Furthermore, since now the two basic constituents of a dialectical unity, the association of producers and the regulatory force of the plan, are divorced from and opposed to one another, the 'force of circumstance' — which is the necessary consequence of this separation rather than its cause, whatever the historically changing social determinants at work — becomes the unqualified cause, indeed the 'inevitable cause'. And since the 'inevitable cause' is also its own justification, the transformation is carried even further, setting itself up as the only possible form of realization of Marx's ideal: as the unsurpassable *model* of all possible socialist development. From now on, since the prevailing form of political rule must be maintained and therefore everything must remain as it is, the problematical notion of the 'force of circumstance' is used in the argument in order to assert categorically that it *could not have been otherwise*, and thus it is *right* that everything should be as it is. In other words, Marx's ideal is turned into a highly problematical reality, which in its turn is reconverted into a totally untenable model and ideal, through a most tortuous use of the 'force of circumstance' as both inevitable cause and normative justification, while in fact it should be critically examined and challenged on both counts.

To be sure, this double perversion is not the product of one-sided theory, though it represents an apologetic capitulation of theory to the 'force of circumstance', which in its turn is brought into existence as a result of immensely complex and contradictory social determinations, including the share of theoretical failure as a significant contributory factor to the overall process. But once this process is accomplished and a uniform praise of the perverted ideal is imposed by the force of law, condemning as 'heresy' and 'subversion' all voices of dissent, critical reflection must assume the form of bitter, self-torturing irony. Such as the answer given by the mythical 'Radio Yerevan' to the question of an anonymous listener who asks: 'Is it true that we have socialism in our country?' The answer is given in an oblique form as follows: 'You are asking, Comrade, whether it is true that luxurious American motor cars will be given away this Saturday afternoon on Red Square. It is perfectly true, with three qualifications: they won't be American, they will be Russian; they won't be motor cars, they will be bicycles; and they won't be given away, they will be taken away.' Cynically nihilistic though this may sound, who can fail to perceive in it the voice of impotence protesting in vain against the systematic frustration and violation of the ideals of socialism? Admittedly, the problems of political power in post-revolutionary societies cannot be solved by simply reiterating an ideal in its original formulation, for by their very nature these problems belong to the period of *transition* which impose their painful qualifications on all of us. All the same, there is a moral for us too in the story of 'Radio Yerevan'. It is that we should never consent to 'qualifications' which obliterate the ideal itself and turn it into its opposite. To ignore the 'force of circumstance' would be tantamount to living in the world of fantasy. But whatever the circumstances, the ideal remains valid as the vital compass that secures the correct direction of the journey and as the necessary corrective to the power of *vis major* which tends to take over in the absence of such corrective.

Political Power in the Society of Transition

Is it possible to identify the necessary socio-historical qualifications which apply the spirit of Marx's original formulations to the concrete realities of a complex historical transition from one social formation to another? How is it possible to envisage this transition in a political form that does not become its own self-perpetuation, thus contradicting and effectively nullifying the very idea of a transition which alone can justify the continued, but in principle diminishing, importance of the political form? Is it possible to have such qualifications without liquidating Marx's theoretical framework and its implications for our problem?

As we have seen, Marx's original definition concerned political power as the direct manifestation of class antagonism, coupled with its opposite: the abolition of political power properly so-called in a fully realized socialist society. But what happens in between? Is it possible to break entrenched political power without necessarily resorting to the exercise of a fully articulated system of political power? If not, how is it possible to envisage a change of course 'halfway through' — namely, the radical transformation of a powerful system of *self-sustaining* political power which controls the whole of society, into a *self-transcending* organ which fully transfers the manifold functions of political control to the social body itself, thus enabling the emergence of that free association of men without which the life-process of society remains under the domination of alien forces, instead of being consciously regulated by the social individuals involved in accordance with the ideals of self-determination and self-realization? And finally, if the transitional forms of political power stubbornly refuse to show signs of 'withering away', how should one assess the contradictions involved: as the failure of a 'utopian' Marxism, or as the historically determinate manifestation of objective antagonisms whose elucidation is well within the compass of Marx's original project?

Marx's assertion about the supersession of political power in socialist society is coupled with two important considerations. First, that the free association of social individuals who consciously regulate their own life-activities in accordance with a settled plan is not feasible without the necessary '*material foundation*, or a series of material conditions of existence, which in their turn are the natural and *spontaneous* product of a *long and tormented* historical development.'[4] The emancipation of labour from the rule of capital is feasible only if the objective *conditions of its emancipation* are fulfilled whereby 'the direct, material production process is stripped of the form of *penury and antithesis*', giving way to the '*free development of individualities*'.[5] By implication, so long as 'penury and antithesis' remain characteristics of the material base of society, the political form must suffer their consequences and the 'free development of individualities' is hindered and postponed.

The second consideration is closely linked to the first. Since overcoming the conditions of 'penury and antithesis' necessarily implied the highest development of the forces of production, successful revolution had to be envisaged by Marx in advanced capitalist countries, and not on the periphery of world capitalist developments (although he touched upon the possibility of revolutions away from the socio-economically most dynamic centre, without however entering into a discussion of the necessary implications of such possibilities). Inasmuch as the object of his analysis was the power of capital as a world system, he had to contemplate a breakthrough, under the impact of a profound structural crisis, in the form of more or less simultaneous revolutions in the major capitalist countries.

As to the problems of political power in the period of transition, Marx introduced the concept of the 'dictatorship of the proletariat'; and in one of his later works, *The Critique of the Gotha Programme*, he addressed himself to some additional problems of a transitional society as manifested in the politico-legal sphere. While these elements of his theory certainly do not constitute a system (the sequel to *Capital* which was supposed to develop the political implications of Marx's global theory in a systematic way was never even sketched, let alone fully worked out), they are important signposts and must be complemented by certain other elements of his theory (notably the assessment of the relationship between individual and class, and of the structural interdependence between capital and labour) which have a significant bearing on the strictly political issues, as we shall see in a moment.

It was Lenin, as we all know, who worked out the strategy of revolution 'at the weakest link of the chain', insisting that the dictatorship of the proletariat must be considered as the only viable political form for the entire historical period of transition that precedes the highest stage of communism, in which it finally becomes possible to implement the principle of freedom. The most significant shift in his analysis was envisaging that the 'material foundation' and the supersession of 'penury' could be accomplished under the dictatorship of the proletariat in a country which sets out from an extremely low level of development. Yet Lenin saw no problem in suggesting in December 1918 that the new state will be '*democratic* for the proletariat and the propertyless in general and *dictatorial* against the bourgeoisie' only.[6]

There was a curious flaw in his usually impeccable reasoning. He argued that 'thanks to capitalism, the material apparatus of the big banks, syndicates, railways, and so forth, has grown' and 'the immense experience of the *advanced countries* has accumulated a stock of engineering marvels, the employment of which is being hindered by capitalism', concluding that the Bolsheviks (who were in fact confined to a *backward country*) can 'lay hold of this apparatus and set it in motion'.[7] Thus the immense difficulties of a transition from one particular revolution to the irrevocable success of a global revolution (which is beyond the control of any one particular agency, however class-conscious and disciplined) were more or less implicitly brushed aside by voluntaristically postulating that the Bolsheviks were capable of taking power and 'retaining it until the triumph of the world socialist revolution'.[8]

Thus, while the viability of a socialist revolution at the weakest link of the chain was advocated, the imperative of a world revolution as a condition of success of the former reasserted itself in a most uneasy form: as an insoluble tension at the very heart of the theory. But what could one say in the event that the world socialist revolution did not come about and the Bolsheviks were condemned to hold on to power indefinitely. Lenin and his revolutionary comrades were unwilling to entertain that question, since it conflicted with certain elements of their outlook. They had to claim the viability of their strategy in a form which necessarily implied anticipating revolutionary developments in areas over which their forces had no control whatsoever. In other words, their strategy involved the contradiction between two imperatives: first, the need to go it alone, as the *immediate* (historical) pre-condition of success (of doing it at all); secondly, the imperative of the triumph of the world socialist revolution, as the *ultimate* (structural) precondition of success for the whole enterprise.

Understandably, therefore, when the actual conquest of power in October 1917 created a new situation, Lenin exclaimed with a sigh of relief: 'It is more pleasant and useful to go through the "experience of the revolution" than to write about it.'[9] And again: 'The October 25 Revolution has transferred the question raised in this pamphlet from the sphere of theory to the sphere of practice. This question must now be answered by deeds, not words.'[10] But how deeds could themselves answer the dilemma concerning the grave difficulties of accomplishing all the necessary 'material groundwork' which constitutes the prerequisite of a successful socialist transformation, without 'words' — without, that is, a coherent theory soberly assessing the massive potential dangers involved, and indicating at the same time, if feasible, the possibilities of a solution to them — Lenin did not say. He simply could not envisage the possibility of an objective contradiction between the dictatorship of the proletariat and the proletariat itself.

While in March and April 1917 Lenin was still advocating 'a state *without* a standing army, *without* a police opposed to the people,

without an officialdom placed above the people',[11] and proposed
to 'organize and arm *all* the poor, exploited sections of the population in order that they *themselves* should take the organs of state
power directly into their own hands, in order that *they themselves
should constitute* these organs of state power',[12] a significant shift
became visible in his orientation after the seizure of power. The main
themes of *The State and Revolution* receded further and further in
his thought. Positive references to the experience of the Paris
Commune (as the *direct* involvement of '*all* the poor, exploited
sections of the population' in the exercise of power) disappeared from
his speeches and writings; and the accent was laid on 'the need for a
central authority, for dictatorship and a united will to ensure that
the *vanguard* of the proletariat shall close *its ranks, develop the state*
and place it upon a new footing, while *firmly holding the reigns of
power*'.[13] Thus, in contrast to the original intentions which
predicated the fundamental identity of the '*entire armed people*',
[14] with state power, there appeared a separation of the latter from
'the working people', whereby '*state power* is organizing large-scale
production on *state-owned* land and in *state-owned* enterprises on a
national scale, is *distributing labour-power* among the various
branches of economy and the various enterprises, and is distributing
among *the working people* large quantities of articles of consumption
belonging to the state'.[15] The fact that the relationship of the
working people to state power manifested as the *central distribution
of labour-power* was a relationship of structural subordination did
not seem to trouble Lenin, who bypassed this issue by simply
describing the new form of separate state power as 'the proletarian
state power'.[16] Thus the objective contradiction between the
dictatorship of the proletariat and the proletariat itself disappeared
from his horizon, at the very moment it surfaced in reality as a
centralized state power which determined on its own the distribution
of labour-power. At the most generic level of class relations — corresponding to the polar opposition between the proletariat and the
bourgeoisie — the contradiction did not seem to exist. The new state
had to secure its own material base and the central distribution of
labour-power appeared to be the only viable principle for achieving
this, *from the standpoint of the state already in existence*.* In reality,

*The extent to which the newly constituted state organs were structurally
conditioned by the old state should not be underestimated. Lenin's analysis
of this problem in his stock-taking speech on the NEP is most revealing. 'We

however, it was 'the working people' themselves who had to be reduced to and distributed as 'labour-power': not only over immense geographical distances — with all the upheavals and dislocations inevitably involved in such a centrally imposed system of distribution — but also 'vertically' in each and every locality, in accordance with both the material dictates of the inherited production structures and the political dictates inherent in their newly constituted principle and organs of regulation.

Lukács's Solution

No matter how problematical his conclusions, it was Lukács's great intellectual merit to have highlighted this dilemma in a most acute form, in one of his relatively unknown articles, written in the spring of 1919. The issue is important enough to warrant the long quotation which is needed to reproduce faithfully the train of his thought: 'It is clear that the most oppressive phenomena of proletarian power —

---

took over the old machinery of state, and *that was our misfortune*. Very often this machinery operates against us. In 1917, after we seized power, the government officials sabotaged us. This frightened us very much and we pleaded: "Please come back". They all came back but *that was our misfortune*. We now have a vast army of government employees, but lack sufficiently educated forces *to exercise real control over them*. In practice it often happens that here *at the top, where we exercise political power*, the machine functions somehow; but down below government employees have arbitrary control and they often exercise it in such a way as to *contradict our measures*. At the top, we have, I don't know how many, but at all events, I think no more than a few thousand, at the outside several tens of thousands of our own people. Down below, however, there are hundreds of thousands of officials whom we got from the Tsar and from bourgeois society and who, partly deliberately, and partly unwittingly, work against us.' (*Collected Works*, Vol.33, pp.428-9, emphasis added.) The new state power was constituted and consolidated through such tensions and contradictions, which deeply affected its structural articulation at all levels. The old heritage, with its massive inertia, was a factor that weighed heavily on successive stages of Soviet development. Not only in the sense that 'state officialdom placed above the people' could counteract the 'good measures' taken at the top where political power was being exercised, but even more in that this type of decision-making — a far cry from the originally advocated alternative described in *State and Revolution*, with reference to the principles of the Paris Commune — turned itself into an *ideal*. From now on the problem was identified as the conscious or unwitting obstruction of state authority by local officials and their allies, and the remedy as the strictest possible form of centralized control over all spheres of social life.

namely, scarcity of goods and high prices, of whose immediate consequences every proletarian has personal experience — are the direct consequences of the slackening of labour-discipline and the decline in production. The creation of remedies for these, and the consequent improvement in the individual's standard of living, can only be brought about when the causes of these phenomena have been removed. Help comes in two ways. Either the individuals who constitute the proletariat *realize* that they can help themselves only by bringing about a voluntary strengthening of labour-discipline, and consequently a rise in production: or, if they are incapable of this, *they create institutions which are capable of bringing about this necessary state of affairs.* In the latter case, they create a legal system through which the proletariat *compels* its own individual members, the proletarians, to act in a way which corresponds to their class-interests: *the proletariat turns its dictatorship against itself.* This measure is necessary for the self-preservation of the proletariat when correct recognition of class-interests and voluntary action in these interests do not exist. But one must not hide from oneself the fact that this method contains within itself *great dangers for the future.* When the proletariat itself is the creator of labour-discipline, when the labour-system of the proletarian state is built on a *moral* basis, then the external compulsion of the law ceases *automatically* with the abolition of class division — that is, the state withers away — and this liquidation of class-division produces out of itself the beginning of the true history of humanity, which Marx prophesied and hoped for. If, on the other hand, the proletariat follows another path, it must create a legal system which cannot be abolished automatically by historical development. Development would therefore proceed in a direction which *endangered the appearance and realization of the ultimate aim.* For the legal system which the proletariat is compelled to create in this way *must be overthrown* — and who knows what convulsions and what injuries will be caused by a transition which leads from the kingdom of necessity to the kingdom of freedom by such a *détour?* ... It depends on the proletariat whether the real history of humanity begins — that is to say, *the power of morality over institutions and economics.*'[17]

This quotation shows Lukács's great power of insight as regards the objective dialectic of a certain type of development, formulated from a rather abstract philosophical point of view. Lenin, by comparison, preferring 'deeds' to 'words', was far too busy trying to squeeze out the last drop of practical socialist possibilities from the objective instrumental set-up of his situation to indulge in theoretical anticipations of this kind in 1919. By the time he started to concentrate on the dreadful danger of an ever-increasing domination of the ideals of socialism by the 'institutions of necessity', it was too late — not only for him personally, but historically too late — to reverse the course of developments. The idea of autonomous working-class action had been replaced by advocacy of 'the greatest possible centralization'.* Both the Soviets and the factory councils had been deprived of all effective power, and in the course of the trade-union debate all attempts at securing even a very limited degree of self-determination for the working-class base had been dismissed as 'syndicalist nonsense'[18] and as 'a deviation towards syndicalism and anarchism',[19] seen as a direct threat to the dictatorship of the proletariat. The cruel irony of it all is that Lenin himself, totally dedicated as he was to the cause of the socialist revolution, helped to paralyse the selfsame forces of the working-class base to which he tried to turn later for help, when he perceived the fateful danger of those developments in Russia which were to culminate in Stalinism. Against this background, it is pathetic to see Lenin, a genius of realistic strategy, behaving like a desperate utopian from 1923 to the moment of his death: insistently putting forward hopeless schemes — like the proposal to create a majority in the Central Committee from working-class cadres, in order to neutralize the Party bureaucrats — in the hope of reversing this dangerous trend, by now far too advanced. Lenin's great tragedy was that his incomparable, instrumentally concrete, intensely practical strategy in the end defeated him. In the last year of his life, there was no longer a way out of his almost total isolation. The developments he himself, far more than anybody else, had helped to set in motion had made him historically superfluous. The specific form in which he lived the unity of theory and practice proved to be the limit even of his greatness.

What was extremely problematical in Lukács's discourse was the

---

*'Communism requires and presupposes the *greatest possible centralization* of large-scale production throughout the country. The all-Russia centre, therefore, should definitely be given the right of *direct control* over *all* the enterprises of the given branch of industry. The regional centres define their functions depending on local conditions of life, etc., in accordance with the *general* production directions and *decisions of the centre*.' Anything short of such centralization was condemned as 'regional *anarcho-syndicalism*'. See Lenin, *Collected Works*, Vol.42, p.96 (emphasis added).

suggestion that the acceptance of the need for higher productivity and greater labour discipline — as a result of the philosopher's direct moral appeal to the consciousness of individual proletarians — might avert the danger so graphically described and render the creation of the institutions of necessity superfluous. What degree of labour discipline is high enough under the conditions of extreme urgency of the necessary 'material groundwork'? Is 'correct recognition of class-interest' *ipso facto* the end of all possible objective contradiction between individual and class interest? These and similar questions did not appear on Lukács's horizon, which remained idealistically clouded by postulating an individualistic yet uniform moral base of social practice as an *alternative* to collective necessity. Nevertheless, he clearly spelled out not only the possibility of the proletariat turning its dictatorship against itself, but also the anguishing implications of such a state of affairs for the future when 'the legal system which the proletariat is compelled to create in this way *must be overthrown*'.

Was it this early thought, perhaps, which Lukács tried to amplify in much greater detail, in the light of subsequent developments, in an unpublished 'political testament' he wrote in 1968, following his bitter condemnation of the military intervention in Czechoslovakia? Be that as it may, the dilemma remains as acute as ever. What were those objective and subjective determinations which produced the submission of the proletariat to the political form through which it assumed power, and is it possible to overcome them? How is it possible to avoid the potential convulsions associated with the imperative need of changing in depth the prevailing forms of political rule? What are the conditions of transforming the existing rigid 'institutions of necessity', by means of which dissent is suppressed and compulsion enforced, into more flexible institution of social involvement, foreshadowing that 'free development of individualities' which continues to elude us?

Individual and Class

This is the point where we must put into relief the relevance for our problem of Marx's considerations on the relationship between individual and class. For in the absence of a proper understanding of this relationship, the transformation of the transitional political form into a dictatorship exercised also over the proletariat (notwithstanding the original democratic intent) remains deeply shrouded in mystery. How is it possible for such a transformation to take place? The ideas of 'degeneration', 'bureaucratization', 'substitutionism' and the like not only all beg the question, but also culminate in an illusory remedy, explicit or implied: namely, that the simple overthrow of this political form and the substitution of dedicated revolutionaries for party bureaucrats will reverse the process — forgetting that the blamed party bureaucrats too were in their time dedicated revolutionaries. Hypotheses of this kind idealistically transfer the problem from the plane of objective contradictions to that of individual psychology, which can explain at best only the question of why a certain type of person is best suited to mediate the objective structures of a given political form, but not the nature of those structures themselves.

Similarly, it would be very naive to accept that the new structures of political domination suddenly and automatically — and just as mysteriously — come into existence following the refusal of proletarians to accept an intensified labour-discipline and a self-sacrifice that have been dictated to them. On the contrary, the very fact that the question can be raised in this form is itself already evidence that the structures of domination are in existence before the question is even thought of. Admonitions and threats are empty words if they do not issue out of material power. But if they do, it is an idealistic reversal of the actual state of affairs to represent *material dictates* as *moral imperatives* which, if unheeded, would be followed by material dictates and sanctions. In reality, material dictates are internalized as moral imperatives only under the exceptional circumstances of a *state of emergency*, when reality itself rules out the possibility of alternative courses of action. To identify the two — i.e. to treat material dictates as moral imperatives — would mean to lock the life-processes of society into the unbearably narrow confines of a permanent state of emergency.

What are the structures of domination on the basis of which the new political form arises, which it must get rid of if it is not to remain a permanent obstacle to the realization of socialism? In discussions of Marx's critique of the state, what is usually forgotten is that it is not concerned simply with the termination of a specific form of class rule — the capitalist — but with a much more fundamental issue: the full emancipation of the social individual. The following quotation makes this amply clear: 'the proletarians, if they are to assert themselves as *individuals*, have to abolish the hitherto prevailing condition of their existence (which has, moreover, been that of all society up to then), namely, *labour*. Thus they find themselves directly opposed to the form in which, hitherto, the *individuals*, of which society consists, have given themselves *collective expression*, that is, the State. In order, therefore, to *assert themselves as individuals*, they must overthrow the State.'[20] Try and remove the concept of 'individuals' from this reasoning, and the whole enterprise becomes meaningless. For the need to abolish the State arises because the individuals cannot 'assert themselves as individuals', and not simply because one class is dominated by another.

The same consideration applies to the question of individual and class. Again, discussions of Marx's theory as a rule neglect this aspect, and concentrate on what he says about emancipating the proletariat from the bourgeoisie. But what would be the point of this emancipation if the individuals who constitute the proletariat remained dominated by the proletariat as a class? And it is precisely this relationship of domination which *precedes* the establishment of the dictatorship of the proletariat. There is no need to establish anew the domination of the proletarians by the proletariat, since that domination already exists, though in a different form, well before the question of taking power historically arises: 'the class in its turn assumes an *independent existence as against the individuals*, so that the latter find their conditions of life *predetermined*, and have their position in life and hence their personal development *assigned to them by their class*, thus become *subsumed* under it. This is the same phenomenon as the *subjection* of the separate individuals to the division of labour and can only be removed by the *abolition* of private property and of *labour itself*.'[21]

To be sure, this aspect of class domination holds in all forms of class society, irrespective of their specific political superstructures. Nor could it be otherwise, given the existence of irreconcilable inter-class antagonisms; indeed, the submission of the individuals to their class is a necessary concomitant of the latter. Moreover, this condition applies just as much to advanced capitalist countries as to their more or less underdeveloped counterparts. It would, therefore, be illusory to expect that the political consequences of this objective structural contradiction could be avoided simply in virtue of some undeniable differences at the level of the legal-political superstructure. For the contradiction in question is an objective antagonism of the *socio-economic base* as structured according to a hierarchical *social division of labour*, though, of course, it also manifests itself at the political plane. Underneath any so-called 'elected dictatorship of Ministers' (or, for that matter, under whatever other form of liberal democracy), there lies the 'unelected dictatorship' of the hierarchical-social division of labour, which structurally subordinates one class to another and at the same time subjects individuals to their own class as well, predestining them to a narrowly defined position and role in society in accordance with the material dictates of the prevailing socio-economic system, and thus unceremoniously ensuring that, may Ministers come and go as the electors please, the structure of domination itself remains intact.

Paradoxically, this dilemma of the structural domination of individual by their own class becomes more rather than less acute in the aftermath of the revolution. In the preceding form of society, the severity of inter-class antagonism gives an apparently — and to a significant extent also objectively — benevolent character to the subjection of individuals to their own class, in that the class does not champion only its own interests as a class but, simultaneously, also the interests of its individual members against the other class. Individual proletarians accept their subordination to their own class — though even that not without deep-seated conflict over objective sectional interests — since class solidarity is a *necessary prerequisite* of their emancipation from the rule of the capitalist class, although it is an astronomical distance from being the *sufficient condition* of their emancipation as *social individuals*. Once the capitalist class is defeated and expropriated, however, the objective structural contradiction between class and individual is activated in its full intensity, since the dampening factor of inter-class antagonism is effectively removed, or at least transferred to the international plane.

It is this contradiction between class and individual which is intensified in the aftermath of the revolution to the point that it may indeed, in the absence of adequate corrective forces and measures, endanger the very survival of the dictatorship of the proletariat and revert society to the *status quo ante*. What we witness, however, at the level of political ideology and practice is the misrepresentation of a necessary prerequisite of class emancipation as the sufficient condition of full emancipation, which is said to be hindered only by 'survivals from the past', or the 'survival of the class enemy'. Thus the rather intangible 'enemy within' becomes a mythical force whose empirical counterpart must be invented, to fill with millions of common people the emerging concentration camps.

One cannot emphasize too strongly that the ideological-political mystification does not feed on itself (if only it did, for that would be relatively easy to overcome), but on an objective contradiction of the socio-economic base. It is because 'the condition of existence of individual proletarians, namely labour', is not abolished as Marx advocated — because in other words, hierarchical social division of labour remains the fundamental regulatory force of the social metabolism — that the antagonism, deprived of its justification through the expropriation of the opposite class, intensifies, creating a new form of alienation between the individuals who constitute society and the political power which controls their interchanges. It is because the dictatorship of the proletariat cannot remove the 'contradictions of civil society' by abolishing both sides of the social antagonism, including labour — on the contrary, it has to envisage enhancing the latter, in function of the absolutely necessary 'material foundation' — that 'the proletariat turns its dictatorship against itself'.[22] Or, to be more precise, in order to maintain its rule over society as a class, the proletariat turns its dictatorship against *all* individuals who constitute society, including the proletarians. (Indeed, including the party and state officials who have a mandate to carry out determinate functions and not others, following the imperatives of the system in existence and not their own exclusive sectional interests, even if by virtue of their privileged location with regard to the machinery of power they are in a position to appropriate a greater portion of the social product than other groups of individuals, whether or not they actually do so.)

Since one side of the antithesis Marx speaks of — labour — cannot be preserved on its own, under the new conditions of the post-revolutionary society a new form of manifestation must be found for the other side as well. The expropriation of the capitalist class, and the radical disruption and alteration of the normal market conditions which characterize the functioning of commodity society, impose radically new functions on the proletariat state. It is called upon to regulate, *in toto* and in small detail, the production and distribution process, directly determining the allocation of social resources, the conditions and the intensity of labour, the rate of surplus-extraction and accumulation, and the particular share of each individual in that portion of the social product which it makes available for consumption. From now on we are confronted with a system of production in which the *extraction of surplus-labour is politically determined* in the most summary form, using extra-economic criteria (ultimately the survival of the state itself) which, under determinate conditions, may in fact disrupt or even chronically retard the development of the productive forces. Such a politically determined extraction of surplus-labour — which, under the conditions of extreme penury and in the absence of strictly economic regulatory forces and mechanisms, may indeed reach dangerously high levels, whereupon it becomes self-defeatingly counter-productive — inevitably sharpens the contradiction between individual producers and the state, with the gravest implications for the possibility of *dissent*. For under these circumstances dissent may directly endanger the extraction of surplus-labour (and everything else built upon it), thus potentially depriving the dictatorship of the proletariat of its material base and challenging its very survival.

By contrast, the liberal state, under normal conditions, has no need to regulate *directly* the extraction of surplus-value, since the complex mechanisms of commodity-production take care of that. All it has to do is to ensure *indirectly* the safeguard of the economic system itself. Therefore, it need not worry at all about the manifestations of political dissent, so long as the impersonal mechanisms of commodity-production carry on their functions undisturbed. Of course, the situation significantly changes at times of major crises, when the forces of opposition cannot confine themselves any longer to contesting only the *rate* of surplus-value extraction, but have to question the very *mode* of surplus-value production and appropriation. If they do this with any success, then the capitalist state may be compelled to assume very far from 'liberal' forms. Similarly, under the conditions of present-day development, when we can witness as a trend that the whole system of global capitalism is becoming extremely 'disfunctional', the state is forced to assume increasingly more direct regulatory functions, with potentially serious implications for dissent and opposition. But even under such circumstances, the respective structures are fundamentally different in that the political involvement of the capitalist state applies to an all-pervasive system of commodity-production, and the underlying aim is the reconstitution of the self-regulatory function of the latter, whether it can be successfully accomplished or not. By contrast, the · post-revolutionary state combines, as a matter of *normality*, the function of overall political control with that of securing and regulating the extraction of surplus-labour as the new mode of carrying on the material life-processes of society. It is the close integration of the two which produces apparently insurmountable difficulties for dissent and opposition.

Breaking the Rule of Capital

All this puts sharply into relief the dilemma we have to face when we try to envisage a socialist solution to the underlying problems. In 1957 a gifted young German writer Conrad Rheinhold had to flee the DDR, where he used to run a political cabaret in the aftermath of the Twentieth Congress. After he had had some experience of life in West Germany, he was asked by *Der Spiegel* to describe the main difference between his old and new situations. This was his answer: 'In the East political cabaret is supposed to change society, but it is not allowed to say anything; in the West it is allowed to say whatever it pleases, so long as it cannot change anything at all.' (*'Im Osten soll das Kabarett die Gesellschaft ändern, darf aber nichts sagen; im Westen kann es alles sagen, darf aber nichts ändern.'*) Is there a way out of this painful dilemma? If there is, it must be through the maturation of the objective conditions of development to which political movements can relate themselves, greatly accelerating or powerfully frustrating their unfolding. In this respect, it matters very much whether or not post-revolutionary societies represent some new form of capitalism ('state capitalism', for example). For if they do, with the advent of the revolution nothing has really happened: no real steps have been taken in the direction of emancipation, and the allegedly monolithic power of capitalism which prevails in all its forms makes the future look extremely gloomy.

Marx wrote his *Capital* in the service of breaking the rule of *capital*, not just *capitalism*. Yet, strangely enough, it is on the assessment of this innermost nature of his project that the misconceptions are the greatest and most damaging. The title of Book I of *Capital* Volume One was first translated into English, under Engels's supervision, as 'A Critical Analysis of Capitalist Production', whereas the original speaks of 'The Process of Production of Capital' (*Der Produktionsprozess des Kapitals*), which is a radically different thing. Marx's project is concerned with the conditions of production and reproduction of capital itself — its genesis and expansion, as well as the inherent contradictions which foreshadow its supersession through a 'long and painful process of development' — whereas the mistranslated version speaks of a given phase of capital production only, while confusingly conflating the concepts of 'capitalist production' and 'production of capital'.

The concept of capital is much more fundamental than that of capitalism. The latter is limited to a relatively short historical period, whereas the former embraces a great deal more than that. It is concerned, in addition to the mode of functioning of the given capitalist society, with the conditions of origin and development of capital production, including the phases when commodity-production is not all-pervasive and dominating as it is under capitalism. On the other side of the radical socio-historical line of demarcation drawn by the breakdown of capitalism, it is equally concerned with the forms and modalities in which the need for capital production is bound to survive in post-capitalist societies for a long and painful historical period — until, that is, the hierarchical social division of labour itself is successfully superseded, and society is completely restructured in accordance with the free association of social individuals who consciously regulate their own life-activities.

The rule of capital, rooted in the prevailing system of division of labour (which cannot conceivably be abolished by a political act alone, no matter how radical and free from 'degeneration'), thus prevails over a significant part of the transitional period, although it must exhibit the characteristics of a *diminishing trend* if the transition is to be successful at all. But this does not mean that post-revolutionary societies remain 'capitalist', just as feudal and earlier societies cannot be rightfully characterized as capitalist on the basis of the more or less extensive use of monetary capital and the more or less advanced share which commodity-production, as a subordinate element, occupies in them. Capitalism is that particular phase of capital production in which 1. *production for exchange* (and thus the mediation and domination of use-value by exchange-value) is *all-pervasive*; 2. *labour-power* itself, just as much as anything else, is treated as a *commodity*; 3. the drive for *profit* is a fundamental regulatory force of production; 4. the vital mechanism of the extraction of surplus-value, the radical separation of the means of production from the producers, assumes an *inherently economic form*; 5. the economically extracted surplus-value is *privately appropriated* by the members of the capitalist class; and 6. following its own *economic imperative* of growth and expansion, capital productions tends towards a *global integration*, through the intermediary of the world market, as a totally interdependent system of economic domination and subordination. To speak of capitalism in post-revolutionary societies, when out of these essential defining characteristics only one — number four — remains and even that in a radically altered form in that the extraction of surplus-labour is regulated politically and not economically, can be done only by disregarding or misrepresenting the objective conditions of development, with serious consequences for the possibility of gaining insight into the real nature of the problems at stake.

Capital maintains its — by no means unrestricted — rule in post-revolutionary societies primarily through 1. the material imperatives which circumscribe the possibilities of the totality of life-processes; 2. the inherited social division of labour which, notwithstanding its significant modifications, contradicts 'the development of free individualities'; 3. the objective structure of the available production apparatus (including plant and machinery) and of the historically developed and restricted form of scientific knowledge, both originally produced in the framework of capital production and under the conditions of the social division of labour; and 4. the links and interconnections of the post-revolutionary societies with the global system of capitalism, whether these assume the form of a 'peaceful competition' (e.g. commercial and cultural exchanges) or that of a potentially deadly opposition (from the arms race to more or less limited actual confrontations in contested areas). Thus the issue is incomparably more complex and far-reaching than its conventional characterization as the imperative of capital accumulation, now renamed as 'socialist accumulation'.

Capital constitutes a highly contradictory world system, with the capitalist 'metropolitan' countries and the major post-revolutionary societies as its poles related to a multiplicity of gradations and stages of mixed development. It is this dynamic, contradictory totality which makes the possibilities of dissent and opposition much more hopeful than the monolithic conception of the power of capitalism would suggest. Post-revolutionary societies are also post-capitalist societies, in the significant sense that their objective structures effectively prevent the restoration of capitalism. To be sure, their inner contradictions, further complicated and intensified by their interactions with capitalist countries, may produce shifts and adjustments within their structures in favour of commodity relations. Nevertheless, the possibility of such shifts and adjustments is fairly limited. It is strictly circumscribed by the fact that the political extraction of surplus-labour cannot be radically altered without profoundly affecting (indeed endangering) the political power in existence. The systematic frustration and prevention of dissent has its complement in the extremely limited success of recent attempts at introducing strictly economic mechanisms into the overall structure of production. Post-revolutionary societies, as yet, have no such self-regulatory mechanisms which would ensure that dissenters 'say whatever they please without changing anything at all'. Indeed, it would be a Pyrrhic victory if dissent developed in post-revolutionary societies parallel to the reintroduction of powerful capitalistic mechanisms and institutions. Positive developments in this respect may be envisaged only if the system finds some way of achieving an effective, institutionally underpinned distribution of political power (even if very limited in the first place) which does not represent a danger to the prevailing mode of extracting surplus-labour as such — although of necessity it would question its particular manifestations and excesses. In other words, 'decentralization', 'diversification', 'autonomy' and the like must be implemented in post-revolutionary societies as — in the first place — *political* principles, in order to be meaningful at all.

The dynamic, contradictory totality mentioned above is also an *interdependent* totality through and through. What happens at one place has an important bearing on the possibilities of development elsewhere. The demand for a much greater effectiveness of dissent and opposition in the West arises now under circumstances when the capitalist system exhibits severe symptoms of crisis, with potentially far-reaching consequences. The weakening of the essential mechanisms of control of commodity society — which in their normal functioning successfully nullify dissent and opposition without the slightest need for suppressing them — offers more scope for the development of effective alternatives, and the debate on 'pluralism' must be situated in this problematic. At the same time, it is not without a profound significance that virtually all forces of the left have thoroughly disengaged themselves from an earlier uncritical attitude towards the assessment of post-revolutionary developments. This attitude in the past reflected a state of enforced *immobility*, and could not envisage more than repeatedly reasserting its ideal as a 'declaration of intent' about the future, however remote, instead of undertaking a realistic assessment of a historical experience in relation to its own concrete tasks. In a world of total interdependence, if effective achievements result from this critical examination — which is inseparably also a self-examination — that will not be without positive consequences for the development of dissent and meaningful opposition in the post-revolutionary societies.

NOTES

1. *The Poverty of Philosophy*, in Karl Marx and Frederick Engels, *Collected Works*, Vol.6, London 1976, pp.211-212 (emphasis added).
2. *The Holy Family*, in Marx and Engels, *Collected Works*, Vol.4, London 1975, p.36 (emphasis added).
3. *Capital*, Penguin/NLR edition, Vol.1, London 1976, p.173 (emphasis added).
4. Ibid., (emphasis added).
5. *Grundrisse*, London 1973, p.706 (emphasis added).
6. In a section added to the second edition of *The State and Revolution* see *Collected Works*, Vol.25, p.412 (emphasis added).
7. Ibid., Vol.26, p.130 (emphasis added).
8. Ibid.
9. Ibid., Vol.25, p.412.
10. Ibid., Vol.26, p.89.
11. Ibid., Vol.24, p.49 (Lenin's emphasis).
12. Ibid., Vol.23, p.326 (Lenin's emphasis).
13. Ibid., Vol.30, p.422 (emphasis added).
14. Ibid., Vol.23, p.325 (Lenin's emphasis).
15. Ibid., Vol.30, pp.108-109 (emphasis added).
16. Ibid., p.108.
17. 'Az erkölcs szerepe a komunista termelésben' (The Role of Morality in Communist Production). The translation here is my own, but see George Lukács, *Political Writings 1919-1929*, London 1968, pp.51-52.
18. 'All this syndicalist nonsense about mandatory nominations of producers must go into the wastepaper basket. To proceed on those lines would mean thrusting the Party aside and *making the dictatorship of the proletariat in Russia impossible.*' Ibid., Vol.32, p.62 (emphasis added).
19. Ibid., p.246. And again, 'The syndicalist malaise must and will be cured', Ibid., p.107.
20. *The German Ideology*, in Marx and Engels, *Collected Works*, Vol.5, London 1976, p.80 (emphasis added).
21. Ibid., p.77 (emphasis added).
22. As Lukács put it in the passage quoted earlier.

The State and Bureaucratic Classes, East and West

Francesco Cavazzuti

Francesco Cavazutti, born in 1939, teaches law at the School of Economics and Commerce of the University of Modena. He deals in particular with the relationship between institutions and the economy. He contributes to trade-union publications, il manifesto, *and many other Italian journals and is the author of the book* Capitale monopolistico, impresa, e istituzioni, *Il Mulino, 1974.*

I would like to go back to Bettelheim's report, which I think contained elements that enable us to draw some conclusions about the real situation in the Soviet Union. These conclusions are not the product of a mere inclination towards sociological discussion, but allow for a more comprehensive political approach.

One element of Bettelheim's report, which involves the debate on the nature of the Soviet state, seems to me to acquire considerable importance when related to a theme he deals with in other writings but did not touch on explicitly in his report this morning.

Bettelheim begins from a critique of the formal notion of property in the juridical sense. I would like to recall that even from the bourgeois point of view, there is no great difficulty in recognizing that when one talks about property rights one is using an expression that summarizes a system of power. What exists is not property in the abstract, but property owners. Property in the abstract is embodied only in the rules of the game drawn up by the property owners.

What does this mean when translated into a system of what Bettelheim calls state capitalism? It means that although there are situations which may be described by the summary expression 'state capitalism', the problem of whether or not capitalists exist remains to be analyzed.

In other words, how are we to define these ruling groups, these social classes, which do not possess the means of production through the formal legitimacy of property in the traditional sense, but nevertheless command power in a manner that subsumes nearly all the content of traditional property rights?

In one of his works Bettelheim used another concept, that of 'possession'. This morning, when he talked about disposition, it occurred to me that the economic constitution of nineteenth century liberalism was fully inherent in the Napoleonic code; possession was described precisely as the power of disposition over goods.

There is, then, a situation in which power over the means of production is exercised by social classes who derive their legitimacy from the fact that they belong to a given political structure and from the role they play in it.

And here we have an element whose importance, in my opinion, has always been underestimated by the entire left when analyzing the state and the extension of the functions of the state (and we may regard the Soviet Union as a model in this): the emergence and development of social classes created by the very functions of the state itself. In other words, the state is not an abstraction; the growth and expansion of these classes are inherent in the nature of the state itself.

The relevance and importance of the considerations raised by Edoarda Masi in regard to the Chinese situation thus become evident.

I would like to recall that during the discussion on the state in China around 1974, Chiang Chiung Chiao, one of the supporters of the 'gang of four', wrote an article analyzing the survival of capitalism, of capitalist forms, in socialist society. He clearly explained that here he was not referring to the survival of the traditional capitalist forms described by Lenin — shopkeepers, peasants, and so on, which are remnants of history, left over after the transition. Rather, he maintained, it was important to investigate how the public action of the state itself creates these classes.

The result, then, is the rise of classes that derive their power not from the wellspring of property rights, but from their membership in certain institutions.

I believe that this is an enormously important element not only in the debate on the situation in the Soviet Union and the socialist countries, but also in grappling with the theoretical and political difficulties of the left in the West.

The problem of state capitalism and the role played in it by classes that draw their power from institutional affiliation must, I believe, be one of the elements of our current political debate. Overly facile syntheses and comparisons are inadmissible, of course, but there is no doubt that the expansion of public activity engenders the growth of such classes even in the West. Italy, I would say, can play an important part in our analysis of this point. What all this means is that when the left thinks about the state it may find that the Soviet Union is not only an object of examination but also a mirror reflecting possible trends of development of the relationship between the state and the economy in the West.

Why do I insist on this point? Because in past months there has been a great debate on the state in both Italy and France. And we have seen, for example, that the reality of existing socialism has been used in important and authoritative expositions of the crisis of the classical liberal state. I am thinking, for example, of Noberto Bobbio. Pointing to the expansion of the role of the state and the idealization of the historically developed socialist world as a model, these people maintain that the system of bourgeois-democratic rights, of traditional liberties, must be reaffirmed, along with all their corollaries, or better, along with all the elements that underlie their existence. Hence the problem of the market, of freedom of enterprise, and so on. This is a problem to which the left has not always been able to offer clear, exhaustive, and cogent answers. I believe that both the Communist left and the new left face a real impasse relative to these provocations, the limits and importance of which we cannot grasp by dealing with purely particular problems.

One may, of course, reply that the system of free enterprise and the market — which lies at the root of bourgeois-democratic rights, institutional pluralism, and the parliamentary system — is in crisis because of the processes of capitalist concentration and the integration between the state and the economy. But we often realize that we are unable to go beyond this observation and fashion a political theory and theory of the state which deal in a non-regressive way with the processes of modification occurring in the capitalist state itself.

I would say that one of the fundamental elements of this modification is precisely the existence of those classes engendered by the state already referred to. I remember the discussion during the fifties about the de-personalization of capitalist property, the birth of managerial bureaucracies. There was a similar discussion in the thirties about the Soviet Union and the attempts at planning in the

West. Now the same discussion is arising again, but in a different guise: the alleged objectivity of any enterprise managed by a neutral bureaucracy; for isn't this what lies at the root of all the various co-management proposals now being bandied about in the West?

And these proposals, apart from their ideological aspects, are always accompanied by constitutional formulas; i.e. formulas at the level of relations between institutions and individual liberties, formulas which have an authoritarian flavour in that they always place the emphasis more on organization than on concertation.

This would raise another point as well: criminalization and normalization. Here the Soviet Union is a burning issue among the left not only as a great disappointment, but also as a moment of reflection on our own history, a possible image of the future, of a state in which economics and politics are welded together completely, a state in which the establishment of consensus becomes the fundamental objective of all the forms of political or economic aggregation.

Hence the reflection on the role of the trade unions. It must not be forgotten that one of the turning points in the change in the political and constitutional basis of the Soviet Union occurred precisely over the debate on the unions in the early twenties.

For all these reasons, then, the discussion on the Soviet Union involves our very destiny in the West. We must formulate a project for transition that does not simply mimic the roads of planning *tout court*.

Another element that must be re-examined is the significance of the presence of the Soviet Union beyond its borders, not only in the usual terms (so-called social imperialism and the sorts of problems raised by the polemics of the Chinese), but also keeping in mind that the Soviet model is nothing if not easily exportable. Indeed, it has been exported to many countries of the third world in which the state bourgeoisie now constitutes the dominant class, as a bourgeoisie that draws its legitimacy not from private property in land (I say land because these are countries in which the products of industry are rather meagre) but from the institutional role played by the single party.

In some cases we have seen the development of a new 'comprador' state bourgeoisie, a state bourgeoisie in which private property tends to flourish again, at least in those countries in which it is permitted by law. The mechanism is quite simple: the state is used as an instrument of private accumulation of capital, and this capital is invested in real estate. In these countries the old tribal or colonial landlords are being replaced by new landlords recruited from the membership of the secretariats of the various single parties that rule these countries.

Here again, the important thing is not to fashion an abstract model, but to grasp how this question of the classes which use the state as the source of their legitimacy in reestablishing class rule remains one of the central themes to be dealt with when examining the state. This is especially important for the parties in the West that want to develop a strategy for the transition to socialism.

Class Struggle, East and West

Elio Giovannini

Elio Giovannini, born in Rome in 1929, directed student work for the youth commission of the Italian Socialist Party until 1950. He was later a leader of the PSI federations of Varese and Como and became a member of the Central Committee in 1957. When the PSI split in the early sixties, he joined the PSIUP, and later the PDUP. A trade-union leader and former member of the national secretariat of the metalworkers' union, since 1970 he has been national secretary of the General Confederation of Italian Workers. (CGIL).

I believe that we are all aware of how difficult it is to deal with the hypothesis Rossanda defined in her introduction, one which has the merit of placing the entire workers' movement before the problem of really re-examining its attitude toward the post-revolutionary societies of Eastern Europe.

The difficulty arises from the fact that we stand in the tradition of struggle of the western workers' movement, a fact whose importance is not always appreciated by the East European comrades. This movement, not only in its Communist, Third Internationalist expression, but also in its Socialist expression (here it is sufficient to recall the positions taken by Otto Bauer in his book *Between Two World Wars*) has long considered the Soviet Union a society which, although deeply afflicted by dramatic contradictions (and we have refused to ignore the terrible denials of general liberties), represented a 'bulwark' of the international class struggle, as we used to put it during the period between the two world wars and again after the Second World War. Critical reflection on the great processes of regression in Soviet socialist society has been, to some extent, sacrificed on the altar of this assessment.

But alongside this old tradition, we must also confront a new position on the Soviet Union that has cropped up in the Italian left in recent years, especially among the historic left. This is a wholly apologetic historicism which tends to view the processes that led to October as so closely linked to Russian backwardness, to the political immaturity of the Russian proletariat, as to render unintelligible the international context in which the Russian Communists made the revolution.

These days, this historicism, if we may call it that, is expressed in the supposition that the allegedly socialist structure of the East European countries and the Soviet Union will eventually modify the unfree superstructures and effect the transition from an embryo of socialist society, which supposedly already exists in the East, to a completed socialist society.

The most negative element of this position, apart from its content, lies, in my opinion, in its tendency to consider the processes under way in the Soviet Union and Eastern Europe as processes which should be examined without the interpretive criteria and guidelines with which the workers' movement in Italy and the other countries of Western Europe organizes its struggle and determines its perspectives.

And there is another sort of proxy attitude which is also part of the historic legacy not only of the old left, but of the new as well. Here the solution to the problems of Soviet society and the societies of Eastern Europe is delegated either to an idealized Chinese revolution which would automatically correct the model of socialist revolution and socialist transformation of the state or to a western revolution which, by causing a breakthrough in the West, would automatically unravel the historic knots of the crisis of the Soviet Union and the countries of Eastern Europe.

This attitude implies a certain sort of advice to the East European comrades and workers: that they not disturb the western tacticians too much and that they seek to soften the liberal demands of the intellectuals, situating them more firmly in the framework of a hypothetical world revolution, previously completely delegated to the central role of the Soviet Union in the world anti-imperialist struggle, now, equally hypothetically, hinged on a revolutionary breakthrough in the West which would supposedly trigger a crisis in the eastern societies from without.

We must heed the call of comrade Rossanda, who has performed a useful service for the entire left by issuing this call: We must seek to go beyond an examination of the ideas of the intellectuals of the workers' movement and must cease to view the history of these countries exclusively through the prism of the history of the party central committees and the internal debates among the ruling groups. Instead we must strive to study the real class processes more closely, employing a critical approach to fashion a new Marxist analysis of the post-revolutionary societies.

We probably have more information about the political significance of the struggle between the blues and greens at the Constantinople circus or about the role of the *colonat* in the crisis of the Roman Empire than we do about the class processes that have occurred in the Soviet Union during the past thirty years.

It is incumbent upon us in the Italian and western left to forge, within the limits of the immense difficulties we face, a new interpretation that does not simply replace the old list of axiomatic certainties with a new one, but offers a comprehensive analysis, a theory of the development of the class struggle in the East European countries. Our aim must be to improve our understanding of the relationship between the real processes in our countries and those in the East, to be able to evaluate more accurately, for example, the significance of the relationship between the repression of Ukrainian nationalism and the development of the class struggle in the Ukraine, to take the example cited by Plyushch.

In substance, it seems to me that what we are saying here is that the relationship between the western left and the left in the post-revolutionary societies must be based on the real level of maturity of these processes. Here, of course, we must take account of the great differences between Eastern Europe, China, and the Soviet Union, but we must also accept the correct assertion of comrade Franz Marek that the most revolutionary position we can ask the comrades of Eastern Europe to adopt at this point is to demand the immediate and concrete development of some liberty as a precondition for the opening of any real breach in the bureaucratic societies.

We must fully realize that the breach in these societies will not occur in accordance with any ideal model designed beforehand in China or Western Europe. It will inevitably develop in the thick of great social turmoil and will involve things we like and things we like less, things that are new and things that are quite old in these societies. But it is only in this turmoil, only in the context of a process of this kind, that it will be possible to really amass the preconditions for a new rise of class initiative by the workers, by the advanced and revolutionary forces of these countries.

We will not make the error of asking our East European comrades to make us the concession of throwing in a bit more Marxist terminology, of waving a few more red flags when describing the tragic conditions under which the political struggle is developing in their countries.

I believe that what we can and must instead ask of these comrades is that they help us to understand the basic processes at work in their societies, and not only the processes unfolding in the heads of a few intellectuals. In this manner, as comrades, as intellectuals, we will develop a more sweeping view and interpretation of the ongoing processes of struggle, conscious that whenever breaches have opened in the bureaucratic societies, the workers' movement has been able, albeit with great difficulty, to conquer some room for action, as it did during the Prague spring, through the first steps towards the construction of trade unions, the development of councils, the initiation of a process of political regroupment leading to a new leading role for the working class. The same thing happened during the convulsive days in Budapest in 1956, when these phenomena arose in embryonic form in the activities of the factory council at Cepal, and the same lessons were confirmed by the famous Polish October in 1956 and again by the workers' mobilizations of 1976.

What we must ask of these comrades is that they help us to take up the struggle for liberty, precondition for any process of renovation in the East, in the form of a struggle for power for those who have it least, a struggle for a regime that challenges the social divisions in this society.

To claim, as some have, that the New Economic Policy was an ideal solution balancing the private market against state control of the economy, is to forget that by the time Lenin opted for the NEP, the decision to reproduce and intensify the capitalist division of labour both in the factories and in the relations of production more generally had already been made. The Taylorist model had already been adopted as the mode of organization of the economy and of life in the factories in the Soviet Union. The model of the German factory-barracks had already been adopted as a possible model of construction of the socialist state.

For this reason, I believe that rejection of the mechanism of exploitation of labour-power and rejection of labour-power as a commodity can realistically lead, through a long and exacting process, to the rise of a challenge to bureaucratic society from the left, to a new rise of the class struggle in these countries.

But this is not a problem solely for the comrades of Eastern Europe; it is also a focus of activity for us. And here I detect an ambiguity in this gathering which ought to be cleared up.

I cannot help thinking about another congress also held in Venice, twenty years ago, when important events were unfolding in Eastern Europe, like the revolt in Budapest, the challenge to the old order in Poland, and so on. Important new thinking was then beginning in the Italian workers' movement — about socialism, the state, power, and democracy. And I cannot help remembering that this reflection was unfortunately used quite negatively: the self-criticism of what we had not done in the East was stated perfunctorily, while what we were doing in the West was criticized rather radically so as to pose, in terms that can now be described as quite erroneous, the idea of a process of 'democratization' of the class struggle in our countries.

I believe that it would be an incredible and disgraceful deception of the comrades now struggling so laboriously in Eastern Europe to entertain any notion that a more critical attitude toward the eastern societies should be accompanied by any toning down of our critical attitude towards the western societies.

This is a problem that concerns us alone, especially the trade unions, and not the East European comrades. I agree that we in the CGIL should not travel to Prague to commemorate the tenth anniversary of the Prague spring by attending an international trade-union congress. But I also believe that we must declare with equal clarity that we are not prepared to travel to Washington to become a cog in the world imperialist sub-government established by a certain type of American international trade unionism.

The left cannot welcome social conflict in Poland while seeking to extinguish it in Italy. We cannot denounce co-management between

Soviet trade unions and company directors while proposing the extension of German models of co-management in this country, as is now being done in one large Italian city. One cannot wish for the liberation of the working class in the East while asking for the reconstitution of the mechanisms of accumulation and exploitation in the West.

I believe that Edoarda Masi is right, the world is rather more united than might seem. Despite old or new attempts to exorcise it, the class struggle remains the basic motor force. We must therefore make every political effort to bring out the contours of this class struggle more clearly in the East; but at the same time, comrades, we must not obscure them in the West.

How to Change things for Good? What is to be Done? With Whom?

K S Karol

Of Polish origin, K S Karol lived for a long time in the Soviet Union and served in the Red Army during the war. Journalist and writer, he is the author of several books: Visa for Poland; Guerillas in Power; Mao's China: The Other Communism; The Second Chinese Revolution.

My short contribution will also be in the way of a personal testimony. Chance has it that I am the oldest of the Soviet speakers present: in 1939, the year in which both Plyushch and Weil were born, I received what I thought would be a definitive Soviet passport. Poland no longer existed. But I was not averse to the idea of becoming a Soviet citizen, since I deeply identified with the new socialist fatherland. My experiences were doubtless very different from Plyushch's and less extensive than Boris Weil's. Unlike them, however, I did fight in the war.

Furthermore, having lived in the West for the last thirty years, I have gained some experience of what people here know and think about the countries in the East. I have learned how to talk with comrades over here, and also how to talk about the West with comrades from the East. I would therefore like to draw on this personal history in making my contribution — not so much in order to speak of the past, but to raise a few questions that have occurred to me about the present.

First, how is it that the new ideas and forms of struggle which have enriched both the traditional and the new Left in the West have not seeped through to the East? Sitting here in the front row is comrade Gianni Usai from Fiat Mirafiori. And when I see him, I cannot help thinking that exactly the same Fiat exists in Togliattigrad, built according to the same model, with if anything an even more hierarchical structure than in Turin. There is certainly no shortage of relations between the two factories, of people going back and forth. So how is it possible that nothing is known in the USSR about the resounding struggles and demands in Turin, which have become part of the heritage of all Italian metal-workers? Of course, we know that there are problems in obtaining news, and Plyushch was absolutely right to stress the importance of information. But we also know that when someone feels a compelling need to find things out and when there are ideas already in existence, then he will eventually discover them and force them into the open.

Now, things are not like that in the Soviet Union: it is as if there were no interest in such ideas. Some time ago at a meeting with the Paris press, Agnelli was asked to explain the difference between Fiat Turin and Fiat Togliattigrad. He answered with typical bosses' humour: 'In Togliattigrad, they work as fast as in Naples on a freezing-cold day.' Not a very happy reply, by the way, since there are quite a few Neapolitan migrant-workers at Fiat Turin! But the real difference has nothing at all to do with the climate. It is rather that low labour productivity is the only form of resistance open to Soviet workers. The characteristic features of struggle in Turin — qualitative demands, egalitarian labour organization, forms of political class independence — do not manage to penetrate the passivity of the Togliattigrad work-force.

The second mystery is the fact that various Chinese proposals, especially those which made up the Cultural Revolution, do not seem to have got through to people in the Soviet Union. I agree with a lot of what Edoarda Masi said yesterday; and Edoarda would agree with me that the USSR does not compare with China as regards either the model of development or the system of values. The fact is that, in China, they have raised the questions of egalitarianism, ending the social division of labour, and the differences between manual and intellectual labour or between town and country. And even if Chinese propaganda is detestable, obscure and burdened with Stalinist ambiguity — such that its form, in particular, is frightening to the East European masses — this does not explain why the USSR has remained completely impervious to its basic problematic, which has roots and echoes in every revolutionary culture. In theory, people in the Soviet Union ought to be more open to the Chinese debate than we are, since they started out at the same point. They were in a better position to understand the mistakes which China was trying not to repeat, the spectres with which it was grappling, the meaning of their stress on mass struggle, or the necessity of criticizing the Party. However poorly disseminated these ideas may have been, they rapidly opened a breach in the western labour movement. So why did they not do the same in the USSR? I do not think that lack of information was the only factor involved. A deeply-rooted ideological screen also served to cut off this society, which is in a real sense different from that of China.

Now, Boris Weil rightly urged us to stop talking of 'existing socialism' or socialism in inverted commas. We do indeed have to define the nature of Soviet society. But I am not sure that it is adequate to define it as a species of state monopoly capitalism. Although it may be in the process of becoming one, it would still have to attain a degree of structure and cohesion much greater than that which exists today. Anyway, however we may like to rig it out, this society quite clearly exhibits relations of exploitation very similar to ours — with the difference that they function in the framework of another ideology. We should by no means underestimate this last point: it was for a long time the case in the West, and it still is in certain countries, that the exploited masses accept their allotted role by thanking the boss for the very possibility of work. No doubt in the USSR, where property was abolished and there were no more factory-owners, the ideology underlying the relations of production could not be the same as in the West. Yet why is there a social division of labour? It could not, of course, have been abolished overnight; but could society not have been oriented towards its gradual reduction? Sixty years after the October Revolution, what is the principle by virtue of which one person is a manual worker, another an office worker, another an intellectual? Why has social mobility been so reduced, and the choice of work so limited?

Stalinism was an attempt to give an ideological foundation to the continuing division of social relations. In the name of development, it promoted an ideology of producer competition masquerading as service to the country. In this respect, Stakhanovism was at once a bonus system and a conception of society. And yet, I hope Plyushch and Weil will believe me when I say that this ideology never really served its purpose as a crack-proof cement. It is not true that the Soviet Union lived until Stalin's death in a state of voluntarist mass fanaticism, and that everyone became cynical and disillusioned only after 1956. Things were not like that. From the beginning the workers put up a stubborn class resistance in peculiar 'individual' forms: each one tried to protect his labour-power as best he could, even without knowing that it was a commodity. (Such Marxism is not to be learnt in Soviet schools: it has to be sought in secretive reading of the texts themselves, just like that done by Boris Weil.) In reality, this opaque society does not allow itself to be understood by its own citizens, even though it declares Marxism to be the official state philosophy.

However, if Stalinist ideology did not succeed in cementing society together, this was not because it lacked internal coherence, but because its regime never managed to give a basis in reality to the corresponding economic mechanisms. During the transitional years separating revolution and war communism, on the one hand, and Stalin's decision to introduce planning on the other, Soviet power fell to wavering between leaps forward and reversions to previous policies. (In Volume Two of his *Les Luttes de classes en URSS, 1923-1929*, Charles Bettelheim provides an instructive account of the difficulties faced in constructing a different system of production, money and exchange.) By the end of that transition, although it would have gone against the wishes and hopes of October and the soviets, a system of state monopoly capitalism could have been imposed without massive recourse to terror, provided that a way was found to unify and regulate society. Such a system might have justified the continuing social division of labour, exaltation of the hierarchy ('The cadres decide everything'), and the strengthening rather than withering of the State made necessary by the growth in nationalized property. But it would have done so only if it had proved capable of more efficient regulatory dynamism.

As it happened, the new system was never able to establish a real-world relationship between wages and market supply — if only because it was impossible to repress certain social needs and avoid social compromises with one section of the population against another. And so the leaders very quickly chose what they probably regarded as a temporary solution, according to which the workers were guaranteed a certain number of absolutely indispensable goods and services, and left to sort out the rest by themselves. Two economies immediately sprang up: an official one characterized by fixed prices and distribution mechanisms; and a parallel one governed by the law of supply and demand. Let me give you an example drawn from my own experience. In Rostov at the end of the war, my official wage in a large factory working for national defence would have been enough to live on if the consumer-goods network had been able to supply the promised goods. But since this was not the case, I had to turn to the black-market economy, whose price mechanism was so different that a kilo of bread cost a whole month's wages. Like every Soviet worker, I was faced with the problem of finding the means of exchange that prevailed in this second economy.

The low productivity and high rate of absenteeism are explained by the need to save enough strength to earn something elsewhere. I do not believe at all, comrades, that the low output of Russian workers stems from their peasant origins or so-called 'pre-industrial pattern of behaviour'. It derives from the need to defend oneself against a system (the leading cadres in factory, Party and State) which does not guarantee the existing standard of living, but forces one to adapt to the material play of needs, prices and means of exchange imposed by a reality in contradiction with the regime's official image of itself.

The same is true of the prevailing attitude to 'collective property': if no one respects it, this is not because of some traditional anti-social mentality, but because no one feels that it is really collective. As far as I am aware, no other society carries its burden of theft with such equanimity and such complete lack of blame. When I was studying in Rostov, it was quite normal for a student to come to a lecture and say: 'Damn! I tried to pinch a watch, but I couldn't quite manage it.' To which all the others would calmly reply: 'Pity! What bad luck!'

This conception of work and property grew up and persists hand in hand with the parallel economy. Whenever I have gone back to Moscow — in the late fifties or during the seventies — someone has informed me as if it were something new: 'You can't understand us unless you realize that there is now an official economy number one and a parallel economy number two.' But things have always been like that, and everyone has always known it full well. It is obvious that people do their regular shopping at the *Univermag* and the rest at the *tolkuchka* to be found in every town, however small. It is not clear exactly how the shop is supplied, but a little gold will winkle out anything down to the most exotic of goods. We can see how old the system must be, if we recall Zoschenko's tale about a crowd's reckless pursuit of an escaped zoo-monkey in the hope of selling it off to the *tolkuchka*. Of course, the monkey is rather an extreme case, and this story reflects the years of exceptionally harsh shortage. But still today, even in areas inhabited by leaders and state functionaries, it is a fact that staircase light-bulbs are protected by wire-netting. Otherwise, they would unfailingly pass through someone's pocket to end up on the black market.

This reality of everyday life unsettles the country, nourishes scepticism, and sometimes reaches a point bordering on insanity. So great is the compulsion to take anything in reach that people even risked their life during the war. When I was in the air force, the still unperfected aeroplane engines had to be cooled with a special mixture of alcohol and glycerine so that they would not freeze above a certain height. One day, someone had the idea of seeing how it tasted; and from then on, despite the officers' warnings not to waste an ounce since the safety of both crew and aeroplane was at stake, no aircraft ever took off with even a drop of this mixture in the reserve-cans. It had been re-baptized 'chassis liqueur'.

Now, what was it that Plyushch said? He said that all this is part of a massive, reciprocal and circular lie, known to both sides as such, by means of which the rulers lie to the ruled. But it is really a social phenomenon — one that is undermining the foundations of the country. One evening, Althusser and I were dining with a Moscow intellectual who, like so many others, spoke to us about this 'pilfering' with all the pleasure of someone telling a joke. At one point Althusser remarked: 'But this is a serious social problem.' Surprised, the other man replied that it was not a 'social phenomenon'; and he justified himself by adding: 'After all, it's not legal. You can go to jail if you are caught.' As if it were not a social phenomenon for that very reason! As if 'sociality' did not include the specific way in which the prospect of 'going to jail' is regarded in the Soviet Union! In fact, it has become something familiar and, at the same time, has lost its gravity. Repression was so excessive and so normal in the past that it is no longer a means of individual dissuasion. As long as Soviet citizens were convinced in themselves that every city had been ordered to deliver 50,000 men from time to time for the dirty jobs that no one wanted to do, as long as they believed that the KGB was therefore obliged to make up the total more or less at random, they lived with the nightmare of repression and the kind of fatalism that arises when there is no way of rationally defending oneself. The only chance was to avoid exposing oneself to too many risks. But now that repression has abated and become more selective in character, the Soviet people, who have never been a docile lot, are escaping ever more the control of those in power. They evade these controls through such forms as a second job, trafficking in various goods, and certain patterns of consumption; they organize, on the fringes of official society, a parallel, underground, 'secret' life which has become the nightmare of the leadership.

Bettelheim and myself got to know the famous sixties 'reformers': the Liebermans and Nemksimovs. When they came to Paris, they used to talk about nothing else than the urgent need to unify and rationalize the economy and suppress its wild, uncontrolled mechanisms. That was their nightmare: they were perfectly aware that no society can be half-planned; and that, unless things were put back in order, all their planning would be divorced from reality. But this task of unification was not accomplished. The parallel economy is now thriving to such a degree that even leadership cadres tell the following joke: 'Socialism was supposed to turn us all into producers; but instead, it has turned us all into petty-traders.'

The western Left, and above all the New Left, regarded these economic reform projects as essentially a back-door attempt by the Soviet leadership to reintroduce capitalist market mechanisms to the benefit of the 'new managerial class' and its technocratic allies. In my opinion, however, the question was more complicated than that. If the reforms had been implemented, they would have given a modicum of transparency to Soviet society: they would have thrown light on its hidden but all too real machinery, allowing various social figures — from enterprise director to shop-floor worker — to become aware of their objective roles, instead of maintaining these mystified official functions that only appear not to conflict with one another. It is no accident that the political system had difficulty in taking the risk. But that is not the problem under discussion here. I would simply like to say that, in my opinion, the economic 'reforms' were a failure at least partly because the currently privileged layers had an interest in preserving the old system. Why was this so?

Yesterday, Daniel Singer produced a series of facts and figures to remind us that Soviet economic growth is in sharp decline, and that, on the leadership's own admission, the prospects are becoming less and less rosy with every day that passes. Now, whether it occurs in the East or the West, such a phenomenon is never completely reducible to the economic sphere, but immediately gives rise to reduced social mobility, fewer job-openings for young people, and the development of inflation. In the West, inflation breaks into the open; whereas in the East, especially in the Soviet Union, it is integrated into the system. Besides, what is that economy number two if not a form of permanent inflation erased from the official landscape so as not to spoil the picture?

Possibilities of social advancement have considerably declined since the period when I was living in the USSR. Let's be serious: no one likes to be a worker, even in the Soviet Union. Even if productivity is low and work-rhythms less harsh, factory labour is never a cushy number. In my time, at least the high growth rate allowed greater social mobility, and made it possible for someone to leave the shop-floor or hope that his son would not also be a worker. Today, things are no longer like that. We should not give too much credence to statistics about the number of workers' sons attending Soviet universities. After all, Brezhnev's own son figures in the official total, since his father was once a worker. In reality, selection for higher education takes place in an implacable manner: the entrance examinations are very stiff, and the schools which prepare future students are very different from one another. It is one thing to go to school in a 'rich' part of Moscow, quite another to go to one in a working-class suburb of Kiev.

Thus, the Soviet education system, which was created in order to lift the country out of illiteracy and give equal opportunities of social advancement, has become a potent instrument for passing on privileges both big and small. A higher education diploma is now an essential qualification for any leadership position whatsoever, while the implacable selection of entrants puts it further and further beyond the reach of people with modest incomes.

The double economy itself provides another example of principles established to benefit 'the weak' and later turned to their own advantage by the strong. Everyone at the top of the social ladder enjoys all the social aspects of the wage: more or less free services, very low rents, ridiculously cheap public transport, as well as privileged access to state shops with low, fixed prices. In addition, he can use specially reserved shops and go to the top of the queue for a whole range of things, including loans for buying a flat or *dacha*. It is not surprising that, since their salaries are continually increasing, the money left to top cadres can be used to sweep up the majority of goods available on the parallel market. And, of course, this in turn pushes up prices in·the *tolkuchka*.

Even the figures relating to the rise in average consumption need to be closely examined and clarified. Boris Weil said yesterday: *my yescho nye nayelis*, we have not yet had our fill. Who is we? Those who queue up in the shops, who cannot afford to buy food in economy number two, who cannot find meat or even vegetables — in short, the ordinary run of mortals. In the Soviet Union, people have a joke for everything: 'Voronezh? That's an heroic town. They've had no meat for three years, and still they don't surrender!' It is not that the distribution plan (*raznaryadka*) has overlooked the existence of Voronezh, just that the town's meat allocation is only enough for the tables of those with the titles, positions, prestige, wages and priority cards.

Of course, that is not the whole story. Some categories of the work-force are well paid, and full employment (or rather the shortage of labour) allows workers to seek out jobs which carry the highest wages and which make it easiest to live outside the factory. To some extent, this system continues the Stakhanovite tradition (piece-work is still the rule both in the Soviet Union and in the people's democracies); to some extent, it also stems from the difficulties in recruiting labour for regions with an unhealthy climate. In Siberia, for example, where three-quarters of the country's natural wealth is concentrated, forced labour has not been employed on a massive scale since 1953. And nor is it possible to use politically motivated volunteers. Those who go to Siberia therefore have to be given higher pay in the form of productivity bonuses and numerous material benefits. The same is true in technologically advanced industries crucial for export or national defence. But there are no precise rules or criteria in all this: nothing is explained or discussed in the open; no one seems to be familiar with the real mechanisms of this 'jungle'.

What people can see very well is the rivalries generated by a system that paralyses society and prevents nearly all its members from recognizing themselves in it. If you talk to an average intellectual in Moscow (or in Prague or Warsaw), he will show you some 'overpaid' workers and ignore the fact that the great majority are underpaid; he will then attack the traditional poverty and low remuneration of such social layers as doctors (except the increasing number who 'cope' by giving private treatment for higher and higher fees). The wall separating intellectuals from the workers and the broad mass of the population arises out of this material situation, rather than being rooted in the lack of trade-union or political traditions among the Russian working class, or more generally in certain national peculiarities. The eastern intelligentsia has internalized Stalin's anti-egalitarian concepts, believing that it is itself socially indispensable and 'superior' to manual workers. It does not think twice before calling itself a 'middle class' (as Andrei Amalrik has written black on white); and it openly calls for the hierarchy of income and privilege to be still more heavily and rigidly weighted in its favour.

However, even the intellectuals strike one by their combination of discontent and reserve. There is little identification with the regime, even among those who are actively involved in its functioning. Thus, members of the government themselves speak of the existing power as if it were something external: they talk about *them*. (In Poland, a member of the Party Secretariat once said to me: 'Oh, don't let's give up hope. *They* won't be here for ever.') Nor is this all: since the higher intellectual and technical personnel have greater access to information, their discontent is increased, elaborated and even grounded on interesting analyses. And yet they remain reserved and resigned. In my opinion, this is because no one thinks any more in terms of a painless self-correction of the system, and many are therefore afraid of what will happen if it suddenly collapses. The Medvedev brothers are the only two idealists I know who still hope that the Party will be able to change itself. I do not criticize them for that: their point of view is worthy of respect, even though it is shared by very few people and is very difficult to accept. The general impression is, on the contrary, that the inner-party struggle has fallen back since Khruschev's time, and that we are now witnessing a dispute about which nothing is known and from which only a worsening of the situation can be expected. Brezhnev's successor will make fewer speeches and be even harsher — that is what people feel. And no one can see a way forward except through wild movements of revolt that will be just as wildly repressed.

This has to be understood if we are to grasp why society is at a dead-end. In the western workers movement, people talk about reforms and revolution, but they do not see revolution as a bloody settling of accounts; its image no longer has anything in common with a Jacobin, minority-based or, as Plyushch would say, 'Chekist' seizure of power. In the Russian historical memory, by contrast, revolution is synonymous with the seizure of the Winter Palace, the civil war, the Gulag archipelago. Any perspective of social explosions appears to them as a re-run of October — a re-run all the more violent and primitive in that, this time, it would not be mediated by a highly intelligent leading group like the Bolsheviks. The Party no longer produces revolutionaries; and the remaining climate of pure anger involves a simmering revolt which, although feared by the intellectuals, does not burst out into the open among a population unable to speak. This lack of confidence in the possibility of reforming the system, combined with fear of revolutionizing it, leads to a complete absence of perspectives. All that remains is the struggle for civil rights: a pressure whose aim is to secure a little room for freedom and legality.

But such an orientation does not face up to what is really choking the Soviet Union. It does not answer the central question: How to change things for good? What is to be done? With whom? And that, comrade dissidents, seems to us to mark the limitation of your struggle. Of course, it is not difficult for us to support you: to sign your appeals and espouse the cause of civil rights in the USSR. Indeed, we have been doing that for a number of years and shall continue to do so. But no one will ever give you civil rights in the Soviet Union, just as no one handed them on a platter to the western working class. It was not at all a question of a gift from a generous parliament or from Oliver Cromwell, the father of all parliaments. Such rights are the fruit of the long social struggles which forced the ruling classes to concede them. The right to form trade unions was also won through a long and bloody historical struggle. By all means let us demand civil rights in the USSR, and with even greater energy than we have shown so far. But do not imagine, comrades Plyushch and Weil, that they will blossom forth as the result of *our* external pressure. That has never happened anywhere in the world. The road towards civil rights will be opened only through mass political action — not just through a profound change in the way the regime functions, but through a process whereby the people will enter into conflict with it and become a genuine and unavoidable interlocutor. Until that day arrives, your slogan will remain unnoticed.

Time is pressing: the dangers are mounting in the USSR and the Soviet bloc. The split between rulers and ruled was already there when I was in the USSR. I could talk for hours on end about the inability of 'those on top' to win the sympathy of 'those below'; about Stalin's fears and lack of illusions concerning the effectiveness of the 'personality cult'; and about the real unpopularity of Stalin and the poor functioning of the regime in his time.

Is it possible for such a state of affairs to last for ever? Can this enforced compromise between rulers and ruled be maintained without end? Few people think so. The Chinese believe that Brezhnev or his successors will try to escape from domestic difficulties along the road of expansionism, or even through a military adventure in Europe or elsewhere. Others see a future of uncontrolled explosions, national wars and savage confrontations between the peoples making up the Soviet bloc. I would like to sound a less pessimistic note: not because I underestimate the strength and value of Plyushch's alarming prophecies, but because I believe that, throughout Eastern Europe, the workers' passive resistance may assume more developed class-struggle forms, more like our own, more effective and tomorrow similarly victorious.

We are here to study the nature of these societies and investigate their specific mechanisms of exploitation, oppression and integration. But we do not seek merely to advance our understanding. We are militants who are fighting for things to change both here and there — so evident is it that our fates are interlinked. It matters little whether the more correct thesis is the one which analyses these societies in terms of state monopoly capitalism or the one which sees them as a peculiar form of capitalism within which political contradictions occupy the dominant place. The important thing is that the workers should organize and struggle for their rights, dignity and freedom, wherever class divisions remain and wherever there is blatant and scandalous injustice. Through the comrades who live in these countries, we shall try to pass on not so much the elements of a platform held in common with the western workers movement — for the differences are too great — but at least a part of the heritage of mass struggle gained here over the last few years. This is really something that can help the masses in the East to recognize and reorganize themselves. I know how many difficulties that will involve. But unless the peoples of the USSR attain a broader perspective, they will certainly find it difficult to mobilize for the conquest of those rights and freedoms which — we all agree — are not the attribute of bourgeois democracy, but quite real and permanent values. For I think indeed that 'there is no freedom without equality, and no equality without freedom'. And with these words, borrowed from F. Fortini, I shall end my contribution.

Liquidate the Heritage of 'Patristic Marxism'

Alfonso Carlos Comin

Alfonso Carlos Comin, a Catholic well known for his participation in the anti-fascist struggle in Spain, was formerly a leader of the Bandera Roja group. He has since joined the PSUC (the Communist Party in Catalonia) and is a member of its executive committee. He is also one of the four Catalan members of the executive committee of the Communist Party of Spain (PCE).

I must confess that during this colloquy I have been reminded more than once of the feelings we Spaniards had for years when we were waging the underground struggle against fascism. We used to come to public initiatives abroad, naturally under false names, to explain what was happening in the anti-fascist struggle in Spain.

We offered our direct testimony and sought to convince the international left that the Workers Commissions, the Communists, the democratic forces, were making progress and that there were grounds for hope against a system that had lasted forty years, more than a generation. This system may not have seemed like a colossus in 1939, but it later became one, over the bodies of the tens and hundreds of thousands of Spaniards murdered, tortured, and imprisoned.

The persecution and repression were inflicted in the name of fascism and Francoism — the reactionary forces that had been defeated during the Second World War but nevertheless remained in power in Spain. And they remained not only because of the social base or consensus the Francoists had succeeded in welding together, not only because of the ferocious and intelligently applied repression, but also because of a certain degree of international passivity.

We were conscious that it was our task to defeat Francoism, but we also knew that we had to call upon international solidarity to advance our struggle.

After listening to the testimony of the comrades from Eastern Europe, one is at once perplexed and deeply moved, because so much of the testimony we have heard resembles the testimony we Spaniards used to present at conferences like this. In these countries, however, the repression is inflicted in the name of socialism, of what this gathering has dubbed 'existing socialism'. We could put it another way: this oppression is exercised in the name of the deepest hope of contemporary humanity, the complete emancipation of the exploited classes.

Of course, it is not my intention to voice purely ethical and historical thoughts. I must assume full responsibility for my role as a militant and leader of a Eurocommunist party. I will speak, then, in the name of the Catalan Communists of the PSUC and the PCE. At the end, however, I hope you will allow me a brief digression on some problems relating to Christianity, for I am a Christian Communist.

Towards the end of the press conference this morning, when everyone was getting tired and hungry, a journalist from *Corriere della Sera* questioned Fernando Claudín and me about the central theme of this gathering. When he asked us what was our position, as Eurocommunists, on dissent in Eastern Europe, I had to ask myself what was our role in the Brechtian scenario Fortini evoked with such great effect.

As far as Spain and Catalonia are concerned, Eurocommunism represents a hope which, like so many others, could be presented as a historic utopia. But I firmly believe that some gains can be made today, and, without any apologetic spirit, which is wholly alien to me, I can cite some features of the evolution of the PCE and the Catalan Communist Party.

In 1968 our parties unambiguously condemned the annihilation of the Prague spring. I must remind you that at the time we were underground, weak and persecuted, many of our cadres in prison or exile. We were aware of the difficulties this position was likely to cause us in the international communist movement. And there was no lack of difficulty with respect to the solidarity we needed in our struggle against fascism.

I think that was the beginning — or perhaps the acceleration, for it had been building up for some time — of the dynamic towards profound changes within our Eurocommunist parties. We, along with other parties of the Mediterranean area, have affirmed that there is no single model for the construction of socialism, and we further maintain that the rejection of a single model in no way engenders any conceptual crisis of the character of socialism itself.

The fact is that the official language of the Communist Parties, which, like the church, have a history of their own, is a language imbued with a Catholic wisdom, as Salvadori would say; it uses terms whose full consequences can never be mastered. When we said that there was no single model and upheld the idea of national roads to the construction of socialism, we also introduced a dialectical criticism of the Soviet model.

But we did not express this latter element clearly enough, and, as I said at the press conference, I think we should go further in our critique of the social nature of the East European countries. All of you, of course, are familiar with Santiago Carrillo's book *Eurocommunism and the State*,[1] which expresses the views of one individual, but an individual who happens to be the national secretary of our party. It contains both direct and indirect criticisms of the single model and of conditions in the East European countries.

You also know that this book provoked considerable discord with the Soviets. But my point here is not so much to defend the book of our national secretary as to explain the difficulties we still confront when we try to exercise free political criticism within the international communist movement.

I think I should mention another point too. Our party emerged from illegality only about six months ago. Only one and a half months after legalization, on 15 June 1977, we faced elections, the first ever for many of us. Our democratic credibility in the election campaign, in the articles published in the press, and during our discussions throughout the Iberian peninsula, depended to a large extent on the distance we had taken from the single model.

We had to demonstrate, after forty years of fascist propaganda, that we were a genuinely independent party, that we were not controlled by an outside centre, and that we were seeking our own road to socialism and democracy.

I also think that we have made an effort within our own party to restore democratic rights to a position of fundamental and substantial importance, indispensable if we are to talk of genuine socialism. For my part, I can never use the term 'real socialism' to apply to a system that persecutes the toilers, does not respect the right to strike, does not allow the trade unions to organize independently, does not permit free expression, and so on.

We have therefore made an effort to see that socialism reappropriates what had already been part of the patrimony of the people: the democratic rights won in the French revolution, not only because of the struggle of the bourgeoisie, but also through the participation of the popular forces.

We have said that forty years of struggle against Francoism, forty years during which we were denied liberty day after day, have given us a deep taste for democratic rights. We could never agree to separate the words socialism and communism from democratic rights.

We are here, conscious of the approach of this congress, in solidarity with our dissident comrades and friends. Our solidarity is not only human and ethical, but also historical and political, and we assume it in all its breadth, while conscious of its limitations.

Our friend Franco Fortini spoke of a Brechtian tragedy. I imagine that he did not intend this to be a static, fixed scenario, but a dynamic one. We must ask ourselves how many acts it will have, how many scenes there will be, how many steps forward and backward. I am sincerely convinced that this conference itself marks some important steps forward. The left, respecting the pluralism evident here, is now dealing with a fundamental problem, the analysis of the nature of the societies we have referred to as 'existing socialist'. Naturally, this position has various limits, one of which is the international situation. Our analysis is based on a Marxist, left-wing approach, but I also think, if we want to be completely honest, that we should recognize that not a few of the criticisms which we had rejected twenty and thirty years ago as bourgeois, using this adjective in a Manichean sense, we are in the process of rediscovering for ourselves and acknowledging to be correct criticisms, since, as Marxists, we could not continue to be Manicheans.

There was a period in the historic development of the Third International during which Manichean criteria prevailed in the cultural, scientific, and ideological domains. This transformed the parties of the International into inquisitional churches instead of genuinely revolutionary forces.

In this sense I believe that when Louis Althusser recalled that we in the international communist movement have managed belatedly to acknowledge errors, instances of repression, betrayals, etc., even errors of the dimensions of the Lysenko affair, this in itself is an important step forward. We have made the so-called self-criticism, but have we been able to go all the way back to the roots of these evils?

The historic parties, Socialist and Communist, must go more deeply into the analysis of the causes of the errors that have been made in the international historic process, in East-West relations, and in the criticism of developments in the countries of 'existing socialism'.

We must strive for a deeper, perhaps somewhat less prudent, analysis. Here I will include some personal considerations, since even though I am a member and leader of a party, I do not consider the party a horizontal relation among people who must always think alike. Parties must provide for the common enrichment of thinking people, and thinking people inevitably think differently.

During the fourth congress of Catalan Communists we affirmed that the period of unanimity within our Communist Parties in Spain had ended. Various motions were voted, and only one achieved unanimity. There were minorities and majorities. I cannot say that we have achieved complete internal democracy, but I do think we have introduced a number of elements that bring us nearer this goal. How could we come to this conference, speak to the comrades of Eastern Europe, tell them that they must struggle for the conquest of democratic rights in their respective countries, and discuss a multiparty system, trade-union autonomy, universal suffrage, and socialism in democracy, if the party apparatus itself was not being liberalized in the deepest sense of the word, if the party had not succeeded in grasping the richness of the contribution of each and every one of its militants, who, if they are Marxists — and they are — will inevitably bring up differences, conflicts, and debates which cannot be resolved in purely administrative ways?

On various occasions we have stated that the best expression of solidarity we could offer the dissident comrades, the comrades struggling in the Eastern countries, the working classes whose condition has been described so disquietingly here, would be to advance our own revolution. Allow me to present a hypothesis: I believe that the greatest reason for concern in the USSR about the possible advances of Eurocommunism is precisely the threat of contagion in the East European societies themselves.

When I visited Poland I saw that the youth were extraordinarily interested in the reconciliation of the two great words of which Karol spoke: liberty and equality. They wondered whether it was possible to achieve an identification of socialism and liberty.

We all know that what the Soviet leaders found most disturbing about the Prague spring was the possibility that it could spread to other countries, although I would not go so far as to say that this threat was the only reason why the tanks were sent into Prague. What is certain, however, is that the Soviets do uphold the policy of the single model.

Before moving to the second part of my report, I would like to say that our parties, especially the older generations, remain marked by many of the traditions of the Third International, both good and bad. And I, as a Christian, bear the full inquisitional tradition of the church. I often say that I am bound to feel a sense of solidarity with what has happened in my church, both good and bad. Similarly, as a Communist, I feel a sense of solidarity with all that has happened in the complexity of the class struggle throughout history. I think that the discussion which was opened yesterday obliges all of us to liquidate the legacy of patristic Marxism, which I would define as scholastic and which prevents some sectors of the European left from making progress in spite of facts and analyses that leave no room for doubt.

At this point I would like to deal with the question of the relationship between Marxism and Christianity, on which we heard the very beautiful report of Girardet yesterday. He centred on the institutional aspect of the problem, referring to the evangelical Baptist church, etc.

After his intervention, mention was made of Christians of Protestant tradition and even some Catholic minorities who take part in the struggle alongside dissidents of Marxist origin. I think this is a point of extreme importance in what we may call the cultural dimension of Rossana's introductory report. And I don't see how we could conduct a real cultural debate if the question of the relationship between Marxism and Christianity were dealt with solely in institutional terms (the relationship between the church and the parties) and not also in cultural and ideological terms. This is not simply a formal dialogue between Catholics and Marxists, a celebration of friendship of the sort that occurred in Salzburg or Marienbad before 1968. A much more advanced process must be initiated, introducing a cultural debate into the party itself. This presupposes reconsideration of the Marxist critique of religion, officially accepted not only in the East but also in the West. Both the PCE and the Catalan Communist Party have dealt with this problem in programmatic declarations explicitly affirming that it is necessary to go beyond Lenin's theses on the privatization of faith. We have clearly stated that our parties admit Christians — progressives, socialists, Marxists, of course — as full members who maintain their faith. We have decided that faith is not an overcoat that the believer can leave in the cloakroom before entering a party meeting only to don it again upon leaving. If the party intends to assemble all those progressive cultural values enunciated in the Gospel and incorporated into the great socialist project — equality, brotherhood, truth, solidarity, etc. — those values for which great masses have struggled and are struggling not only in Latin America but also in Spain in the fight against Francoism and in Italy and France side by side with the forces of the left, then things cannot be left at the level of a formal dialogue between party leaders and bishops. The conscience of the Christian Communist and the ranks of the party itself must be addressed.

Obviously, these programmatic declarations have consequences, which I will not discuss here. But when we call for this cultural debate; when, during lunch today, we discussed this problem with Plyushch and Weil; when I discussed with comrades of the PCF and the PCI, comrades who maintained that we Spanish Communists had proceeded too hastily, I affirmed (and I think that I speak for the entire party in this) that in countries in which there is a Christian tradition, like ours, this is a crucial question in the building of the mass party, since there is a Christian tradition of struggle for the construction of socialism. The Communist Parties must therefore seek to reap the harvest of this entire tradition of socialist struggle, which constitutes a genuine historic fact.

In this regard, I generally cite Bloch as a decisive turning point in the development of the Marxist critique of religion. I maintain that before Bloch the Marxist critique of religion had not helped the construction of socialism. Many of our Marxist authors understood nothing of the Gospel, remained prisoners of the sociological image presented by the church of their epoch. But especially after the Second World War, this phenomenon should have been dealt with more dynamically by communist and socialist circles.

I would like now to conclude with two brief remarks and the reading of a short text. One of the dissidents who has sent a message to this conference, Adam Michnik, a dissident of Marxist origin who has written several works on the struggle in Poland, found himself repelled by the official ideology of state atheism (which is the confessional version of the ideology of the state resulting from the identification of the state apparatus with the party) and also found that some Christians were struggling for the same goals as he.

Michnik has written a very beautiful text about this, a short text from which I would like to quote the following words: 'when men undertake the struggle for the great values of democracy and socialism, atheists discover that the great values of humanity and the struggle against obscurantism, the struggle for liberty, justice, and equality, are not alien to genuine Christians, but are part of the deepest roots of Chistianity'.

In conclusion, I would say that if we are able to de-ideologize the scholastic Marxism inherited from a particular historical process and to de-ideologize a Christianity monopolized by the bourgeoisie for centuries, and if we are able to lead this process of convergence forward, then an interpenetration of Marxism and Christianity could occur through a cultural debate that would advance the class struggle both East and West. For if this problem were dealt with in Madrid, Rome, or Paris, it could not be ignored in Moscow, Prague, or Warsaw. It is a problem that affects both the international communist and socialist movement and the churches, which, as Girardet said, are also international in the historic sense of the term. I am satisfied with the attention that has been devoted to this theme here. I call upon both sides to overcome dogmatism, and I am convinced that both in our countries and in Eastern Europe the recovery of the progressive power contained in the words of the Gospel would represent a contribution to the construction of the genuine socialism we all want to build.

NOTES

1. Santiago Carrillo, *Eurocommunism and the State*, Lawrence & Wishart, London 1977.

Eurocommunism and Marxist, Socialist, and Democratic Currents of Dissent

Rosario Villari

Rosario Villari, a Communist member of parliament and histor-ian, is a professor at the University of Florence. He is the author of many historical works, particularly on southern Italy. He is the editor of Studi storici, *the journal of the Gramsci Institute, research centre of the Italian Communist Party, and wrote the preface to the Italian edition of the book* Was the Soviet Revolution Inevitable?, *by the dissident Roy Medvedev.*

An evaluation of the Soviet system inevitably constitutes one of the basic components of socialist reflection and action in our countries. Today, in the midst of the deep crisis racking the structures of the capitalist world, which poses a series of new and dramatic problems for the workers' movement, our commitment to deepening our analysis and to sweeping away the myths and schemas of the past has become especially urgent.

I must say, however, that we are not exactly starting from scratch, as may seem to be the case for those who look at things from the narrow vantage point of a particular organized grouping. I do not mean to take any credit away from the organizers and promoters of this conference, but it must be recognized that it is part of a political and ideological process of reflection that has been under way for some time now. Today, more than ever before, the forces and forma-tions of the left have been drawn into this process.

Yesterday Jiri Pelikan expressed some surprise that this initiative had not been organized by the largest force on the left, the Italian Communist Party. I do not believe that by this he meant to accuse the PCI of any desire to avoid the necessity to reflect and take positions on the problems that have been raised in this conference or, especially, to avoid a meeting and open confrontation with comrades and democratic exponents of dissent in the East European countries. Indeed, what is important is not the form, not the choice of one or another particular initiative. There is no need for me to recall the circumstances and modes in which dialogue and confrontation has developed, directly and indirectly, between Italian Communists and representatives of dissent, whether or not they have been close to Marxism and socialism. But above all, beyond the particular circumstances and events, the Italian Communist Party has directly participated in the development of analysis and discussion on questions involving the socialist countries, and has often been the promoter of such discussion. Granted, one cannot and ought not to remain silent about the delays in this work, or the gaps, uncertainties, and contradictions which remain in the assessment of Soviet reality as a whole and of particular aspects of it.

The correct point of departure in evaluating the PCI's position on the Soviet Union and the East European countries, however, must be the contribution of Italian Communists to the elaboration of a new strategy for the advance of socialism in Western Europe. You are well acquainted with the terms of this view of the socialist revolution in the West: the central point is the affirmation that democracy, liberty, and socialism are inseparable. It is the conviction that the conquest and full realization of democracy, and of social, political and civil liberties leads to the transformation of society in a socialist direction. It is the recognition that this process cannot occur without the convergence of democratic and popular forces of varying inspiration, each maintaining its own independence and specificity. This is not the place to examine the storehouse of political and ideological elaboration and practical activity that lies behind the line and strategy of so-called Eurocommunism. The elaboration of this vision of socialism has generated a great number of problems regarding the very structure of the party, its political action, its relations with other parties and with Italian society as a whole, its relations with the state and so on. These problems have been only partially resolved; they constitute the object of broad new theoretical and political reflection. Among other things, this has entailed the beginning of a process of re-thinking of the historical process of development of democracy in the contemporary world, as well as a critical re-examination of the concept of 'bourgeois democracy', which

Plyushch mentioned in his first intervention yesterday.

Plyushch hopes that the USSR will undergo a reversal of the terms of the historic process as we have normally viewed it: a sort of 'bourgeois-democratic' revolution *after* the socialist revolution, as a completion and verification of the socialist revolution. In reality, considering the general terms of the development of contemporary history, it should be clear that the conquest and realization of democracy were not the fruit of a natural and spontaneous evolution of the liberal-bourgeois system, nor were they concessions from the bourgeoisie. Rather, they were the result of a multiform and enormous struggle of the popular classes, and in particular of the development of the organized workers' movement and the shift in the relationship of forces resulting from this development.

An analysis of this question would lead us far afield. It seems to me sufficient to point to it as one of the problems we face. To stick more closely to the theme of this conference, however, I would like to mention, rapidly and briefly, the implications of Eurocommunism for the re-examination of Soviet reality and the reality of the socialist countries and for our relationship to this reality. Tracing the line of development of this re-examination very schematically, one may say that the Italian Communist Party has moved from a phase in which all its efforts were directed at rejecting the Soviet model as such, to a second phase of asserting the independence of its own conception of socialism, to a third phase of stressing the original character of the democratic road to socialism, and now to a phase wherein it is affirming the universal value of democracy as a foundation of socialist society. Each phase was accompanied by a certain assessment of the history and vicissitudes of the USSR after the revolution. This assessment has never questioned the enormous historic import of the October Revolution and its progressive influence both internationally and within Soviet society as such. But on the basis of denunciation of the errors and deviations, it has ever more clearly located the fundamental nub of the contradictions and even tragedies of Soviet society in the authoritarian and bureaucratic structure of the regime and in the lack of development of political democracy. The position we have now arrived at, which was recently expressed synthetically but quite meaningfully by Enrico Berlinguer in Moscow, undoubtedly must be further developed and deepened. This can occur only through a confrontation with other political and cultural forces, fully conscious of the world dimensions of the problem facing us and of the effect, equally for the development of the internal situation in Italy, of relations with the United States, the Soviet Union, and other European countries. The Italian Communists maintain that this analysis must be conducted without reticence and without sugar-coating, but also without creating new divisions among the parties that claim allegiance to the working class and socialism. Each tendency must defend its own autonomy, but without withdrawing into isolation and without renouncing the possibility of holding and expressing divergent positions. There must be no useless and detrimental encounters and no faint-hearted hopes for world revolutions or palingeneses; it must be borne in mind that the workers' movement of Western Europe can contribute to the renovation of the existing socialist societies primarily by waging the struggle on its own terrain. In this context, we must also consider open recognition of the full legitimacy of the cultural and political dissent now being manifested in the USSR and the other socialist countries, whatever its ideological, political, and religious character, as well as the validity of those forces in the socialist countries that are expressing the demand for a profound democratic reform of the state. It seems to me that the testimony and reflections which have been presented here by the comrades and friends from Eastern Europe all converge on one point: recognition that although the discussion on whether these societies are socialist or non-socialist threatens to remain abstract and generic or to lead us astray, the real and fundamental problem is the full development of democratic structures and of liberty, the essential condition for the complete realization of the immense economic, cultural, and political potential created by the October Revolution. It thus appears to me that in this sense there is a convergence between Eurocommunism and the Marxist, socialist, and democratic currents of dissent, a convergence that does not rule out differences of opinion on other fundamental questions, but which seems to me important precisely because it is born of very different experiences. I believe that this, too, is a confirmation of the way in which Eurocommunism is moving and of its capacity to forge links with democratic and socialist elements which have developed in situations quite different from our own. There must be no illusions about the difficulty of the road to be travelled. But it may be that precisely because of this new research, more favourable conditions are now being created for dealing with both the crisis of capitalism and the internal problems and contradictions of socialism.

Politics and Economics in Capitalism and in 'Actually Existing Socialism'

Ursula Schmiederer

Ursula Schmiederer is Professor at Osnabruck University in the German Federal Republic and works closely with Links, *the review of the Sozialistisches Büro. Together with R Rotermundt and H Becker-Panitz she is the author of* Detente, Competitive System and Existing Socialism.

In speaking of the left opposition in the Soviet Union and the other countries of 'actually existing socialism', comrade Weil stressed the importance of the rediscovery of Marxism — Marxism, that is to say, understood as scientific socialism, working-class theory and the science of class struggle. For Marxism to bear fruit once again, it has to be freed from 'Marxism-Leninism'. Sixty years of 'actually existing socialism' have turned a science of struggle into an ideology of legitimation, such that these years appear today as a historical crust to be removed. It is not Marxism that is in crisis (as Althusser maintains) but 'Marxism-Leninism'.

Now, the application of old categories to new realities is an unproductive procedure. I agree with Karol when he rejects as inadequate Bettelheim's use of the concept 'state capitalism' to refer to the society of 'actually existing socialism'. I even think that it is false, since it defines the western working class in the same terms as those of the East. If this conception were valid, the relationship of exploitation and alienation analyzed by Marx would exist for the proletariat in both social contexts. Indeed, as far as I am aware, that is precisely the view of Rossana Rossanda.

It is important to clear this matter up, and to define the

revolutionary subject that is the social and political bearer of emancipation. The perspectives and fate of the intellectual opposition in the countries of 'actually existing socialism' are closely bound up with the way in which the process of 'reconquering class consciousness' is posed for the producers. (See Rossanda's essay on 'Gierek and the Polish workers'.) We need to know how and where the social contradictions of 'existing socialism' will reach the point at which the producers will explode onto the social and political arena. Thus, given the necessity of a systematic analysis, we must ensure that the social processes are not masked by false concepts.

I do not agree with Rossanda when she talks about a 'capitalism without capitalists'. If we were to accept this term, the producers of 'existing socialism' would be defined as mere wage-labourers and we would find ourselves in the presence of the antagonistic contradiction between wage-labour and capital. In reality, however, the relationship of exploitation and alienation characteristic of capitalism is different from that which exists in Soviet-type societies. In the latter case, there is no 'inner nexus' giving cohesion to society through the law of value. One of the peculiar features of capitalist society is the fact that economic laws operate 'to the detriment of the producers' yet seem to go without saying and impose themselves with natural immediacy (except when the cohesion is weakened by a great crisis). Now, it is precisely the lack of such internal social cohesion which entails that Soviet society *is not capitalist*: the character of both labour and domination is different.

We cannot talk [when referring to the Soviet Union] of capitalist wage-labour, but nor either of a free association of men in a classless society. It is rather a question of a species of *forced labour*. When labour assumes the form of compulsion, it indicates the existence of direct domination such as prevailed in pre-capitalist societies. This also explains why, under 'actually existing socialism', the State *cannot* slacken but *has to grow continually stronger*. Since the economic cohesion of such societies is in no sense 'natural', it can be realized only in a *political* manner. Under capitalism, *society* lives according to laws of its own, and the *State* has only to back them up and ensure the conditions for social reproduction. Under 'actually existing socialism', by contrast, 'society' does not exist in that sense: it is both created and maintained in a *political* fashion. Hence the need for institutions of domination like the police, the armed forces, the secret services, or even law and ideology. Here too, the bureaucracy finds its *raison d'être*.

In order to maintain its domination, the bureaucracy has to impose *its* model of socialism ('development of the productive forces', 'catching up and overtaking capitalism') as if this were socialism itself. Any kind of alternative is intolerable, since it threatens to shake the whole structure of domination and endanger the very existence of society. This is why the bureaucracy cannot allow other models of socialism to be discussed (whether it is a question of the Chinese model, the Prague Spring or a model of council communism). This is why every opposition has to be repressed.

As I said, the coercive character of labour entails *domination*; and wherever there is domination, there is oppression. The existence of oppression signifies that the producers are kept in a minority position. The Party, having to uphold its firm monopoly over models of socialism and impose 'socialism' as the emanation of the producers, itself becomes the 'substitute for socialism'. Through 'its' socialism, the Party and state bureaucracy prevents the real emancipation of the producers in a free association, and cements the relationship of alienation within the production process. We are further confronted with a permanent social crisis — conflict and contradiction being the very stuff of 'actually existing socialism'.

The immaturity of society and the alienated living and working conditions of the producers are expressed in another, equally alienated form: the immature producers comfort themselves as consumers. They demand a greater scope for consumption and free time at work — in other words, that alienated satisfaction of deformed needs which follows from alienated conditions of labour and production. Thus, producer resistance assumes first of all the form of 'consumer protest'. In the Soviet Union, there is undoubtedly a relationship between the cycles of social and economic crisis and the multiplication of disorders revolving around such question: for example, in the early sixties, with the failure of the Khruschev reforms; and in the late sixties, when it became clear that the grand economic reforms intended to establish 'the economic system of socialism' were incapable of overcoming the permanent social crisis. (As Karol reminded us, the 1963 events in Novocherkassk resulted in hundreds of deaths; other disorders took place in Odessa, Gorki, Rostov and so on; in the late sixties, there was a new wave of strikes and disturbances, especially in Sverdlovsk, Gorki, Kaunas, Tashkent and Kiev; and in 1972, bitter struggles broke out in the industrial regions of the Ukraine — most notably in Kiev, but also in Dniepropetrovsk and Dnieprodzerzhinsk.) The immediate causes are problems of supply, the general *form* 'consumer strikes' and 'food disturbances'. The 1970-71 Polish dockers' strikes testified to *the relationship between form and content*: although food prices were at the origin of the strike, the workers behaved as emancipated producers when they summoned Gierek and indirectly demanded that the Party and State should bow to their interests as workers. Even if they did not yet realize it, they were thereby calling into question the domination of the bureaucracy. Once this struggle is conducted in a conscious manner, the transition from 'existing socialism' to real socialism will come on to the agenda.

The bureaucracy is bogged down in the following dilemma: it cannot overcome the permanent crisis without changing its model of socialism. Consumer needs cannot be satisfied so long as priority is given to sector one (heavy industry). Not only does the cycle of reform and crisis not resolve the structural problems, but the bureaucracy (no longer believing in a transitional society) has exhausted all its recipes for reform since it created the 'system of advanced socialism'. Since the late sixties, in fact, the bureaucracy has centred its management of the crisis on two axes: *first*, an offensive on the world market designed to close 'the technological gap' and make up for the lethargic pace of domestic innovation through importing capitalist technology; *and second*, a growth in productivity. Imported together with capitalist technology is the capitalist organization of labour. 'A growth in productivity' means quite simply an intensification of labour. Both axes therefore involve squeezing the labour force to a greater extent — increased exploitation of the workers. And since consumer supply cannot at the same time be substantially improved, the producers remain unsatisfied as consumers and new conflicts stand out on the horizon. For what is the point of working more and harder when one does not thereby 'live better'? These social contradictions will become sharper in a subsequent period.

We can here observe a peculiar dialectic with directly political consequences for socialists both in the East and the West. The fact that the bureaucracy hopes to resolve social problems through import and export on the world market does a lot to explain its interest in detente. Thus, the measures of political detente adopted at the Helsinki Conference on European Security were supposed to create the institutional framework for economic exchange; while in the capitalist countries, the onset of crisis has led to a growing interest in new markets and new openings for investment. Thus, on either side, the rulers have an interest both in attenuating the crisis through increased economic relations, and in strengthening their political domination through perpetuation of the social status quo. This also entails that social contradictions should be kept under control and the class struggle damped down.

Now, comrade Plyushch was undoubtedly right when he cautiously voiced the hope that detente in Europe will eventually create positive conditions for the left opposition in the countries of 'existing socialism'. For the intellectual opposition, detente does carry certain advantages: greater publicity in the West for the protests and petitions of intellectuals; greater chances of containing the bureaucracy's harsh repression, and thus a decrease in open terrorism. (Although maybe psychiatric clinics are precisely the form of repression best 'suited' to a cynical era of East-West detente?)

Our task as western socialists is therefore to indicate a strategy and political way out of this dialectic. There is absolutely no reason for us to go along with some vague detente euphoria. For each of the two systems, detente and 'competition' are instruments for maintaining the status quo and blocking the class struggle. Even if detente is useful to the intellectual opposition of 'existing socialism', we cannot shut our eyes to the fact that it hinders resistance among the producers and shackles the development of class consciousness. And this problem has not yet been resolved.

The more the intellectual opposition of 'existing socialism' becomes socialist and takes into account the relationship between its own struggle and the birth of proletarian resistance (as Rudolf Bahro does very acutely in his analysis), the stronger will become the possibility of a united socialist policy pointing, both in the East and the West, towards the emancipation of the working class.

Psychiatry as an Instrument of Repression

Hrayr Terzian

Hrayr Terzian is a psychologist of Armenian descent. He is the director of the neurological clinic at Padua University, a member of the leadership of Psichiatria Democratica *since 1976 and a close collaborator with the CGIL trade union federation in the health field. He has had published in Europe and the Americas more than one hundred scientific works and papers.*

In this conference on power and opposition in the post-revolutionary societies, it would have been unthinkable that no mention, however brief, be made of that instrument of repression which psychiatry has become in the East. The only information we have is of a general, I would say journalistic character, and it is not always first-hand. This prevents us from contributing a really satisfactory analysis to the debate over psychiatric oppression in the East, and especially in the Soviet Union.

I have not come to this conference only in my own name: I also bring the greetings and support of the 'Psichiatria Democratica' group. In fact, *Psichiatria Democratica* asks you to use this opportunity to agree to set up a separate discussion on the problem of psychiatry both in eastern and western societies. Such a discussion would analyze the practices employed in various countries by relating them to the phenomena which they have created.

As you know, *Psichiatria Democratica* was born out of struggles initiated above all at Gorizia psychiatric hospital. An extremely important threshold was crossed last September at the Trieste conference dealing with alternatives to psychiatry. In Trieste, for the first time in western, and no doubt world history, one of the instruments of psychiatry — the lunatic asylum — has been destroyed; and last

September, four to five thousand people came to see what was involved in closing down a lunatic asylum and definitively releasing its inmates after a hundred and fifty years of incarceration. Having reached this important stage in its development, our *Psichiatria Democratica* realizes that it has not made an analysis of what is going on in the East. It now feels sufficiently strong and capable, and nothing can prevent it from beginning this analysis.

I recently came across two books: a Soviet treatise on psychiatry, whose author — I have forgotten his name — is probably an obscure psychiatrist like so many others, and the volume published by Bukovsky on the expertise suffered by numerous dissident intellectuals in the Soviet Union.[1] They are both haunting books, even for someone working in the most backward sector of western psychiatry. The treatise on psychiatry, which has been translated into French by Editions de Moscou, is a really frightening book, above all as far as the illustrations are concerned. For it selects for reproduction in print faces which not even the most backward psychiatrist would dare to publish in Italy today. Indeed, he would not be able to find and photograph specimen faces such as those presented in this Soviet work. And then, no western treatise reduces man in such a vile manner to the level of an object. The foreword praises a certain Soviet psychiatry which makes a general invocation of Pavlov and Marxism-Leninism. But there is absolutely no trace of either Marx or Lenin in the text.

The book published by Bukovsky contains some expert psychiatric reports which, from the point of view of language and analytical method, would today be unthinkable in the western world. In almost every case the reports conclude by stating that the alleged illness is paranoid schizophrenia accompanied with reform mania. That is the essence of their diagnosis of mental illness.

Now, I do not have any deep knowledge of the question. But in reading the treatise I had the impression that in the Soviet Union (as well as in other countries, I think) there is an initial level of so-called neuro-psychiatric out-patient clinics. First developed between 1919 and 1925, when attempts were being made to clear away psychiatric and many other institutions, these clinics are nevertheless used in a completely negative manner, as a system of control in perfect liaison with the police.

This system is more or less comparable to the one which they are currently trying to establish in Italy through the famous territorialization of psychiatry. Here, official psychiatry is seeking to 'psychiatrize' territory. But according to the rare information we have, the Soviet Union has already carried out a veritable territorialization of psychiatry, albeit without 'psychiatrizing' territory.

A second level in the Soviet Union more or less corresponds to our regional lunatic asylums (although I do not know either their number or their dimensions). These are the so-called university psychiatric clinics, which train the various kinds of specialist. Above this level lie the institutions which roughly correspond to our criminal lunatic asylums, and which are called criminal or penal asylums, or some other such term. It would seem that these are much more numerous and widespread than in the West and that it is not just a few dissident intellectuals who are interned there for forcible treatment but many categories of individual. I have not managed to ascertain the categories involved, nor how they are defined. But these criminal lunatic asylums appear to be nothing other than psychiatrized political penitentiaries, which contain not so-called 'common-law prisoners', but exclusively 'political criminals' and dissidents, and other kinds of oppositionists about whom virtually nothing is known.

I would very much like to overcome our lack of information, so that we may understand the mechanism by which one is passed from one of these three levels to another: from the clinic to the true lunatic asylum, to the psychiatric teaching hospital, and to the criminal or penal lunatic asylum. In fact, the latter are very often departments of a prison; while in other cases, they are separate hospitals provided with psychiatrists who are at the same time police agents. Many of the texts in Bukovsky's book speak of people wearing police uniform under a white coat, or wearing sometimes just the coat, at other times just the uniform.

It is on the basis of such sparse information that we wish to build on the post-1968 movement in Italy in order to analyze psychiatry in the Soviet Union. Our own movement led to the resounding conference in Trieste, where lunatic asylums have been destroyed; and it has not been without an impact, even if the struggle is not easy and too often involves only advanced experiments. Today, the entire Italian psychiatric system is becoming disorganized and can no longer use the instruments it did in the past. Thus, in Italy, even the most wretched psychiatrists have given up employing insulin-induced coma; whereas in the Soviet Union, it is now used on a massive scale, just as it is in Cuba. 'We need to experiment with it for two years in order to see whether it really works or not' — that is how some Cuban psychiatrists justified to me their use of coma treatment in public clinics and at the Havana psychiatric hospital.

Moreover, like electric shock therapy and other such methods, coma treatment is applied in a very violent manner. Curiously enough, we used to take pride in saying that the Soviet Union abolished psycho-surgery in 1950. But it has since been reintroduced without any mention of a change in the law that formally prohibited its use. Psycho-surgical operations were recently still being performed, especially on obsessional patients and we know not how many other categories. Perhaps they are also inflicted on oppositional 'patients'. Here too, we would very much like to have more information.

This reintroduction of much of traditional psycho-surgery is very often presented as treatment for epilepsy. But in reality, it is purely a question of psycho-surgery: that is to say, of altering behaviour.

Another level of Soviet psychiatry is mentioned by the psychologist Giorgio Bignami. Since he was unable to attend this conference, I shall quickly read out a report which he sent me:

'For a number of years I have been working in the field of pharmaceutical research. On the basis of our direct contacts and the medical literature available to us, I can state that, at least in sectors like 'biological psychiatry' and neuro-psychopharmacology, there is no essential difference between the working hypotheses, scientific-cultural schemas, practical objectives and criteria for assessing results that prevail in the Soviet bloc and those which characterize the western-bloc countries. One particular aspect is illuminated by articles published in various international journals concerning the way in which psycho-pharmacological experiments are conducted. The existing methods rule out any consideration of constraint and any attempt to re-establish a balance in the power relationship between appointed specialist and blameworthy patient. Thus, people who have attended seminars organized by Soviet delegations have reported on the way in which the latter cross the frontier between brain operations that can somehow be justified by the presence of a serious and objectively identifiable organic condition, and operations performed in order to suppress symptoms not directly linked to an organic condition. A number of documents take up the growing recourse to psychic drugs — a clear sign not only of the silencing of symptoms in genuinely psychiatric cases, but also of the medical and psychiatric invasion of the daily life of the masses, above all through the use of hypnotic drugs, sedatives and tranquilisers. Judging by innumerable congress reports and the official programmes of cultural and scientific exchange (which involve such public Italian bodies as the Higher Institute for Health, the National Research Council and the universities), it is clear that there is an ever growing symbiosis of scientific sectors in the West and the corresponding ones in Eastern Europe; or worse still, that the latter are more and more frequently falling into step with the former. This is evident, first of all, from the lack of any real critique of the reductionist interpretation of deviant behaviour, or of various mystifying proposals for therapy. The drug, once regarded as suppressing symptoms, is now becoming the cure for a given mental illness. At the same time, there are a growing number of explicit East-West links: programmes of cultural and scientific exchange; joint research based on scientific options developed in the West, on psychological and biological models of mental illness, and on the mechanisms supposed to underlie the curative effects of psychic drugs. The ever closer links with private pharmaceutical monopolies and their scientific figure-heads entail that western psycho-pharmaceutical innovations gain more and more rapid and triumphant access to East European markets.'

Now, although we have little information on the subject, the instrument of psychiatry was profoundly challenged in the Soviet Union in the post-revolutionary period between 1919 and 1925. Many lunatic asylums were completely opened up, if not actually destroyed, and the whole problematic of psychiatry was called into question. After 1925, the institutions reverted to their function as traditional lunatic asylums, very similar to our own. In my opinion, they are now worse than any western asylum, involving as they do the pitiless use of instruments and methods that are less and less employed in the West. It is only a mystification when psychiatrists have recourse to gentler methods, when they try to introduce self-management of psychiatry by the patient himself. It is like those American models in which drug addicts give themselves electric shocks when they feel the need for drugs, without a psychiatric specialist having to step in.

Plyushch said that the criminal lunatic asylum, such as it is employed in the Soviet Union, is a purely Soviet invention which exists in no other country. But I do not think that that is altogether true. Although it is not today used in the traditional Soviet manner, the criminal lunatic asylum also used to play this role in the West. Everyone knows that most of the Paris communards who survived ended up in an asylum, pronounced alcoholics, perverts or homosexuals. And we need only recall Lombroso and his famous reports on numerous leaders of trade unions and worker or peasant leagues — reports which became part of expert knowledge 'Italian style'.

I would like to conclude by simply asking you to collect as many documents as possible: not so much those wretched experts' reports which are not worth even looking at, as a real analysis of the entire psychiatric structure and mode of operation, from the out-patients clinic to the criminal lunatic asylum. I would also like to suggest holding a conference, if possible on the basis of such information, and devoted to comparing our own practices with those employed in the East.

NOTES

1.   V. Boukovski, *Une nouvelle maladie mentale en URSS: l'opposition*, Paris 1977.

The USSR, Past and Present, in Discussions Among Workers at Fiat Mirafiori

Gianni Usai and Marcello Capri

Gianni Usai, a Sardinian metalworker, is a trade-union delegate at Fiat and a member of the executive committee of the factory council at the Mirafiori plant. He has been a member of the central committee of the PDUP.

Marcello Capri, a worker in the Fiat bodyshop, is also a union delegate and a member of the executive committee of the factory council at Fiat Mirafiori.

Gianni Usai

This gathering offers workers the first opportunity to participate directly in a discussion on dissent in the East European countries. There has been some talk about this in the factories lately. But to tell the truth, up to now the process of revision and rethinking that has been launched among the left has involved the leaderships more than the workers. It is difficult for us in the factories to escape the accusation that these discussions play into the hands of the conservative forces. We have not yet succeeded in going beyond the alternative of the fifties, of the period of the cold war: either you're with the Soviet Union or you're with capitalism, imperialism and the United States.

At Fiat Mirafiori, where we act through a PDUP-Manifesto collective, we hung up a wall newspaper commemorating the sixtieth anniversary of the October Revolution. The things we wrote were very modest and general. We said that we had to recover the content of the October Revolution and seek to understand how it developed in order to combat capitalism better and to avoid those practices within the left that lead to degeneration and regression, for which the workers are the first to pay the price. Despite this moderation, we ran into a lot of resistance from the workers.

What is the reason for this? I believe that many of the comrades who fight the employers in the factories day after day and fight the bourgeois conception of life in society too (thereby prefiguring, in their own practice, new and egalitarian relations among people, genuine 'elements of socialism') are the same people who tend to delegate a series of crucial decisions to their political parties, to people who supposedly 'know better about such things'. This process of delegation of authority, which affects such questions as economic policy, reforms, the administration of the state, and the nature of the Soviet Union, is mistaken and dangerous, for it is the real breeding ground of the traditional conception of the revolutionary process as advanced by a small, external, iron-willed vanguard.

We see this contradiction in the factories concretely every day. The councils of delegates still exist. But, to take one example, how much damage has been done at Mirafiori not only by the strategy of the left, but also by this notion of a sort of 'double truth' which everybody lulls themselves with and because of which faith in the possibility of really changing society is declining little by little? There is no lack of initiative in the factories, though. And on this basis, we seek to go forward towards control of economic policy, satisfaction of needs, and decisions on which productive choices to emphasize.

What, however, has really enabled and still enables the factory councils to persist? I think that the workers in struggle consciously feel linked to the long history of class struggle in Italy. In other words, there is a widespread consciousness, which resists all bourgeois manipulation, of being part of this long history, which is made up of many defeats, but also of memories, positive achievements, and future possibilities. I feel myself an integral part of this history; Marcello Capri feels himself an integral part of it too. And yet he and I are different, because we have been formed, as vanguard workers, in two different sectors of Fiat Mirafiori. In this sense as well, our contribution to the subject of this gathering begins from the analysis of the differing levels of consciousness within the working class.

To conclude, I would like to tell you an anecdote from the factory. While leaving work the other day, I was involved in a very tense discussion with a former comrade of the Communist Party who had not renewed his membership because he said he did not agree with the historic compromise. Both of us were angry. The argument was about the wall poster about the sixtieth anniversary of the Russian revolution. This comrade had spent his holidays in Russia this year, and he had come home quite happy. In Russia, he said, there is no unemployment, the transport system works, the medical care system functions; the best we could aspire to would be a society like that. Besides which, he added, 'I talked to several Russians and they told me that these dissidents are all pretty much like Solzhenitsyn'. And then he used a term which I will repeat, because I found it quite striking: 'shit-ass Catholics', people who are objectively against the workers. I answered that some of the dissidents in Russia and the other East European countries are comrades, people fighting for socialism. At that he stalked off, shouting, 'They ought to send the cossacks to straighten things out in Italy too'.

Be careful now. Here is a comrade who has been in the factories for many years; he has paid for the bosses' repression out of his own hide; he knows the kind of working conditions that prevailed at Fiat before 1968-69; he worked in the forced-labour shops Fiat set up at Mirafiori. But despite his past (and his present too, for he is still in the forefront of all struggles, one of the people who organize and promote them), he goes so far as to call for the coassacks. This strikes me as real cause for alarm, exactly because it shows us how much more still has to be done to develop full awareness of a mode of thought, a conception, a class consciousness, that can deal with the comprehensive problem of the revolution in this country.

Marcello Capri
Gianni spoke a bit about the differences among workers. I would like to take this opportunity to introduce a 'clarification' about the first point he made, namely the fact that the workers have been rather slow in taking up the discussion, namely about 'existing socialism'. I would say that there is not so much delay as outright rejection, an automatic defensive reaction, a basic incapacity to confront this problem.

In my experience, this is true primarily among the 'older' workers, those who lived through the tough years of repression at Fiat, who were sustained for years by the myth of the socialist countries as they strove to move forward in a struggle that was supposed to lead, step by step, to a common goal. In fact, this myth has been the cornerstone of their ability to resist; it is therefore enormously difficult to challenge it, to discuss it in any real depth. Moreover, today this discussion is taking place in a particular context which has never arisen in Italy before. The workers' movement, the trade unions and left parties, are taking up ever greater political tasks. Their specific weight is becoming gigantic. At the same time, the contradictions and imbalances are growing too. In sum, exactly because we are closer to a process of profound change of society and the state, the comparison with real historical experience becomes more dramatic. There is no point in hiding this.

If the mechanisms of rank-and-file participation in and control of this process are not strengthened, a bureaucratic regression will become almost inevitable.

I therefore believe that the left organizations must make an effort to devise initiatives that are not disruptive but can maintain and advance the discussion in this direction. We cannot hope suddenly to shatter some of the basic certitudes (correct or incorrect, instrumental or not) which the workers' movement has been nurturing in the factories for years, which have been one of the pillars of its ability to resist and struggle, without simultaneously finding some way to recover the entire historic experience being discussed here today.

I do not believe that this discussion, this gathering, could have been held at any other time. It is occurring today exactly because historic reality compels us to deal with all the dimensions of this problem. We could not have discussed these questions purely in the abstract.

What we are talking about is the struggle of the workers' movement we have built in the West, particularly in Italy, which is different from that which was built in the East European countries, whether during the revolutionary or post-revolutionary phase. Are we dealing with two substantially different and separate truths, or with two truths that do intersect and mutually nurture each other after all?

Would the Italian workers' movement be what it is today without the October Revolution? Conversely, would the discussion on dissent in the East European countries be occurring in its present form without the experience of the Italian or French workers' movement of the past several years?

I believe that a part of the revolution has been made the way we have made it. I do not believe we can acknowledge the existence of two societies, two experiences of struggle, two class movements, that have travelled completely separate paths, each independent of the other.

But what has our experience been during these past years? We have a boss, Gianni Usai said; we have a government that is not the government of the working class; it is a bourgeois government, and this boss and this government work together very closely in running this country. All discussion, then, both within the unions and within the political parties, has always been aimed at achieving unity against the other side, even if only through the violence of the confrontation and conflict. There has always been this dynamic: the left has had to elaborate, discuss, and clash, but ultimately in order to present a united front against the bosses and the government.

Things have been different in the countries which have gone through bloody revolutionary phases, where the seizure of power has occurred, where there is no longer an employer or a democratic government. Here the urgency of unity is lacking, and discussion does not have to result in united and definitive solutions. Perhaps it is exactly because of this lack of participation and ability of the ranks to exert control that the movement finally fell under the hegemony of others.

Naturally, all this is very schematic. Time is very short. But I believe that our main effort must be directed along these two lines: how the movement has developed in the East European countries and what limits (and this is a really enormous paradox) have been created because the East European workers' movement does not have to deal with a capitalist and bourgeois opponent, limits which have resulted in the regression of certain forms of power which now embody bureaucratic administration.

At the same time, I consider it really necessary to rediscover the significance of the experiences of this workers' movement, despite the regression that has occurred. The potential of such an investigation and discussion could lead indirectly to a rise in the level of participation of the working masses in the class organizations.

This is a fundamental point. Otherwise we will go through the same thing again, albeit in attenuated, milder, and less violent forms. I want to insist that we have already reached this situation and are not merely on our way there, and that processes of bureaucratic regression are already evident even within our own class organizations.

This is the basic theme the left must try to deal with today.

The West European Left and the Political and Social Conflict in the East

Real Socialism and Possible Socialism: The Problems of the East European Societies and the European Left

Lucio Magri

Lucio Magri, a theoretician and cadre of the Italian Communist Party, was expelled from the party in 1969 along with the other founders of the newspaper il manifesto. *Since 1971 he has been secretary of the organization that arose around* il manifesto *and then of the PDUP. He is a member of the leadership of PDUP-Manifesto and was elected a member of parliament in the elections of 20 June 1976.*

With your permission, I would like to return to the reasons why we organized this gathering. Or rather, to state them more explicitly. There is an urgent political reason for this, which is as follows:

The European workers' movement has arrived at a new and critical point in its history. Once again it faces great possibilities and great dangers. Capitalist society is again in crisis. Regarding the stagnation of the productive forces, this crisis is as grave as any in the past; but it is deeper and more radical than any other in that it is organic, directly linked to a crisis of the state, of ideology, and of dominant values. It also differs from past crises in that the upsurge of the masses is more intense. It is uneven and confused, but no less potent, and it points toward an extension and new definition of democracy. This mass pressure makes it difficult for the bourgeoisie to assemble its forces and even to muster the resolve required to mount a counter-offensive and reestablish its own power. Whatever the limits and contradictions of past revolutions — and we have been extensively informed of them during this conference — it is incontestable that the general international relationship of forces is different today, not only in terms of the level of consciousness and organization of the working class, but also in terms of the social and ideological reserves the ruling classes are able to mobilize. At least from the vantage point of Europe and Italy, we feel that although the moment of victory is still far off — indeed, the very outcome of the conflict remains undecided — we have not struggled in vain for all these decades.

This is the real underlying situation which, during the past several years, has generated a positive crisis even among some sectors of European Social Democracy which are now realizing the limits of the welfare state and are timidly seeking a policy that would no longer be the mere administration of capitalist society.

More important, this is also the objective basis, the qualifying premise, for Eurocommunism. In several countries the European Communist movement is drawing closer to a role in government, not as a repetition of past Social Democratic experiences, but in the thick of a deep crisis, under the pressure of genuine mass initiative, and having behind it a tradition of struggle that has not been liquidated.

This is the interest of the European situation, which, perhaps for the first time, appears as the most dynamic and advanced front in the world struggle, not in theory but in reality. But this is also where the greatest dangers loom. We know this from the lessons of past history, for we remember the disasters the defeat in the West in the twenties entailed for the entire world. But we can also see it with our own eyes. Indeed, if we look at the events of the past year, we find no grounds for triumphalism, or even optimism.

In France the unity of the left has broken down so completely as to threaten the outcome of the next elections and perhaps much more than that. Hopes for rapid developments have been disappointed in Spain and Portugal, although for different reasons and to differing extents. In Italy, after the great victory of 20 June 1976, we are not only finding it difficult to initiate profound transformations of society but are also seeing the first fissures in the political and social bloc of the left. In Germany we see not only a new shift to the right in general, but also a regression of the Social Democratic Party. Everywhere there are tensions between Socialists and Communists; everywhere the new left is in crisis; and above all, nowhere has the mass movement been able to make the transition from an effective struggle around particular demands to an equally effective struggle for the transformation of the economy and the state.

All these difficulties have a common root, although they find varying forms of expression: the extreme gravity of the crisis of the system. The possibilities of economic and social development which had allowed for an expansion of democracy within the system for twenty years and even made democracy one of the stimulants of the expansion itself, have now dried up.

The survival of the capitalist system (not to mention any recovery) increasingly requires that the positions of strength of the masses be dismantled, that their wage increases be rolled back, and that social and political repression be intensified. Even the democratic thrust of the masses, if it is not transformed into a different manner of producing, living, and governing, threatens to disintegrate into corporatist phenomena or blind revolt.

If the unity of the left is breaking down in France, to take one example, it is not merely because the PCF, for some obscure sectarian reason, is raising the stakes of the alliance around an artificial theme, nationalizations. At bottom, there is a genuine and in certain respects comprehensible 'fear of victory'. Fear of victory, which would mean having to govern a country racked by crisis, without the political unity, programme, or mass support required to sustain the conflict.

If, as I maintain, it is a suicidal error to respond to these difficulties by shirking them — i.e. by declining governmental power, or worse, by preparing to govern merely in order to effect a normalization — then the European left is now compelled by the force of circumstance to pose, well before it expected or desired it, the problem of the transition to a different social system. The problem of the revolution in the most developed countries has thus been placed squarely on the historical agenda again, and if we do not begin to solve it, we will suffer a defeat of unpredictable import and duration on a world scale.

This is where the question of Eastern Europe comes in, as one of our immediate problems. It is our problem because it is unthinkable firstly to propose a transition to socialism in the West without taking account of the reality of existing socialism in the East, without explaining how and to what extent the society we want will be different, secondly to initiate a radical upheaval in the social and political equilibrium in Western Europe without considering what sort of processes this could trigger off in the neighbouring, powerful Soviet bloc.

This is what motivates us in this gathering. It is not a conference on dissent in general. Nor on dissent in Eastern Europe *per se*. It is a conference on the crisis and perspectives of East European society, as an element in a process of theoretical investigation aimed at determining our action and perspectives in the crisis of our society. We are interested not in an international of dissidence but in a new way of discussing proletarian internationalism.

Well then, we must recognize that the European left has been quite sluggish in this matter; indeed, the assumptions on which it has been acting up to now are racked by a serious crisis.

Let us look first of all at the position of the great traditional forces of the workers' movement. During the past several years the Socialist and Communist Parties have acted on a common general line as regards the Soviet bloc, although with understandable tactical differences. This line is rooted in the conviction (similarly maintained by Deutscher and Togliatti, for example) that the Stalinist model, being closely linked to the conditions of backwardness and encirclement in which the Russian revolution developed, was destined to evolve towards democratization as the tasks of industrialization, urbanization, and the extension of literacy were completed and as the process of international détente unfolded.

Even deeper lies the conviction that the political authoritarianism and administrative centralization of the East European countries were primarily institutional phenomena reflecting the delay of the superstructure in catching up with the structure. This is why the Soviet ruling group, as the necessary protagonist of a gradual reform, has remained the interlocutor.

This line, formulated by Togliatti at the time of the twentieth congress of the Communist Party of the Soviet Union in 1956, has prevailed for twenty years now and still represents the predominant approach, not only because it arose out of an old and highly consolidated culture common to the entire workers' movement, but also for political reasons which have not been, and will not be, easy to dispose of. If we do not understand the real reasons for the policy of the historic parties and for its persistent strength, we will be unable to change it.

It does not get us very far to replace real historical processes with definitions of principle. This line arose (and was nurtured) primarily out of a concern for realism, a concern to take account of the strategic balance between the two great world powers, a fear that this balance would be dangerously compromised by any grave crisis of the so-called socialist camp, and the desire to use the international context of Russian-American partnership as a lever with which to avert excessively rapid and dangerous clashes within the European societies (which would have polarized all the intermediary forces to the right again).

Togliatti's line also arose — and this is its second source — from the desire to resolve the problem of the relationship between socialism and democracy in a relatively simple manner comprehensible to the masses. The illusion was that this problem would be easier in the West because of the superior level of development and that it would gradually become soluble in Eastern Europe too, for the same reason. This is why this line has persisted to this day, in spite of such dramatic 'incidents' as the invasion of Czechoslovakia. Hence, even today, not only for the Communist Parties but for the Social Democracy as well, the interlocutor remains the Soviet ruling group, from which one takes one's distance but whose 'positive evolution' one hails.

The new elements that have arisen during past years are certainly not unimportant, however. It is not without significance that Berlinguer stated in Moscow that the question of democracy is a matter not only of national peculiarities but of principle, thus intervening in Soviet affairs themselves. But the underlying assumption remains unchanged: dissidence is considered merely a symptom of the anachronistic superstructure and a stimulus for a gradual evolution of Soviet society; all hopes continue to be staked on this. The relationship between democracy and socialism is reaffirmed primarily in terms of a mitigation of the severity of economic planning through the introduction of market mechanisms or in terms of a correction of the dictatorship of the proletariat through the introduction of parliamentary pluralism.

I think it would be quite foolish to deny the significance of the political options and acts of the Eurocommunists with respect to the Soviet bloc. Not only because mere statements of position in favour of civil rights and liberties acquire quite considerable weight when they are expressed by great parties of the Third International, but also because the question of democracy has now assumed a wholly new and decisive importance in Soviet society (and not only in Soviet society). It is no accident that democracy has been increasingly filled with a workers' and people's content over the past several decades. Because it is only with democracy, even in the most classical sense, that the proletarian social forces can rid themselves of particularist

narrowness, the ideology of subordination, and the sense of resigna-
tion or impotent revolt constantly inculcated in them by their very
position in capitalist social relations. The revolutionary social subject
always needs greater culture, organization, and struggle in order to
hold itself together. And if dissent in the USSR, whether intellectual
or popular, is often expressed in isolated forms of protest — in
particularism, irrationalism, passive resistance — it is precisely
because of the lack of any democratic environment in which it could
grow, define itself, and become a rational alternative.

Democracy allows the intellectuals to express something; but it
also enables the workers and peasants to have something to say as a
class. This is why the sort of pressure Eurocommunism can exert is
important and tends to become an element of great value for the
class struggle.

Nevertheless, I believe that this line, sensible and profitable so
long as the European Communist movement was in opposition and
the capitalist system was stable, no longer holds up in the thick of the
crisis, faced with the test of a process of transition. Primarily for the
following reason: it is not enough to repeat 'we want socialism with
democracy', even if one adds that democracy means the continuous
expansion of mass initiative. The western crisis is again highlighting
what had already been clearly demonstrated by the twenty years that
followed the twentieth congress. For the fact is that both Brezhnev
and the *nouveaux philosophes* are correct on one point: the problem
of the construction of socialism as a higher form of democracy is an
objectively complex one which has yet to be resolved. And not only
because of the backwardness of certain societies or the weight of
their past, but for structural and permanent reasons as well.

Indeed, this is demonstrated by the fact that forty years of Social
Democratic administration in some western countries has not
succeeded in eroding the bases of the system, and also by the fact that
economic development, political stability, and military security have
not sufficed for the USSR to rid itself of its authoritarian institutions.
Why? It is important to realize, as Rossanda and Bettelheim have
explained better than I ever could, that what we are dealing with
here is the restoration of a class society. This is the root of
authoritarianism. But one wonders why in the world this new form of
class rule cannot afford the luxury of even the facade of pluralism
and instead requires a stiflingly repressive apparatus and an authoritarian ideology, even though this creates not a few problems for it.

The fact is that in western capitalist society the market and private property provide both the real mechanisms of repression and the most effective stimulants to activity. Various institutions, so old as to seem like products of nature — the family, the work ethic, religion, the elitist educational system — have guaranteed, so far, a reasonable, almost spontaneous, mass acceptance of the rules. This is the hidden basis of liberal-bourgeois pluralism, the real factor that prevents individualism, competition, and secularism from having disintegrating or paralyzing effects. But when collective property and the planned economy demolish these mechanisms and when subsequent expansion of industrialization dismantles these old basic institutions, then — in the absence of new structures of collective participation, new intrinsic stimulants for the quality and aims of labour, new community values — the only instruments of social cohesion and (illusory) mobilization become political totalitarianism, the ideological state, and the administrative bureaucracy. This is the unshakable source of strength of the present authoritarianism. The same phenomenon, incidentally, may be glimpsed in the crisis of the welfare state in the West.

Hence the vicious circle: political pluralism cannot be reintroduced into a system of state capitalism without going all the way and also reinstituting the market and profit as mechanisms of repression and yardsticks of efficiency; but such mechanisms cannot be reintroduced (indeed, it is difficult enough to make them function properly in the countries where they already exist) without sowing social and political conflicts so intense that they might have to be kept under control through authoritarian instruments.

Thus, the further development of the productive forces has made the relationship between democracy and socialism more complicated, not simpler, precisely because it has removed the unambiguously progressive element from the purely quantitative expansion of material resources, has dismantled those 'internal links' that used to dictate rules of behaviour to the masses, and has generated a surge of new and radical needs.

But that is not all. The present international equilibrium and internal stability of the Soviet bloc are increasingly in question. The attitude the Carter administration has taken towards the USSR (although cautiously) is certainly not accidental, nor, in my view, transitory. It reflects the need of the United States to hew out a new strategy to respond to the crisis that followed the failure of Kissinger's attempt to stabilize the third world through a network of sub-imperialist states and thereby to open new frontiers there.

Further, the United States is beginning to detect some internal instability in the Soviet bloc and to exert some pressure against it. Similarly, the Chinese concern with rising Soviet aggressiveness does not seem to me to be the product of pure ideological schematism. Indeed, I believe that Daniel Singer's observations on the latest crisis of Brezhnevism are quite pertinent here. To be sure, Brezhnev has cleverly been able to construct an internal equilibrium of his own, stabilizing the ruling classes, easing the pressure on the peasants, and patiently seeking some mediation between the working class and the managers.

But there is no doubt that tension is rising. The attempt to acquire a new stability through a rapid rise in consumption conflicts with the relative stagnation of production. To escape from this contradiction would require the rupture of the compromise with the workers. The aspirations — and the strength — of the technical and intellectual groupings are also on the rise. And even more important, the post-Stalinist and post-Khrushchevist solutions to the problem of relations with the masses (depoliticization and corporatism) are now causing social disintegration and rising nationalism.

If these tensions finally explode in their present forms and through the present channels, if they are not transformed, with our aid, into a real political opposition, then they will neither generate an alternative nor even force reformist adjustments. In that event, given the rising disproportion between scant economic and social stability and excessive military power, a dangerous trend toward external aggression cannot be ruled out.

This danger hovering over peace, which we of course want to avert, cannot simply be conjured away by leaving things as they are nor by attempting to exorcise a crisis which is with us anyway, but by trying to prevent in time this crisis from unfolding in a blind and spontaneous way. The lack of interest the European left has shown in the East European situation, the reluctant and even indifferent manner in which it has followed the evolution of dissent, in particular paying little attention to which forms of dissent are spreading within society, thus threatens to become adventurist precisely because of its excessive prudence. It is equally adventurist to continue to wager exclusively on the improvement of Russian-American relations instead of pursuing a more vigorous line of European independence in order to confront possible phases of tension and even to intervene actively and positively in the internal destabilization and transformation of the two camps.

It is for all these reasons that the East European policy of the traditional left has arrived at an impasse, a point of crisis. And this crisis may soon produce a regression towards normalization or impotent libertarian radicalism. We have not forgotten that 'existing socialism' began its regression when and where it had to assume power. The European left is now approaching just this moment of truth. It is therefore reasonable to ask whether 'existing socialism' expresses only our past or whether it still represents a danger for our future, despite the most sincere declarations.

The new left, however, also faces disturbing questions and must re-think many of the suppositions to which it has always clung. Obviously, I am not referring solely to those (and they were many) who reconstructed their own ideological identity after 1968 on the basis of the thesis of the revolution betrayed and the recovery of Leninist orthodoxy or who dogmatically adopted China as a new model. I am also thinking of those, like us, who sought to travel new roads, to seek solutions in a direction that still appears correct to me.

The period immediately before and after 1968 was a great time; it was not merely the time of the invasion of Prague, but also of the struggles of workers and students in the West and of the cultural revolution in China. It was precisely in those experiences that we thought we saw a precious example and a concrete possibility of escaping from the Stalinist model. We always refused to turn the Chinese cultural revolution into a new model to be imitated, for we were not unaware of the great limits imposed on that experience, even at its finest moments, by the objective context of backwardness and isolation in which it occurred. These limits were expressed in the virtually religious use of the ideology and authority of Mao as the necessary other face of the spontaneous and tumultuous contestation of the masses, constantly bordering on voluntarism, moralism, and even corporatism and anarchy. Similarly we made no myth of the ability of the opposition movements in the West to project an immediate alternative, nor did we ignore their utopian limits, linked to their base among social subjects oscillating between revolt and integration. Nevertheless, it appeared to us — and it still appears to us — that a strategic hypothesis was being advanced by these movements, a new idea of revolution which may be defined by the summary formula 'break with Stalinism to the left'. What did this expression mean? Merely that it was necessary to launch a new class struggle against the new privileged classes? No, not only that. It meant that the root of what had to be and could be criticized in the

Soviet model and its authoritarianism lay in the fact that the process of transformation of capitalist relations of production was very quickly halted and then reversed; that socialism was never conceived as a transitional society leading to communism and was never constructed in that way; that the objective of industrialization was therefore adopted as absolute; that the construction of the material basis became detached from the general process of the establishment of communist relations among human beings; that state and society were still separated; that the division between manual and intellectual labour was recreated; that the educational system was erected on the basis of meritocratic selection, and so on.

This, I repeat, seems to me the real point. Democratic administration of planning is not possible in an economy whose market character is not really on the road to disappearance. It is impossible to transcend wage labour unless repetitive tasks are really on the wane, or at least unless the time devoted to them is being reduced and redistributed throughout the body of society. Political equality is not possible, nor is the withering away of the state, unless the social base is refashioned. 'If a cook is really to administer the state, then it is crucial that no one can really be called a cook any longer.' Moreover, if the habits of oppression and the instrumental use of all forms of power are to disappear, then the innermost structure of the institution of the family, which fuels them, must be attacked. Now, what seemed new to us in 1968 was that all this no longer appeared as a lofty Marxist utopia but was a real possibility, an actual process determined by the development of capitalist contradictions and the historic results of revolutionary struggles. For the first time, it was something that had attained historic maturity in the needs and practice of millions of people. There were many subjective and objective reasons for this, but also some very material ones, a few of which may be summarized as follows:

1. The now evident, almost physical, impossibility of guaranteeing any real progress of the productive forces in the third world by resorting, as did the USSR, to the technological models of capitalism, and of the opulent capitalist societies in particular.

2. The increasingly evident negative results of any productive organization whose sole motor force is the quantitative expansion of goods and wage labour, whether through the market or through a plan: rising parasitism and waste, labour absenteeism, destruction of the environment, lack of correspondence between production and needs, etc.

3. The crisis of the efficacy and unifying capacity of the state as a distinct apparatus, increasingly characterized by bureaucratism and technocratic fiefdoms and unable to exercise any real control over the corporatist segmentation of the body of society.

4. The extraordinary growth of productive potential as a precondition for the reduction of necessary labour time and the concurrent rapid expansion of new free and creative forms of social labour.

5. The rise of qualitatively new needs, no longer reducible to bourgeois and consumerist horizons. The common denominator of these needs is the assertion of individual autonomy and creativity, no longer in terms of separate and competing individuals.

6. The mass critique of the division of labour, the stratification of roles, and the neutrality of science and technology, and the rejection of a hierarchy increasingly reduced to the arbitrary assertion of power.

7. The emergence of a new world relationship of forces, not only because of the new balance of power but also because of the entrance of countless masses and entire continents into the real dialectic of history.

We felt that all this could be seen in both the forms and content of mass struggles, especially in places where there were precedents in the traditions of the workers' movement, like China and Italy.

What I want to stress here, at least as a working hypothesis, is the importance of these objective facts, which served as the foundation of the new rise and new quality of the revolutionary project. For we owe at least this both to the comrades of the East European countries who have so dramatically described the oppression they suffer and to the worker comrades who have been fighting for decades here in the West.

We must declare, as far as it is possible for us to do so, that their revolutions and struggles (and their defeats too), even though they have not achieved a genuinely socialist society, even if they do not suffice to shield us from an epoch-making historical defeat, have nevertheless served to advance the front of struggle and now enable us both to learn from their mistakes and to try to avoid repeating them. I think this is a very precise distinction that must be made during our gathering here. We are not here to lament the fact that the October Revolution occurred, that the battle of Stalingrad was won, or that the Eurocentric world has collapsed.

In 1977, however, we must acknowledge that this sort of response to the crisis of the Stalinist model has proven inadequate. Why? The things comrade Masi said yesterday — perhaps with the one-sidedness born of the disappointment of those who had believed (equally one-sidedly) — are quite eloquent. The defeat of the cultural revolution — no matter how partial or total, transitory or lasting — has one especially burning consequence. No one can deny that the masses energetically irrupted onto the scene during the cultural revolution, counterposing themselves to the established regime in a genuinely and not merely ideologically radical manner. Mao's China was not Stalin's Russia. Nevertheless, it was not enough. Indeed, paradoxically, almost as an elementary survival reaction, it triggered a chain reaction which caused the rebirth of a regime and ideology that had perhaps never been seen in revolutionary China before.

It is here, from this new defeat, that the tendency arises, now prevalent among the new left, to move towards a rejection of politics as an organized project and action measuring itself against the relationship of forces, the real historical process, and the current problems of the transformation of the economy, the state, and international relations. This is the root of the temptation to criticize the cultural revolution itself 'from the left', calling for further radicalism, a greater moralistic and voluntaristic deviation.

It is here also that arises the tendency to 'go beyond' Marxism, not by reviewing and criticizing its analytic inadequacies but rather by reducing it to the mere discovery of the class struggle as the motor force of history (a discovery that had already been made by bourgeois culture anyway). History itself is thus reduced, independent of any material factors, to a kind of puppet show in which the poor confront the rich, the servant confronts the boss, Gulag oppresses the individual and everything remains the same until the final day of redemption, the certainty of which becomes a matter of pure faith. The class struggle thus appears primarily as a revolution in the hearts of men, and when this is not enough to respond to the tragic urgency of needs, there is no alternative but to fall back on the shortcuts of terrorism, putschism, or some sort of exemplary gesture.

The impasse in which we find ourselves in regard to 'existing socialism' is therefore grave. It is not my task here to discuss if and how the European left can overcome this sluggishness and escape from this impasse. Frankly I would be quite incapable of doing so.

The analysis I have sought to sketch out, however, does suggest both a direction of research and experimentation and the necessity for a very precise political choice.

1. The direction of theoretical research and practical experimentation is as follows. It is my view that Eurocommunism and the new left make the same error in dealing with the problem of existing socialism. Neither has carried through to the end a serious reflection on the concept of transition, despite the fact that historical experience on the matter is by now rather rich. Indeed the Eurocommunists have reduced this concept to the historicist platitude that the revolution is a process; they have thus renounced the effort to determine scientifically its vicissitudes on a world scale, to define, little by little, the mechanisms and structures that guarantee its course, and to pinpoint the opposite tendencies towards barbarism. The new left, on the other hand, has simply eradicated the problem of transition, claiming that communism is at hand, or at best has reduced it to the mechanical extension of workers' autonomy and the potential of struggle such autonomy can express.

In neither case has any serious effort been made to organize the alternative proposal of the working class into a conscious project. Most important, there has been no effort to translate the most advanced, most radically anti-capitalist aspirations and behaviour of the masses into genuine modifications of the economy, the state, and the forms of organization, so that workers' hegemony could rise and be consolidated in reality — not merely in the political heavens or the intimacy of individual consciousness — and could gradually take shape as a material force. What, for example, has been done to construct the institutional channels and fields of experimentation through which the critique of the neutrality of science or the struggle against the organization of labour could become new science, new technology, new organization of labour? Or what has been done to ensure that the institutions of direct democracy are not limited to coexistence with the traditional institutions but instead become part of a real process of withering away of the state and social administration? What has been done to attack the educational system, not only to paralyze it or sow illusions that it can be reformed, but to heal its separation from society and thereby to socialize a growing portion of intellectual labour?

This, in my view, is the angle from which we must again begin to think about existing socialism and the sort of socialism that is possible. Not by retreating into ideology, but by applying ourselves very concretely to questions like these: given the present level of the productive forces and the present political conditions, what does it mean to go beyond the historically determined capitalist model of development? And what social forces, what organizational structures, can and must be mobilized? In sum, we must develop an equation for the relationship between democracy and communism that maintains their unity but does not subsume one into the other.

Such are the questions that arise from the experience of existing socialism. By confronting them we make a decisive contribution which is, I stress, not ideological and demonstrative, but concrete and political. For, by beginning to modify our model of development in the direction of an exit from capitalism we can offer many of these societies, especially the peripheral ones, the possibility of overcoming their technical and cultural subordination to the American model. It is a matter of seeing that the translation of utopia into science is not a task that is resolved once and for all in one fell swoop.

2. The political choice that appears necessary to me, on the other hand, is to take up an attitude of concrete political struggle in regard to the Soviet bloc. (I say the Soviet bloc not only because this bloc is close to us geographically, but also because I still consider China profoundly different.) Why political struggle? Because there is no longer any sense in assuming that there will be a self-reform of that system. Only the rise of genuine social conflict, of an opposition, can constitute an alternative. To recognize the necessity and urgency of this conflict does not mean to fall into empty revolutionary appeals to a mythical working class in Eastern Europe. On the contrary, it is a question of thinking very seriously about the whole range of interlocutors and allies, of thinking about the immediate objectives around which a crisis of East European society could develop. It is quite probable that a change of regime may not occur in the same way in every country and that it could assume, for example, the complex form of the recent crisis of Francoism rather than that of an explosion. But this makes it even more imperative for the left to define a line and to develop its initiative at the party level and, in the future, at the level of state policy. Between mere condemnations and appeals to pure revolt on the one hand and placid faith in the evolution of the present system on the other, there stands an alternative: political intervention. This is not at all impossible.

I agree with Karol and Singer that it would be a mistake to make Brezhnev out to be stronger than he is. The Soviet regime's history is not one of pure terror. It is subject to real compromises with the working class, both domestic and international. During Stalin's time the Russian workers were guaranteed a social role that was not pure ideological mystification, and, in exchange for terrible sacrifices, they did make certain gains, such as industrialization, literacy, the victory over Nazism. And the regime received the support of millions of people around the world, who saw the USSR, often correctly, as the country of Stalingrad or as the gravedigger of colonialism. More recently, the compromise has been reestablished at a lower level: internally as a moderate consumerism without an excessively exhausting work place, externally through the erosion of American world supremacy.

But the very basis of this compromise is now being shaken. It is clear that the European left could play a role in this if it did not limit itself to increasingly radical ideological condemnations, but selected interlocutors, implemented a policy, and helped dissidence to become opposition and opposition to become a programme and struggle for a different regime.

All this may appear obvious, but in fact it is not obvious at all. The great forces of the left face considerable obstacles. Those faced by the PCI when it comes to discussing the merits of Soviet policy are evident. But those hindering others are also ponderous. It could be accidental, but it does not seem to me that the PSI has manifested as much internationalist dynamism in this gathering as its secretary has demonstrated in running to the aid of Schmidt at difficult moments.

Nevertheless, things are moving. And positively. This conference itself is evidence of that, not only because of what has been said here, but also because of who has said it. Nothing would be more stupid than to think that the comrades of Eastern Europe can be aided simply by assembling the most resolute spirits without striving for a united commitment of the entire workers' movement.

I have finished. Basically, what I wanted to say was simply this: the greatest gift we could grant the enemy when formulating our basic critique of 'existing socialism' would be to renounce what is most vital in Marxism: the conviction that society can change and that it must be changed on the basis of its real contradictions, through the modification of its structures, and not through moral witness.

Bitter experience and theoretical reflection have long innoculated us against historicism and determinism. We no longer believe that communism is the only possible outcome of the historic phase in which we are living. Even now there are clear and powerful pressures towards barbarism and catastrophe. But we also reject the historicism in reverse in fashion these days: resigned belief that the world, and politics in particular, never changes, leading to the tendency to turn one's eyes towards paradise, or, even worse, to suffer the aestheticizing fascination of expiation.

Only Conflictive Democracy Can Guarantee Liberty, East and West

Bruno Trentin

Bruno Trentin was the leader of the metalworkers' union, one of the largest trade unions in Italy, for thirteen years before joining the national secretariat of the CGIL in 1977. He has been a member of parliament and of the Central Committee of the Communist Party. Since the prohibition on holding posts in political parties and trade unions simultaneously, he has devoted himself entirely to the leadership of the union. A protagonist of the great workers' struggles in Italy, he has published his writings of the 1969-77 period in a volume entitled Da sfruttati a produttori.

The value of this gathering seems to me to lie fundamentally in the fact that it has initiated a confrontation, certainly not an easy one, among people of profoundly different experiences. Its participants are seeking a common language, and although they are still having difficulty finding it, they have recognized from the very outset that they face a common set of problems and, most important of all, a common destiny. We must go beyond the affirmation of solidarity, important as it is, with all forces fighting to defend their right to dissent and must move towards free and creative activity that strives to broaden the scope of democracy and individual liberty everywhere.

To be sure, it is correct to emphasize the necessity of supporting every battle to extend liberty and defend civil rights in the countries in which an attempt has been made to begin building a socialist society, in the countries of 'existing socialism'. Because every battle to extend liberty is a battle for socialism, a battle to launch a non-regressive process that would restore to post-capitalist society its character as a transitional society. The appeal addressed to us by comrade Marek can on no account be disregarded.

But I also feel it necessary to emphasize (and here I return to the basic concern that seemed to emerge from Rossanda's report) that it is above all incumbent on the forces of the left in Western Europe to demonstrate in reality — through their critical research and initiatives on the question of the building of socialism in Europe — that the problem of the post-capitalist societies is their problem too. This is certainly the greatest contribution we in Western Europe can make to the advancement of socialist democracy in Eastern Europe.

It has been said that without the beginning of a socialist revolution in the West — a non-Jacobin and non-authoritarian revolution, one that promises to be neither easy nor sudden — the emergence of a new phase in the organization of society and the state in the countries in which a break with the capitalist system of production has already occurred will be difficult.

But this process would give pretty poor results if it was limited to attempts to complement the social organization of the East European countries in some way by grafting the liberal-democratic tradition onto them.

There are various reasons why such an attempt would be both futile and completely misleading.

To begin with, it is increasingly difficult to maintain that the progress of democracy in the world is a product of liberal-democratic thought and on top of that to classify into good and bad the content and form that political democracy has come to assume in the history of the workers' movement. For more than a century and a half now, democracy has been advancing in the world simultaneously with the workers' movement and its struggles. Even the institutions characteristic of democracy as we understand it in the western world now bear the stamp of the battles of the workers. Democracy is again being posed as a universal value precisely because the working class and the class struggle are also tending to become universal facts. There will be no further progress without this fundamental protagonist. The spread of liberty throughout the world thus depends, in ever greater measure, on the concrete history of the workers' movement, its advances and retreats, and certainly not on the fortunes of liberal democracy. Even the institutions of representative democracy, which have become the inalienable patrimony of the transition strategy of the workers' movement, and the multiparty system, which has also become one of the pillars of the workers' movement's conception of democracy, are inseparable from the fate of the class struggle and the political action of the labour movement. The breakthroughs that have been achieved by the anti-capitalist revolutions since 1917 have had an enormous influence on the development of this battle for democracy by the workers' movement.

Second, one of the origins of the crisis of democracy in the countries of 'existing socialism' lies in the profound limitations of the cultural and political patrimony of the western workers' movement itself. These limits cannot be explained by the labour movement's detachment from liberal-democratic thought. Indeed, such an explanation would be overly facile. Above all, it would be false if, as is indeed the case, some of these limitations — the most important ones as it happens — were also found among those components and currents of the workers' movement which have been most strongly characterized by the effort to forge a bond between 'socialism' and 'liberal democracy'.

In making such assertions I am not at all overlooking the fact that the authoritarian regression of many of the societies that have undergone anti-capitalist revolutions in Europe, Asia, and Latin America is also due to the particular historical circumstances and social conditions in which these revolutions unfolded. I believe, however, that we must recognize that they also bear the stamp, to a greater or lesser extent, of a model, a cultural and political matrix, whose origins lie precisely in Western Europe, in the workers' movement of the Second and Third Internationals, in that very same workers' movement that has been the standard-bearer of liberty, democracy, and greater power for the oppressed classes.

We should perhaps concentrate on the fact that the authoritarian regression probably became more serious in certain cases because of the collision of this political and state model of the Second and Third Internationals, rooted in Western Europe, with the fragile civil societies in the countries in which the process of transition took place.

For all these reasons (and because it would be futile to try to shirk responsibility or disavow paternity), we must deal in depth, dialectically and independently, with all the expressions, institutional expressions included, of the countries of 'existing socialism'. This is also why it would be harmful to take the 'logic of the break' to its extreme conclusion, as Villari correctly pointed out in his intervention.

Our relations with the parties and trade-union forces in the countries of 'existing socialism', the unimpeded juxtaposition of experiences and positions — and this, I think, was the value of Berlinguer's presence and intervention in Moscow, of the presence and intervention of the CGIL in the last meeting of the FSL, and of our insistent desire to maintain relations, critical of course, with the East European trade-union organizations — represents a political option that actually expresses something more than mere diplomatic concern. It also expresses our awareness (and many of the comrades who have spoken here have borne this out) that there are tensions in these formations which are of interest to us. We must not fall into a Manichean schema that winds up considering these formations alien to the societies in which they operate. Karol's observation in this regard seems significant to me.

But I want to return to my initial premise: that the fate of these societies involves us directly. This is one of the reasons why I am not overly thrilled by the sort of discussion that could have occupied a good deal of time at this gathering (and it is positive that this did not happen), namely whether or not these societies are socialist in character. This is not only because of the risk of falling into new dogmatism in the course of invective about these definitions, often based on obsolete categories since we lack the requisite new ones, but also because there is a real danger of falling into the trap of thinking that the problem can be disposed of by altering labels. We must go beyond this sort of terminological discussion, which would be completely diversionary today, because we still lack any homogeneous instruments of analysis and elaboration. Instead we must courageously note that socialism, even as a phase of transition, is still an open process, open to our research in struggle and to our knowledge. It is a process with many national aspects, of course, but it also has general, universal features which, at least in part, remain to be defined, redefined, and discovered.

Critical reflection on the East European countries and the historic events that have changed the world over the past sixty years thus requires that we come to grips with the tradition of the workers' movement of the western world, of the Second and Third Internationals. I do not believe that this is an evasive response to the testimony that has been presented here by the comrades from the Soviet Union, Czechoslovakia, Poland, and the other countries. On the contrary, this is the most honest kind of response we can offer these comrades, and we must present it not only in documents but also by bringing to bear the critical reflection and creative force of a genuine movement with mass experience.

One of the thorny problems posed again and again in this critical reflection is that of the relationship between party and trade union. This is not at all a particularist concern. It represents only the tip of an iceberg that has been too long buried in the theoretical debates of the workers' movement.

In his intervention yesterday Bettelheim recalled the enormous negative influence of a restrictive, 'juridical' interpretation of the Marxist notion of 'property in the means of production'. This 'juridical' interpretation has had the effect of separating the act of expropriation, the appropriation of the instruments of production by the state (or by other organs representing the collectivity), from the deeper process of socialization, which in Marx's view also required immediate efforts to overcome the division of labour, a complex and gradual endeavour. This is a well-founded observation. At this point, however, it must be recalled — and Bettelheim knows this very well — that the scission between juridical property in the means of production and the social division of labour to which he refers has quite far-reaching origins (as is attested to by Marx's writings). It can certainly not be imputed to Stalin. To a large extent, it has been assumed as part of the legacy of so-called vulgar Marxism, but particularly of the 'practical' Marxism of the workers' movement of Western Europe.

But it does not seem to me that this heritage, which has distorted some of Marx's fundamental ideas, stops there. We must also consider that for more than seventy years now the West European workers' movement has also adopted a reductive and distorted interpretation of Marx's analysis of the private appropriation of surplus-value. Indeed, until the end of the nineteenth century, this aspect of the relation of exploitation was conceived not only as the characteristic, predominant element of capitalist relations of production, the 'principal contradiction' of capitalism, but also as the *only* one that could be resolved in the short term, at least in part, under a transitional society. Is this not perhaps the origin of the crisis that erupted in the Marxist movement at the beginning of this century? And has this crisis enabled us to resolve this specific problem even today? We must ask ourselves whether this reading of Marx (summary and distorted in my opinion, but nonetheless inherent in the 'practical' Marxism of the Second and Third Internationals and even in the 'crisis' of Marxism opened by the debate around Bernsteinism) has not gradually obscured in the political consciousness of the workers' movement what was increasingly becoming the fundamental contradiction in the productive process, namely the technical division of labour as a factor in the reproduction of a more general social division of labour, or, to put it another way, the constantly repeated expropriation of the means of production and instruments of culture from the producers themselves. In other words, the element of oppression inherent in the system of exploitation. Perhaps here we may find a less artificial explanation of the similarity between Togliattigrad and Mirafiori of Turin and of the fact that the 'German factory' of which Giovannini spoke remained, at bottom, a model even for the societies of real socialism.

In short, we now find that we must come to grips with a theoretical and political vacuum that goes back many decades, one which weighed heavily in the concrete experiments conducted just after the October Revolution.

If such a schema is adopted, then it becomes wholly legitimate to define a socialist society primarily as one in which the distribution of surplus-value (if this is indeed defined as the principal contradiction to overcome) is effected on the basis of conscious choices by the national collectivity, or even the collective at the factory level. Even though wage labour would not necessarily disappear in an initial phase, as it has not disappeared in the Soviet Union, China, or Cuba. But this does not scandalize me.

And it would then be wholly legitimate to admit that the distribution of this surplus-value should no longer be effected (or no longer primarily effected) through the conflictive mediation of the trade union. At most the latter could survive as an instrument for the correction of errors or the removal of bottlenecks in the decision-making process. The entire meaning of Lenin's reference to 'transmission belt' lay precisely in his identification of the trade union as a relatively autonomous instrument of struggle against the bureaucracy during the period of the NEP. Let us not forget this.

In any case, it is clear that once this view is accepted, the antagonistic role of the trade union as an instrument of class struggle, as the agency of the redistribution of the social product, inevitably appears completely outmoded. This function can now be fulfilled more effectively by the conscious action of purely political organs which are also capable of influencing the production of wealth: the party, the state, and even the enterprise councils, which are often mere projections of the state in the factories.

Was the assumption of Taylorism as a 'neutral' instrument in a phase of transition governed by a workers' state tantamount to a 'Lassallean' view of the trade union, reducing it to a 'school of socialism' and *therefore* the party's transmission belt into the working class during the transitional phase? And was this not implicitly tantamount to the renunciation of democracy *of* the producers in favour of democracy *for* the producers? This, it should be noted, had important effects, such as the elimination of democratic tension, of conflictive democracy, as an instrument in the *redivision of surplus-value* through the constant critical verification of the priorities determined by the collective organisms of the enterprises or those supposedly representing the national collectivity.

Just after the Poznan events Di Vittorio made the evident but momentous observation that a transitional society, particularly one being constructed on the ruins of war, would have to plan on difficult sacrifices by the workers. Painful choices would have to be made between 'today' and 'tomorrow'. The basic problem raised by Di Vittorio's harsh criticism was this: what instruments would determine the extent and *quality* of the sacrifices of this 'today'? No one, however, could presume to define these sacrifices 'on behalf of' the working class. Their extent and quality must be determined by the organs of self-government of the working class and by their conflict-ive tension.

This disappearance of the trade union as an instrument of conflictive democracy, as the conflictive moment in the construction of a collective synthesis, therefore had important implications for the very criteria by which the redistribution of surplus-value is deter-mined. But it also led — and this is even more important — to the disappearance of a centre of democratic tension, a real terrain of liberty and of political and cultural creativity, which can potentially produce (as shown by the experience of recent years in the West) constant modifications in the organization of labour, in the hier-archical structure of the enterprises and even of the state, in the technical division of labour in the factories and schools, and consequently in the social division of labour as a whole, albeit in mediated terms.

Indeed, what Marx had seen as a problem in any mature industrial society, namely the recomposition of the labour of the workers — which capitalist restructuration tends to resolve in an anarchic manner but which, through a 'proletarian' use of the schools and cultural institutions, could become a conscious project — was thereby postponed, shunted to another epoch, the phase of the conclusion of the process of building communism. In this manner, I believe, what had been one of the *motor forces* of transitional society was transformed into a mere accessory, a possible complement of the final stage of the revolutionary process.

This reductive conception, inspired by the 'provisional character' of the trade unions and the other forms of organization of civil society (including the many possible forms of decentralized conflict-ive democracy in the economy and culture), inevitably sanctioned a particular relationship between democracy and socialist accumulation. At the same time, the permanence (or at least persistence) of the division between rulers and ruled and of the centralized state and the social division of labour was reaffirmed (and here I am speaking not only of the East European countries but of the West as well).

Such a conception, of course, had inevitable effects on the function and vitality of representative institutions, both old and new, independent of the vicissitudes of Stalinism. Indeed, these representative institutions, parliaments and local assemblies, no matter how irreplaceable (and the workers' movement has reappropriated these instruments and heightened their value), have proven too weak to guarantee, in themselves, without recourse to repression, not consensus (which is still possible in certain periods) but a conflictive democracy of the producers during the phase of transition and of break with the mechanism of capitalist accumulation. Such democracy, however, ought to be the guarantor of liberty (individual liberty included) and the 'motor force' impelling the renovation of society.

The workers' movement in Western Europe is only just beginning to re-think the question of trade unions, the nature of autonomous and conflictive organizations capable of reunifying economics and politics in the factories and workshops, although of course in ways different from political parties, and of therefore contesting not the co-management of an enterprise in microcosm, but the direction of society as a whole, even while remaining 'partial' and not crystalliz-ing into totalizing institutions. We should not forget that this problem aroused a good deal of heat in the various formations of the left and the workers' movement only a few years ago. It is a theme which, even today, is not part of the patrimony of some fundamental forces of the left in many Western countries. It is quite difficult to assert this point, for example, in societies where the Social Democra-tic tradition runs deep, where, if we may put it this way, the prevalent conception of the relationship between party and trade union is wholly derived, albeit in several variants, from the matrix common to Kautsky, Lenin, Luxemburg, and the entire Second International.

But critical reflection on this point inevitably entails critical reflection on many other points as well. That is why I spoke of the tip of an iceberg. Here I would like to limit myself to a few of the implications.

The autonomy of the trade union, understood as the elimination of the 'division of labour' between trade union and party, ineluctably poses the elimination of the model of the single trade union, whether imposed by law or fact. In reality, it poses a profound revision of what has long been a postulate of vulgar Marxism and the tradition of the workers' movement: the assumption that the working class must inevitably equip itself with a *single* class organization, even if only through a long and tortuous process. The autonomy of the trade unions (which can never be wholly confined to the subordinate sphere of the distribution of income, as it is conceived today by very broad sectors of the Italian workers' movement) and the struggle for trade-union unity do not imply any negation of the right to a plurality of organizations with differing political programmes. Rather, they represent a terrain on which new organizations and new projects can emerge at any moment, even within the existing trade-union structures.

Similarly, another old schema is being challenged, one that has been a long time dying: that of the single party. Indeed, we must understand that the notion of the 'single party' and its greater or lesser interpenetration with the state, like the notion of the single trade union, draws it legitimacy *primarily* from the old dogma that every social class must sooner or later endow itself with a *single* political formation, or at least a *dominant* formation. This notion is in turn rooted in another old conviction, now widespread throughout the various ideological tendencies of the West European workers' movement, that a plurality of parties and therefore of political projects within one class somehow reflects an imperfection, an accident of history, or immaturity — in any event, a temporary situation, if not a malicious contrivance of the ruling classes.

The adoption of the model 'one party to a class' makes it fully legitimate for the party that claims to represent the entire working class to establish a one-party state once the disappearance (real or presumed) of other social classes is complete, since all other party formations, supposedly cut off from their classes and therefore lacking any social base, would then be useless at best and downright noxious at worst.

In considering this point, we must deal not only with the distortions in the countries of 'existing socialism', but also with some deeply rooted convictions of the West European workers' movement which have begun to be radically challenged only in recent years.

Now there is a danger that the approach to the revolution in the West initiated by Gramsci and the research undertaken by the Italian Communist Party, which has registered achievements of great significance, could lead to mere tactical adaptation or be reduced to a banal inclination to superimpose the liberal-democratic state on an 'existing socialism' that has lost some of the essential elements of its internal dynamism.

The turning point we have reached in a phase as dramatic as the present one — I refer to the crisis now racking the capitalist West — may perhaps incline us to some optimism about the research we are engaged in here, even though we begin from differing positions and concerns. As Edoarda Masi correctly pointed out, the current period inherently poses all the problems of transition.

On the one hand, we need a strategy for the various sections of the workers' movement which is somehow capable of sacrificing today for tomorrow. This is the ineluctable price of any process of social transformation. This capacity of a society to opt for tomorrow by sacrificing something of today is indeed a sign of life.

On the other hand, a very wide circle of social forces must be drawn into this strategy, all the forces which are affected by the crisis in varying ways but have an interest in change. This therefore involves the political reunification of the working class and the other toiling classes, and with them a vast range of social forces, around a project of transformation, a 'plan'. This is necessary both to permit the transformation of society and to guard against severe divisions within the oppressed classes themselves. But these vital needs, characteristic of the phase of transition, may *objectively* conflict with important areas of individual liberty and therefore creativity (even when there is broad consensus around them), and also may eventually negate themselves as factors of profound and continuing transformation of the social and political basis of society, unless their realization is accompanied by the activation of all the rediscovered forms of liberty and power which can contribute, through a process of conflict, through 'tumult' as Gramsci said, to a new leadership of the state and the factories. What I am speaking of is an ever broader articulation of power, diffusion of democracy, *even in its conflictive forms*, which transforms the political project and planning itself into a process that advances by successive approximations under continuous control which prevents any rigid compartmentalization, any segmentation or corporatization of this liberty and power. There can be no industrial democracy detached from political democracy; a system of co-management of the factories functioning purely in accordance with centralized state planning is unacceptable.

The problem of the hegemony of the workers' movement in the phase of transition is therefore quite complex in the West. Here more than elsewhere the hegemony of the working class must overcome a plentitude of tests in order to avoid a grave crisis of consent within the working class even prior to an economic and cultural stagnation.

Indeed, the stakes involved are not only liberty, and therefore a socialism really open to transition, but also the movement itself: the possibility of mature industrial societies emerging from the crisis by transforming their social base and political system while preserving the indispensable mainspring of conflictive democracy, to wit, the capacity of permanent dissent on the part of a culture free of the old interpretive schemas, the capacity of a composite society to subject the existing models continuously to new tests and challenges.

In a socialist society, a transitional society in which profit gradually loses its role of driving force and incentive characteristic of it during the phase of the rise of capitalism (as is already taking place in the advanced industrialized societies), we can be sure, even if we have no ready-made model, that there can be no mainspring other than the conflictive democracy of the producers. There is no other way to avert regression and guarantee the mobility, and therefore the liberty, of this society.

I believe that it is by deepening our reflection on these themes, by debating our approach to these problems, that we can most honestly repay the heavy debt we owe the various forces struggling in the countries in which anti-capitalist revolutions have taken place, forces which are seeking — albeit in different ways — the road to the extension of liberty and thus also to the development, dynamism, and creativity of these societies.

The Soviet Model and 'Caudillism' in Cuba

Carlos Franqui

Carlos Franqui was one of the principal figures of the Cuban revolution and after the revolution's victory played an important role in the sphere of culture becoming one of the main figures at Radio Rebelde, a radio station in the Sierra, and on the daily Revolución. *However, the evolution in the internal situation and Castro's position in favour of the Soviet invasion of Czechoslovakia decided him to leave Cuba and settle in Europe.*

The Cuban Revolution has gone through three phases: the first, between 1952 and 1958, was anti-militarist and libertarian in character; the second, from 1959 to 1960, anti-imperialist and libertarian; the third, since 1961, so-called socialist. During the first phase, the war and the revolutionary struggle never assumed a terrorist form: prisoners were given medical treatment and then freed, while the thousands of guerrilla and sabotage actions did not produce a single victim. In fact, we associated the word terror with the Batista dictatorship, and that is why the revolution was anti-militarist and humanist. During the next phase, our '26th of July' movement adopted an anti-imperialist platform — one, however, which was not defined in any precise way. Some of us were already Marxists; and since some had belonged to the Cuban Communist Party, they were aware of the dangers and shared the concerns which we are discussing in today's session.

It was during this grandiose phase, so ill defined from both an ideological and organizational point of view, that we created the revolution's initial instruments: labour unions, the student movement, the mass organizations, a revolutionary culture, a revolutionary press. From the beginning, our activity within the contradictory framework of Cuban reality made us aware of the dangers of *caudillism*.

During this second phase, repression was directed essentially against the class enemies — against the defeated bourgeoisie. No doubt there were some acts of injustice, like the twenty-year jail sentence passed on Hubert Matos for resigning his post as *commandante*. (It was precisely there that Matos underwent a long apprenticeship in Marxism: prisons seem always to be schools of revolution, even in the 'socialist' countries.) However, such acts were the exception rather than the rule in Cuba. Thanks to the nationalizations, the Cuban people recovered the natural wealth of their country's lands and seas, as well as of its sub-soil. The Cuban people eliminated the bourgeoisie, the landowners and the capitalist cultural apparatus; it conquered illiteracy and erected new health structures. At first, there was a genuine festival of freedom. The Cuban revolution was, for the first time in history, a revolution made entirely by the people: it destroyed capitalism without having a communist party at its head. In the struggle against Batista, the role of the newly-created institutions proved to be of the greatest significance. This was above all true of the trade unions (where the '26th of July' movement won 95 per cent of the votes, as against the PCC's 5 per cent in the free elections of 1959) and of the press. These institutions ensured that the revolution had a character at once radical and non-repressive.

In the course of this process, Batista's followers took up exile in the United States, believing that a small country would never be able to withstand the American colossus. Their 1961 Bay of Pigs invasion, which took advantage of the fact that we had no air force, was supposed to mark the beginning of a war that would have been extremely dangerous for Cuba. But in reality, it constituted the first disastrous defeat for American imperialism.

These counter-revolutionary activities, which lasted until 1965, never endangered the revolutionary power. They were limited to mindless sea attacks and small-scale, isolated actions within the country that could be easily controlled. Nevertheless, in the year 1961, a merciless repression began to be directed against those who had made the revolution: technicians, workers, peasants, intellectuals and common people. There were two factors involved in this repressive turn: on the one side *caudillism*, on the other the Soviet model.

Caudillism, that old Latin-American disease of an essentially colonial nature, expresses distrust of the masses, legal institutions, laws and popular structures. It signifies power concentrated in the hands of a single person resting on the army and police. Fidel Castro, the most recent American *caudillo*, feels a deep mistrust of the people. He thinks that it is not ripe for socialism (his socialism), and that the revolutionary minority has to impose its dictatorship on the people. Fidel's first act was to wind up the majority '26th of July Movement' that made the revolution, and replace it with a new army.

The Soviet model, imported from the USSR, was immediately concretized in the creation of a state security body and in the recuperation of the old Cuban Communist Party, then quite meagre and discredited. In short, there was a perfect accord between *caudillism* and a Soviet model adapted for use in the 'Third World'.

Castro began by severing the links between the people and the forces which had fought against Batista and the United States. He entered the Communist Party together with ten *commandantes*, while a million revolutionary militants were not allowed to join. From then on, the only people 'entitled' to work for socialism were long-standing militants of the CP.

The first period of repression was characterized by sectarianism. The Ministry of Labour banned trade unions and eliminated their massively supported '26th of July' leaders. Also replaced were the militia leaders and *commandantes* from the time of the Sierra. Even Fidel's bodyguard and his personal secretary, Celia Sanchez, were replaced by PCC militants. The defence committees, nearly all composed of fringe elements, unleashed an implacable repression against technicians, members of the liberal professions, the petty bourgeoisie and even the working class. These marginal people took revenge for all the humiliations they had previously suffered by using their police powers against all and sundry. At the same time, the lands which the revolution had given to the small peasants were taken away from them.

Lunes de revolución, the vanguard review of revolutionary intellectuals as a whole, fell under the thumb of the PCC daily, *Hoy*. Widescale persecutions got under way: following the Girón action (the Bay of Pigs), more than 100,000 people were imprisoned without evidence; whole villages were subjected to forced migration. And then began the campaign against homosexuals, people without a fixed job, religious practices and Afro-Cuban customs and rites. This sectarian conduct disorganized industrial and agricultural production, provoking huge economic chaos. Nationalizations were continued to an excessive degree, coming to embrace more than 80 per cent of all economic resources, land-holdings and other activities.

In order to strengthen his control, the PCC Secretary Anibal Escalante went so far as to send a tobacco-worker into the management of a sugar-refinery, a sugar-worker into a tobacco-factory, a research-chemist into a farm, a peasant into a shoe-factory, or a pharmacist into coffee-production. To this should be added the huge mistakes committed by Fidel himself: in one speech he gave the order for sugar-cane plantations to be torn up (which resulted in a 50 per cent drop in production), and then went on to do the same for coffee and rice.

And yet, it was still possible to struggle: the people had reserves of energy and strength; and we were not ground down by terror. The journal *Revolución* was in the forefront of the struggle being waged by former underground fighters. Popular resistance grew and leaders such as 'Che' Guevara went over to our side. Indeed, in a very sharp speech in March 1962, Fidel Castro himself denounced sectarianism and attributed to Escalante the entire responsibility for what had happened. There was another festival of freedom. However, the deep canker was not completely uprooted, and it was later able to resume its course. Thus, the forced labour camps (UMAPs) set up in 1965 were destined to receive tens of thousands of people.

In 1968, Fidel decreed the complete nationalization of small-scale trade, bars and the land. An extremely harsh law was promulgated against alcohol; the night-clubs were closed down and popular festivals and dance-halls suppressed. In 1971, following the failure of the great *zafra* and the popular protests against this general disaster, a law was enacted against absenteeism. According to official figures, more than 100,000 workers, peasants and youth were sent to agricultural work-camps for several years. Cuban life became more and more highly militarized.

The Angolan War ushered in a new period of repression. Dr Marta Frayde, an old companion of Fidel's who first put him in touch with the communists in 1955 and later became Cuban ambassadress to UNESCO and France, was arrested at the age of sixty and sentenced to 29 years in jail. In Cuba's prisons, thousands of men are serving harsh terms: two communist leaders have died there; and other members of the '26th of July' and the former 'Directorate' — *commandantes*, peasants, workers, revolutionaries, intellectuals — continue to spend long years under inhuman conditions.

What problems does Cuba face today? Soviet domination. Statism. *Caudillism*. Militarism. Sugar monoculture. Complete lack of freedom.

Numerous basic problems have not been solved. Seventeen years after the revolution, Fidel announced nine severe restrictions on goods crucial to the people's standard of living: sugar, coffee, meat, milk, etc.; certain other products, which have been rationed since 1971, are in even shorter supply. Only half of the monthly 3-kilo-gram rice allowance is currently distributed. The already low coffee ration has been reduced by 50 per cent, the meat allowance by 20 per cent. In 1960, the average Cuban consumed 22 kilograms of meat per annum; today the figure is less than 17. And we should not forget that all these goods are produced within the country.

It is true that Cuba has recovered its national resources. But it is one thing to recover them, quite another to know how to utilize, administer and develop them; one thing for the state to own these resources, another for the people to do so.

The Cuban military-caudillist state was founded on the bureau-cratic Soviet model — in contradiction with the Cuban people. The power apparatus comprises a million people out of a total population of ten million. The army, police, secret services, defence committees — in short, the repressive apparatus — number more than half-a-million members. The other half-million is made up of administra-tors, bureaucrats, Party functionaries, new technicians, members of the liberal professions, and hand-picked students. This bureaucratic bourgeoisie enjoys the privileges taken from the capitalist regime: houses, beaches, villas, motor-cars, restaurants, trips, a higher standard of living. And in addition, it has the privilege of giving orders and being obeyed. The people works and obeys: it can neither think nor criticize.

All forms of opposition, resistance and dissidence have been wiped out. A power without historical precedent is concentrated in the hands which hold all the means of production, the sole economic power, the single Party, the single ideology. These hands control the state, the army, the police, and the apparatus of mass instruction and information.

This situation has given rise to a number of contradictions. Although capitalist power has been destroyed, the face of the new power is far from clear. Workers, peasants and intellectuals have witnessed the disappearance of the boss, the landlord and the bourgeois cultural apparatus; but in their place have emerged new administrators calling themselves representatives of the people. Factory, land and culture do not belong to the workers, peasants and intellectuals, any more than they did under the old bosses. The confusion becomes total when an external threat and internal reaction are added to these elements. Many years were necessary in order to perceive the character of the new power. But as we are beginning to see in the case of the USSR and Eastern Europe, this is a regime in which the people is methodically depoliticized and confined to the fringes of political life: it becomes the object and no longer the subject of history. For the objective contradiction between the people and the new oppressor state to become clear, it is necessary to overcome the inertia born of confusion, terror, depoliticization and lack of information.

It is for these reasons that the phenomenon of dissidence is of such great importance. It provides a certain awareness of society, breaking the conditioned reflexes of obedience, impotence and terror set up by the apparatus. All revolutions in history have been preceded by art, literature and philosophy. (This was true of the French Revolution, the fall of Tsarism, and so on.) The key question is not whether Balzac was a conservative or whether Solzhenitsyn is a reactionary: what matters is the reality of their books. The western Left must think seriously about what will happen on that distant yet inescapable day when revolution will break out in the socialist countries.

Some people fear that there may then be an attempt to restore the power of the old, vanished property-owner. But that is completely out of the question. Capitalist dangers arise from the established power, not from the opposition. In the event of revolution, there will be a great moment of truth. It will be necessary to invent new forms of ownership of the means of production, change the state and create new political and cultural institutions. We have heard Plyushch talk about the reality of the Soviet Union. But there have also been the Prague Spring and the Polish workers' strike (related by Baluka) which was supported by the people and attacked by Gierek's police and army. These demonstrate the character of the class struggle in the 'socialist' countries: who stands for the present and who for the revolutionary future; who is being born and who is dying.

If we identify the present regime with socialism, if we persist in this enormous misunderstanding, we shall not succeed in sealing our alliance that is so crucial for the history of the world and of revolution. For this alliance has to be directed against the three forms of capitalism existing in the world today: industrial capitalism, colonial capitalism (its legitimate heir), and the new state capitalism in which the means of production are in the hands of a bureaucratic bourgeoisie (hiding behind an old mask of socialism), and in which an ever stronger state oppresses an ever weaker people.

Women, 'Real Socialism', and the Autonomy of the Political

Anna Maria Crispino

Anna Maria Crispino, born in Naples in 1951, graduated from that city's Oriental Institute with a thesis on international politics. She now teaches English language and literature in a Naples secondary school. She began her political activity in the student movement in Naples in 1968, later joining Manifesto, *in which she remained until 1976. She was among the founders of the feminist movement in Naples.*

In my opinion this gathering constitutes an acknowledgment, an irrevocable recognition, that we have left too many questions unanswered and that the problems we now face as Marxists with regard to the nature of the post-revolutionary societies are, in the last instance, no different from the unresolved problems faced by the left concerning the capitalist countries, despite the diversity of histories and conditions.

The crisis of Marxism today results essentially from the inadequacy of the political categories and framework, derived from Marx, that the left has fashioned for itself; categories which do not allow us to account for the elements of unity and simultaneity of the different upsurges and demands of the various subjects; in short, from the poverty and narrowness with which reality is being apprehended.

It is the crisis of a theory that no longer expresses the thirst of the masses for *radical change*, because it does not give any adequate and credible answers to the questions raised by the historically new subjects, and has not succeeded in closing the gap between the daily, material fact of oppression and the idea of communism.

If we consider the history of Marxist theory, not only the way in which 'real socialism' has been built but also the way the inter-national contradiction between socialism and capitalism has been articulated in the western left, we note a process of accentuated theoretical and practical cleavage between daily consciousness, both individual and collective, on the one hand and the representation of this consciousness in theory on the other hand. It is a theory which posits politics as independent of needs rather than as their synthesis and expression. It posits the state separate from and against civil society. It deals only with the material aspect of the economy, separating off the social, the unconscious, the emotional, the sexual, and the corporeal as 'superstructural', secondary, and sometimes even non-existent. In the end, this theory joins battle on terrain chosen by the bourgeoisie, and thus formulates a policy founded neither on the interests of the individual nor on the complexity of the needs the individual expresses.

In my opinion we must pose the questions differently if we want to obtain different answers.

Here I would like to tackle two questions, closely linked from my point of view as a woman, feminist, and communist. I confront this theme with great difficulty, even personal difficulty. The practice of feminism, the rejection of categories that do not belong to us because they do not include us, leads us, as women, to use another language. This bilingualism in turn raises real difficulties of communication and comprehension and gives rise to the idea that feminism and communism, for the moment at least, are two parallel paths which never meet. But neither can ignore the existence of the other. I will therefore be compelled to make logical transitions that will probably appear arbitrary and schematic, because they are not yet the patrimony of the entire movement. Moreover, what I propose is perhaps a particular point of view; in my opinion, however, it is neither partial nor marginal with respect to the questions now before us.

The first question concerns the sort of daily life resulting from the present organization of Soviet society, which, as has been pointed out, is based on the division of labour in the economic domain. I ask myself what has been the weight and significance of the massive presence of women on the job. This participation of women in productive activity is fully consistent with the policy of maximally utilizing all available human resources; in fact, during the period of the two wars, it was the labour of women that enabled the Soviet economy to keep going.

For women, however, this entry into the world of labour meant their admittance to masculine labour in terms of the mode, tempo, and organization of labour itself. It therefore became the fundamental determinant of the daily lives of women, as it is for men. But given the persistence of social relations of production based on the division of labour, the determinant of the family also came into play, first for women and then for everyone.

The family, which in the initial moments of the October Revolution seemed fated to disappear as the fundamental social nucleus (and the 1917 measures on marriage and illegitimate children confirmed that the family structure would be provisional), once again became, in a process which ran parallel to the loss of real power by the soviets, the sole mode of organization of the lives of individuals.

Labour and family were rendered compatible for women by the establishment of state-run social services for child care. These services were conceived and organized as complementary to the family structure, which was reassigned the tasks of education and socialization of children and the management and maintenance of the physical location of daily life, namely the home. (I say children and not babies for the same reason that, given the existence of the family, one must say mother and not woman. Mother/daughter instead of woman/child redefines the roles and functions of the bourgeois family, even terminologically.) Thus, the Soviet woman works, and social services take care of her children during her working hours. Then she goes home, where she performs the domestic chores required to maintain the family. This robs her of three of the five hours of free time remaining after her 'real' job.

The testimony offered by Baranskaya in her book *A Week Like Any Other* inclines me to believe that women pay a very high price for their emancipation through labour, regardless of what official statistics may say. Behind the dim greyness of these official pronouncements, we discover an oppressive and exhausting daily life in which the male-female contradiction is obliterated by the failure to take account of the differences in the condition of each.

There are two disquieting facts. The first is that, although women do attain the same level of skills as men on the job (because of the high educational standards and because they continue their careers after having children), and although 54 per cent of intellectual workers are women, there are very few women in the rank-and-file structures of the Communist Party and virtually none in the top leadership. Given the absolute predominance of the Communist Party in all social choices, this means that women are effectively excluded from the administration of power, probably because their daily schedules leave them no time for politics. And this, in turn, is not unrelated to the sort of dissent being expressed in the USSR today.

The other fact is the insistence with which the regime is again fostering the ideology of the family and motherhood. The campaign launched in the early seventies under the slogan 'three babies in every family' is not merely an attempted response to a demographic problem which is becoming disturbing, but also an attempt to resolve the crisis of the family. This crisis is ascribed primarily to the emancipation of women, not only because they work, but also and more particularly because they seem to be adopting the same attitude as men towards family obligations and sexual mores. And how can the family function if it is not based on the subordination of women, on their double work day?

This argumentation brings me to the second question I wanted to touch on briefly. In a society like Soviet society, in which the economic models are based on the productivity of the various institutions, how are sexuality, love, personal relations, and the desire for happiness experienced? These problems are not extraneous to Marxism and were dealt with in the discussions of the Bolshevik Party, in particular in the positions of Kollontai. The discussion on the family, on 'winged Eros', on the emancipation of women, dealt with real problems of Soviet society in its transition from semifeudal economic-cultural and social conditions to the establishment of an order that was endeavouring to be socialist. Now, the emancipation of women through labour has not resolved the contradictions which, although they may appear dormant today, are actually inherent in the mechanism of the family and in the male-female relationship. Why and for whom should children be produced if maternity is negated in practice by the combination of external labour and domestic chores and is therefore experienced as a burden and an impediment? Why are Soviet women tending to adopt male attitudes towards sex, denying their own sexual specificity? Why is the love relation reflected only in the family? The lack of solutions to these problems, indeed the conscious decision to reproduce bourgeois forms of existence, has consequences on the daily lives of all citizens, not just women. The roles defined by labour, like those defined by the family (father, mother, child, wife, husband), define functions rather than real and whole individuals.

Yesterday one comrade said that people in the Soviet Union do not seem to be fed up yet and cited this as the reason why dissent was still not very extensive. If we think about this point as women, if we recall that feminism in the West was born of the consciousness of emancipated women who drew the conclusions from their own experience that this emancipation was wholly incompatible with the existing social order, then we may assume that these sorts of contradictions will also sharpen in the East European countries, just as they did during the Chinese cultural revolution, because everyone increasingly sees socialism as the need for liberty, equality, and a different quality of life.

The feminist movement has much to say about these problems, although it consciously and correctly does not pretend to be a 'scientific' theory. Its materialist rationality lies in its rejection of the modality and logic of a policy which rests on so-called reason alone, masculine and bourgeois even if leftist, in its affirmation that the relationship between self-interest and whatever contradicts it is political, in that it begins from a daily oppression which is material even in those of its aspects which are not visibly and directly economic. It is the wholly Marxist refusal to be the sex to which the irrational and negative pole of persistent western and bourgeois dualism is ascribed, in order to demand, for women and for everyone, the materialist unity of the subject.

To stand outside the organizational methods and language of Politics, Rationality, and the State; not to accept the priorities and decisions on compatibility determined by others; to reject any regulation of social conflict, i.e. power; to rely on one's own specificity in order to find modes, instruments, language, and time to construct a communism that leaves no one out and excludes no part of ourselves — such is the reason and consciousness of women; but it can be the consciousness of others as well.

Eurocommunism and 'the antagonistic societies of a new type'

Fernando Claudin

Fernando Claudin was an important figure in the Spanish CP until 1964. Following differences over what attitude to adopt towards the USSR and over the line of the PCE in Spain itself, he was expelled from the Party at the same time as the writer Jorge Semprun. He works with Il Manifesto. *Claudin is the author of a key book analyzing the history of the Third International:* The Communist Movement. From Comintern to Cominform *(Penguin, London 1975). In 1978 his book* Eurocommunism and Socialism *appeared (NLB); a third book, a detailed study of Marx and Engels and the Revolution of 1848, has still to appear in English.*

I completely agree with Rossana Rossanda and other speakers when they underline the political importance of this conference. The very fact that it is being held at all seems to indicate that although the prospects for socialism in Europe are still rather dismal, they are not as bleak as some people suggest. In pessimism, as in other things, a certain moderation is required.

Not since the revolution failed in the West, leaving the Russian Revolution isolated and creating one of the basic preconditions for its subsequent degeneration, has the struggle for socialism East and West seemed so closely interlinked and interdependent as it is today. As in the twenties and forties, the historical basis of this convergence is the world crisis shaking capitalism — only this time it is combined with the crisis (whose mechanisms are not identical) that is shaking the new class society born of the October Revolution, the Chinese Revolution and other revolutions on the periphery of the imperialist system. Never before, at least in modern times, has human society been plunged into such a deep and generalized crisis — even though this does not involve us in a situation of world-wide conflict. Not only do the conservative forces of the old and new social systems confront problems which they are unable to control, but even those forces aspiring to radical change are not very clear about where they are going. And we are no exception, surrounded as we are by extinct myths, failed experiments, unrealized predictions, theoretical and practical dead-ends. It is as if we had to start from scratch by clearing the building-site of its old debris.

One of the elements that made this meeting possible (and not merely necessary) is undoubtedly the awareness or nascent awareness of this situation. The hour of illusions has passed: all the conditions are now present for the critical inspiration of Marxism to be reinstated. Such a resurrection of Marxist criticism alarms the ruling groups in the East. For they are representatives of a new ruling class that has turned Marxism into its opposite — into the justificatory ideology of a new society based on class oppression. Their reactions to the Eurocommunist phenomenon show just how much the rulers of these societies fear the domestic impact of every step towards a theory and practice capable of unblocking the present impasse and advancing towards socialism.

Whatever the limitations and inconsistencies of Eurocommunism, its criticisms are feared by bureaucrats in the East much more than those coming from other sections of the Left. For since it is precisely the communist parties that were appointed sole agents of Marxism-Leninism in the West, their criticisms and initiatives are all the more difficult to reject and even appear credible to members of the ruling communist parties. We cannot ignore the fact that they can have a much greater and more disturbing impact in the East. It is thus of great importance that Comin and Villari have made themselves heard at this meeting. Comrades from the socialist opposition in Eastern Europe have frequently reminded us of the major stimulation and assistance which the Eurocommunist phenomenon represents for their difficult struggle. Even though the results have so far for the most part fallen below their expectations, I think it would be wrong to draw over-negative conclusions. Despite certain ups and downs, the split in the western communist movement will grow deeper and deeper.

In any case, it is becoming clearer every day that a socialist-oriented political and social transformation of these countries will require the active political solidarity and theoretical collaboration of socialist forces in the West. Now, although Eurocommunist initiatives for the moment have a more effective impact than those coming from other sources, it cannot be expected that Eurocommunism will exhibit great theoretical audacity in studying the problematic of the eastern bloc. In this field, other sectors of Marxism are undoubtedly able to make a more important contribution.

It is also becoming more and more evident that unless there is an initial *modicum* of liberalization or democratization in the East, and unless the satellite countries gain a certain degree of autonomy, any attempt at a socialist-type transformation in the West will remain blocked and threatened, just as the October Revolution was sixty years ago. Any such attempt will be threatened in the military sense as well. Indeed, in formulating our strategic theories and tactical options, we should not forget for a single instant the existence of Russian military power. The irony of history is such that the Russian gendarme, which used to be Marx's great obsession, has reappeared a century later in Marxist-Leninist uniform ready to bar the way to socialism.

The importance of every criticism of the eastern systems originating from Eurocommunism should not lead us to show any inhibitions or indulgence when dealing with its inconsistencies and waverings. Quite the contrary. Precisely because of the weight of the criticisms they may make, we should insist on dialogue and discussion with every level of the Eurocommunist parties concerning the problems of the countries in the East. This is so regardless of the differences which separate us from the national leaderships of these parties, and even if it is not always congenial to differentiate ourselves from them on this question.

So far, all the Eurocommunist parties (including those, like the PCE, which have gone furthest in breaking with Moscow) have contented themselves with limited verbal protests against the most scandalous cases of political repression in the East. In fact, we have hardly done much more ourselves. As Rossana pointed out, with the exception of some very small groups or certain isolated individuals, the European Left as a whole has until recently maintained an attitude towards the regimes in the East that I would describe as one of complicity. We have thus run up a sizeable debt with the revolutionaries and the workers of these countries.

Aside from its inability to make a revolution of its own, the European Left has been the main accomplice of Stalinist repression against the best revolutionaries of Central Europe and against millions of workers. It has been the accomplice of the *gulag*. Although the greatest responsibility undoubtedly lies with the communist parties, the socialist parties and other sections of the Left are by no means free of blame.

There are many reasons why this has been so, and some of them have weighed very heavily. The fact itself, however, is undeniable. And this fact has in turn had grave consequences, being at the heart of those elements determining the present crisis of the struggle for socialism. To be sure, this same fact also has something to do with the present weakness of the socialist opposition in the East, especially in the USSR, and with the influence of certain reactionary currents in (above all) the Soviet opposition. Nor should we forget the weight of the veritable lag in the struggle for socialism in the West — a lag at once historical, theoretical and practical.

As long as Marxism served to obscure such basic truths instead of prompting us to understand them, it was very difficult to make a sure step forward in any direction whatsoever. Rossana said that although the Left knew for a long time the real character of 'actually existing socialism', it continued to take sides with it in the inter-war period, and later during the Cold War and the colonial revolutions. Was there, then, no imperialism on the other side?

I do not wish to deny the importance of this latter factor. But I think that the majority of the Left had until very recently (and a not insignificant section still has) a mistaken analysis of 'existing socialism'. This was above all true of the communist parties. A whole series of elements of its pseudo-Marxist ideology — elements which I do not have time to specify here — made possible this ideological alienation.

It should not be ruled out in advance that a new connection may be established between 'existing socialism' and anti-imperialist struggles. Indeed, such a development seems to me quite likely. A link of this kind can perfectly well go together with the non-socialist character of 'existing socialism', just as it did in the past. For between 'existing socialism' and this or that capitalist power (especially American imperialism) there are real contradictions which are much more real than the reality of that socialism. Whoever takes up the struggle for socialism, whether in Europe or in the rest of the world, cannot forego utilizing these contradictions whenever such a course proves to be possible.

These contradictions have various roots, including what are called 'great power interests' (an ambiguous concept that may embrace diverse contents). But in my opinion, one of these roots is the difference in nature between the social systems — in other words, the fact that the eastern systems, without being socialist, are not assimilable to western capitalism.

We come here to a key problem that lies at the heart of our whole debate. What is the nature of these new social formations? The theoretical answer given to this fundamental question will essentially determine whether, from the Elbe to the Pacific, it is possible to engage in a struggle for socialism that is neither a blind revolt nor an explosion without perspective. The problem is of crucial importance because the theoretical solution will also decisively affect all progress in defining 'socialist society', in escaping the situation to which Rossana referred, whereby no one is quite sure any more what is being talked about when socialism is mentioned.

During the last few years, some progress has been made in this field and we have clarified the initial question of whether these are socialist societies or not. All of us here agree that they are not socialist. Even the communist parties have, in practice, come to the same conclusion by stating, on the one hand, that socialism and democracy are indissolubly united and, on the other hand, denouncing the lack of democracy in the eastern countries.

It is true that they still define these systems as socialist, but in so doing they fall into a blatant contradiction that is bound to explode sooner or later. This has already happened in the case of the Spanish Communist Party, and it is probably just a matter of time and circumstance before the same happens with the other Eurocommunist parties. In order to bolster their existing position, the Eurocommunists have fallen back, as it were, on the old Trotskyist position according to which the relations of production in these countries are socialist and the political superstructure non-socialist. I shall not pause to argue against this thesis: I have done so elsewhere, and Bettelheim and others have already spoken about it. Besides, the real discussion begins once we have denied the socialist character of these formations. For if they are not socialist, what exactly are they?

We are already familiar with the two opposing theses: for the first, they represent a peculiar kind of capitalism, a state capitalism, or monopoly state capitalism; for the second, they are a new type of class society with antagonistic interests — one that is neither socialist nor capitalist. In order to remove any doubt, I should make quite clear that such analyses do not refer to a species of 'advanced democracy' or to a form of pseudo-transition between capitalism and socialism. (I here use the concept of socialism in the Marxist sense of a transitional social formation between capitalism and communism.)

At the moment, my own hypothesis converges with the second of these two. I believe that we are facing a new type of antagonistic class society that cannot be assimilated to the capitalist model. Public discussion on the two hypotheses has already taken place on various occasions, most notably between Bettelheim and Sweezy. Personally, I feel closer to Sweezy's positions. But maybe the important historical research now being done by Bettelheim will lead me to change my views.

To put things very schematically, at present I think that in those societies where private property has been liquidated and where the means of production are in the hands of the state there really are a number of forms analogous to capitalist relations of production. But does this similarity correspond to an identity in kind? To what extent and within what limits does the law of value operate? Up to what point is the wage really a wage? How accurate is it to speak of a labour market in the capitalist sense of the term?

In reality, there are no longer numerous independent capitals in these countries, but only a single capital. Similarly, there are neither independent factory directors really owning the means of production, nor workers able quite independently to 'sell' their labour-power outside the place to which they have been allocated.

All such relations are subject to the law of political authority. This law finds expression not only in the plan, but also in a series of rules and obligations representative of that single, abstract capital within which the economic and the political attain a high degree of fusion. In this system of relations, the relationship between state and production unit is itself a determining production relation which relegates the law of value to an ever more subordinate role.

Society is not inherently socialist just because there is a mechanism regulating it. Only if power at every level belongs to the workers' collective does such regulation have a socialist character; for then its criterion is the satisfaction of social needs. But if power is in the hands of a corpus of functionaries and administrators dominating the workers' collective and escaping its control, then this corpus becomes the *de facto* holder of the means of production. It thereby increases its capacity to control the means of production — that is, to exercise effective control over the mechanisms of social regulation. But it does so in its own interests and for the perpetuation of its position as the dominant class.

I shall not spend any more time on this problem for the moment. It will require fresh research and discussion, and we obviously cannot find a solution today. The debate is unquestionably not academic in character, but is of the utmost theoretical and political importance. On the other hand, I did not understand very well the dilemma posed by Rossana at the end of her talk. If, she argued, these are new social relations in which the persistence of capitalist relations is a secondary factor, then it is possible to address our appeals for greater liberalization to the governments concerned; whereas if we are faced with capitalist formations, then we should not address the governments themselves and we should call for resumption of the class struggle rather than for democratization or the defence of civil rights.

In my view, we should be talking about class struggle in either case, even though the mechanisms of the two kinds of social formation are different. In either case, they are societies containing antagonistic class interests, where, consequently, it is a question of class struggle. In either case, I think that the struggle for democratic freedoms, civil rights and so on is an objective of prime importance. I would even say that it is the first objective of any class struggle destined to open the way to the socialist transformation of these countries — whatever their present features may be. Whether we should address governments on specific occasions is a purely tactical question. The strategically significant point is that the fight for democratic liberties remains of prime importance in any struggle for socialism whatsoever.

The Crisis of Marxism

Louis Althusser

I shall limit myself to a brief reflection on the situation which we are living through. Because our interest in the exiles from Eastern Europe is not only based on a need for information, nor just a manifestation of solidarity. What is happening in the Eastern countries involves us directly. For what is happening there is also happening to us. Everything which goes on in these countries is of immediate concern to us, and has an impact on our perspectives, the objectives of our struggle, our theory and our practice.

I must apologise in advance for presenting my comments, in the space of a few minutes, rather roughly and schematically — without the necessary nuances. But for a certain time now people have been starting to talk among themselves about a *crisis of Marxism*. In her opening remarks Rossana Rossanda used this phrase.

There are phrases which have played such a dubious role in the history of social struggles that one hesitates to use them. For a century, the phrase 'the crisis of Marxism' has itself been used over and over again by the enemies of the labour movement — but for their own purposes, in order to predict its collapse and death. They have exploited the difficulties, the contradictions and the failures of the labour movement in the interest of the class aims of the bourgeoisie. Today they are exploiting the horrors of the Soviet camps and their sequels against Marxism. Intimidation also has its place in the class struggle.

We must meet the challenge of this intimidation by taking up the phrase 'the crisis of Marxism', but giving it a completely different sense from collapse and death. We have no reason to be afraid of the term. Marxism has experienced other periods of crisis, for example the one which led to the 'bankruptcy' of the Second International, its desertion to the camp of class collaboration. But Marxism survived. We must not be afraid to use the phrase: it is clear from many signs that today Marxism is once again in crisis, and that this crisis is an open one. Which means visible to everyone, including our enemies, who are doing everything in their power to exploit the situation. But we are accustomed to these diversionary tactics. We, ourselves, can not only *see* the crisis: we are *living through it*, and have been for a long time.

What is this crisis of Marxism? A phenomenon which must be grasped at the historical world level, and which concerns the difficulties, contradictions and dilemmas in which the revolutionary organizations of struggle based on the Marxist tradition are now involved. Not only is the unity of the International Communist Movement affected, and its old forms of organization destroyed, but its own history is put in question, together with its traditional strategies and practices. Paradoxically, at the moment of the most serious crisis which imperialism has ever known, at a moment when the struggles of the working class and of the people have reached unprecedented levels, the different Communist Parties are all going their own separate ways. The fact that the contradiction between different strategies and practices is having its own effects on Marxist theory itself is only a secondary aspect of this profound crisis.

Something which has 'snapped'

At its most direct, most obvious level, this crisis is expressed in remarks like those made here yesterday by our comrades, the workers of Mirafiore. They said: for many of us, something has 'snapped' in the history of the labour movement between its past and present, something which makes its future unsure. And *it is a fact* that it is no longer possible today, as it used to be to 'integrate' the past and present, to 'integrate' October 1917, the enormous world role of the Soviet Revolution, as well as Stalingrad, with the horrors of the Stalin regime and the oppressive Brezhnev system. These same comrades said that if it is no longer possible, as it used to be, to hold the past and present together, it is because there no longer exists in the minds of the masses any 'achieved ideal', any really living reference for socialism. We are told that the countries of Eastern Europe are socialist countries, but nevertheless, for us, socialism is something quite different.

This simple fact did not of course pass by unnoticed: it gave rise to the shock-effect of the 20th Congress of the CPSU, and was taken up and expressed in the repeated declarations of the leaders of the western Communist Parties to the effect that 'there is no single model of socialism', that 'we reject the idea of models', etc. That is all true, but it does not provide an answer to the question posed by the masses. For you cannot really hope to *grasp* the present situation simply by arguing that there are 'several paths to socialism'. Because in the last resort you cannot then avoid the other question: what will prevent this 'different type of socialism', arrived at by a different path, from ending up just like the existing forms of socialism? And the answer to this question depends on another: why and how did Soviet socialism lead to Stalin and to the present regime?

But this last, key question, has not been properly answered.

The crisis which we are living through has been aggravated by a special circumstance. Not only has something 'snapped' in the history of the Communist movement, not only has the USSR 'moved on' from Lenin to Stalin and Brezhnev, but the Communist Parties themselves, organizations of class struggle claiming to base themselves on Marx, have not really provided any explanation of this dramatic history — twenty years after the 20th Congress of the Soviet Party! They have either been unwilling or unable to do so. And behind their reticence or politically motivated refusals, behind the ridiculous phrases which we know only too well ('the personality cult', 'violations of socialist legality', 'the backwardness of Russia', not to speak of the way in which we *have been repeatedly assured* that 'the USSR has built the foundations for democracy — just wait a little longer and it will come to flower'), behind all this there lies something more serious: that is, the extreme difficulty (everyone working seriously on the problem knows this very well) and perhaps even, in the present state of our theoretical knowledge, almost the impossibility of providing a really satisfactory Marxist explanation of a history which was, after all, made in the name of Marxism! If this difficulty is more than imaginary, it means that we are now living through a situation which is revealing limits in Marxist theory, and behind these limits some critical difficulties.

I think that we should go so far as to say that the crisis of Marxism has not spared Marxist theory: it does not take place outside of the theoretical sphere, in a purely historical domain of chance, accidents and dramas. As Marxists we cannot be satisfied with the idea that Marxist theory exists somewhere in pure form, without being involved and compromised by the hard tests of the historical struggles and their results, in which it is directly concerned as a 'guide' to action. It would be quite idealistic, as Marx ceaselessly pointed out, to consider that Marxist theory is, as a theory, responsible for the history made in its name: it is not 'ideas', not even Marxist ideas, which make 'history', just as it is not 'self-consciousness' (the self-application of the name 'Marxist') which defines a person or an organization. But it would be equally idealistic to consider that Marxist theory is not involved in and compromised by a history in which the actions of organizations of class struggle inspired by Marxism or calling themselves Marxist have played an important or determining role. A Marxist only has to take seriously the argument concerning the primacy of practice over theory in order to recognize that Marxist theory really is involved in the political practice which it inspires or which uses it as a reference: in its ends and means. The forms and effects of this involvement necessarily reflect back on the theory, provoking or revealing conflicts, changes, differences and deviations: these forms and these effects themselves have a political dimension. It is in this sense that Fernando Claudin spoke, as long as eight years ago, of a 'theoretical crisis', in order to analyse the crisis of the International Communist Movement, and that Bruno Trentin referred a short while ago to organizational questions (the relation between party and trades unions) as themselves having a theoretical meaning and importance.

It is in this profoundly political sense that we are forced today, it seems to me, to speak of a theoretical crisis within Marxism, in order to clarify the ways in which it affects what is called Marxist theory itself: and in particular the fact that a number of apparently infallible principles inherited from the Second and Third Internationals have now been placed in doubt. It is only too clear that we cannot escape from the shock-effects provoked by the crisis of the International Communist Movement, whether open (the Sino-Soviet split) or veiled (between the Soviet and Western Communist Parties, since the invasion of Czechoslovakia), nor from the questions posed by the ceremonial or silent abandonment of principles as important as that of the 'dictatorship of the proletariat' without any demonstrable theoretical or political reason, nor again from the problems posed by the uncertain perspectives of the present struggles. The obvious political dead-ends, the diversity of strategies, their contradictions, the confusion produced by different ways of speaking and different references — all these have an evident political significance, which must have an impact on Marxist theory itself. This in fact poses a number of problems for Marxist theory, not only with regard to the contradictions of the present historical situation, but also with regard to its own character.

Three reactions to the crisis of Marxism

If we leave aside the exploitation of Marxism by its enemies, we can, very schematically, distinguish three reactions to this crisis.

1. The first reaction, characteristic of certain Communist Parties, is to close one's eyes and to keep quiet: in spite of the general disaffection from which it suffers among the masses and young people of Eastern Europe, Marxism continues to be the official theory and ideology there. Officially there is no crisis of Marxism, it is an invention of the enemies of Marxism. Other parties take account of the problem, and in a pragmatic manner take their distance on certain selected points, or on others 'abandon' a number of 'embarrassing' formulae, but always keep up appearances: they do not call the crisis by its name.

2. The second consists in absorbing the shock of the crisis, in living through it and suffering under it, while at the same time looking for genuine reasons for hope in the strength of the labour movement and the movement of the people. No-one among us can entirely avoid this reaction, which is accompanied nonetheless by many questions and doubts. Because you cannot go on forever living without a minimum reflection on a historical phenomenon of such great importance: the power of the labour movement is a reality, that is true, but it cannot alone take the place of a proper explanation, perspective and distance.

3. The third type of reaction is precisely to view the matter with sufficient historical, theoretical and political perspective, in order to try to discover — even if the task is not easy — the character, meaning and implications of the crisis. If we succeed in this, we can then start talking in a different way, and, emerging from our long history, instead of stating that 'Marxism is in crisis', we can say: 'At last the crisis of Marxism has exploded! At last it is in full view! At last something vital and alive can be liberated by this crisis and in this crisis.

This is not just a paradoxical way of presenting the question, nor merely an arbitrary way of turning it on its head. In using the term 'finally', I mean to draw attention to a point which is in my opinion crucial: that the crisis of Marxism is not a recent phenomenon; it does not date only from recent years, nor even from the crisis of the International Communist Movement, which opened publicly with the Sino-Soviet split and has been deepened by the 'differences' between the Western and Soviet Communist Parties; it does not even date from the 20th Congress of the CPSU. Even if it has only come to public attention since the crisis of the International Communist Movement broke out, the crisis of Marxism is actually much older.

A blocked crisis

If the crisis of Marxism has exploded, if it has now, at the end of a long process, become visible, that is because it has been hatching for a very long time but within forms which have *prevented* it from exploding. Without trying to go back into history in order to find the first steps or causes of this crisis in a more distant period of history, we can say that *for us*, very schematically, the crisis of Marxism emerged in the thirties — and at the same time as it emerged was suppressed. It was in the thirties that Marxism — which had been alive, living from its own contradictions — became blocked, entrenched in 'theoretical' formulae, within a line and in practices imposed by the historical control of Stalinism. In resolving the problems of Marxism in his own way, Stalin imposed 'solutions' whose effect was to block the crisis which these solutions had themselves provoked and reinforced. In doing violence to what Marxism had been, with its openness as well as its difficulties, Stalin in effect provoked a serious crisis within it, but in the same act he blocked it and prevented it from exploding.

The situation which we are living through today does therefore have this advantage: that at the end of a long and tragic history, this crisis has indeed finally exploded, and in conditions which oblige us to take a fresh view, and may allow new life to be breathed into Marxism. Of course, not every crisis contains in itself, of itself, the promise of a new future and liberation. Nor can a mere understanding of the crisis guarantee that this future will ever arrive. That is why it would be wrong to relate the 'explosion' of the crisis of Marxism simply to the dramatic history which led to the 20th Congress of the CPSU and to the crisis of the International Communist Movement. In order to understand the conditions which led to the 'explosion' of the crisis, to its becoming a living force, we must also look at the other side of the matter: not only what is dying off, but what is emerging to take its place: the power of an unprecedented mass movement of the workers and of the people, which has at its disposal new historical forces and potentialities. If today we are able to refer to the crisis of Marxism in terms of possible liberation and renewal, it is because of the strength and capacity to make history inherent in this mass movement. It was this movement which forced a breach in our hermetic history. Through its repeated sallies (such as the Popular Front and the Resistance), its defeats and its victories too (Algeria, Vietnam), finally, through the audacity of May 68 in France, Czechoslovakia, and struggles in other parts of the world, it swept aside the accumulated obstacles and provided Marxism in crisis with a real chance of liberation.

But these first signs of liberation are also a warning. We cannot content ourselves with turning backwards to the past, towards positions which we consider to have been simply distorted or betrayed. The crisis through which we are living forces us to change something in our relation to Marxism, and in consequence, to change something in Marxism itself.

We cannot get round the problem simply by invoking the role of Stalin. We cannot consider our historical, political and even theoretical tradition as a *pure* heritage, which was distorted by an individual called Stalin, or by the historical period which he dominated. There is no original 'purity' of Marxism that only has to be rediscovered. During the whole testing period of the 1960s when we, in our different ways, went 'back to the classics', when we read or re-read Marx, Lenin and Gramsci, trying to find in them a living Marxism, something which was being snuffed out by Stalin-type formulae and practices, we were all forced, each in our own way, even within our differences, to admit the obvious — namely, that our theoretical tradition is not 'pure'; that, contrary to Lenin's over-hasty phrase, Marxism is not a 'block of steel', but contains difficulties, contradictions and gaps, which have also played, at their own level, their role in the crisis, as they already did at the time of the Second International, and even at the beginning of the Third (Communist) International, while Lenin was still alive.

The contradictions in Marxism

This is why I am tempted to say: we are now faced with the vital necessity of reviewing very closely a certain idea which we formed, in history and in the struggle, of Marx, Lenin, Gramsci and Mao — an idea obviously rooted in the demand for the ideological unity of our parties, an idea which, *in spite of our critical efforts*, we have depended on for too long and which we still sometimes cling to. Our chosen authors provided us with a set of theoretical elements of an unprecedented and priceless kind. But we must remember Lenin's perfectly clear phrase: Marx 'gave us the corner-stones ... '. None of the classics gave us a unified and finished whole, but a set of works comprising a number of solid theoretical principles and analyses, *mixed up with* difficulties, contradictions and gaps. There is nothing astonishing about that. If they provided us with the beginnings of a theory of the conditions and forms of the class struggle in capitalist societies, it is nevertheless absurd to consider that this theory could have been born in a 'pure' and complete form. Besides, for a materialist, what could the idea of a pure and completely theory mean? And how could we imagine that a theory of the conditions and forms of the class struggle which denounced the hold and the weight of the dominant ideology could completely escape, from its first moments, from this very ideology, without being marked by it in some way, even in the struggle to break with it? How could we imagine that, in its political and ideological history, this theory could have escaped from any back-lash, from any contagion by the dominant ideology? The break with this ideology is a struggle, but it is a struggle which never comes to an end — a truth which we had to pay for dearly in order to learn. And since even the unpublished papers and the mere study notes of the classic authors are now being dug up, to justify a certain required idea about these authors, let us be honest enough to recognise that these men, who were advancing in unknown territory, were — whatever their qualities — only men: they were searching and discovering, but also hesitating, exposed to the mistakes, to the constant need for correction and to the errors bound up with all research. There is nothing surprising, therefore, in the fact that their works bear the mark of the ideas of their 'time', that they contain difficulties, contradictions and gaps.

It is very important today to realise that these last do exist, and to take full and clear account of them, for certain of these difficulties touch precisely on vital points of the present crisis.

In order to make the point clearer, I shall give some very rough examples.

Exploitation, State and class struggle

In the work of Marx himself, particularly in *Capital*, there exists a theoretical unity which — as we are beginning to see quite clearly — is in large part fictitious. I am not just referring to the fact that

Marx thought it necessary to begin ('every beginning is difficult [...] in all sciences') with an analysis of commodities, therefore of value (which itself poses many problems), but to the effects of this beginning and of a unity of thought imposed on *Capital* which manifestly corresponds to a certain idea Marx had of the kind of unity which ought to be displayed by a true theory. One of the most important of these effects is connected with the question of surplus value. When you read Section 1 of Book 1 of *Capital*, you find a theoretical presentation of surplus value: it is an arithmetical presentation, in which surplus value is *calculable*, defined by the difference (in value) between the value produced by labour power on the one hand, and the value of the commodities necessary for the reproduction of this same labour power (wages) on the other. And in this arithmetical presentation of surplus value, labour power figures purely and simply as a commodity. It is clear that this arithmetical presentation of surplus value conforms with the order of exposition followed by Marx. It therefore depends on his 'starting point' and on subsequent distinctions (constant capital transferring a part of its value to the commodity, variable capital invested in labour power). *Even if* we were to accept this starting point, this beginning, and these distinctions, we should still be forced to note that the presentation of surplus value as a mere calculable quantity — which thus completely ignores the conditions of extraction of surplus value (conditions of labour) and the conditions of the reproduction of labour power — may lead to a very strong temptation: *for this* (arithmetical) *presentation of surplus value may be taken for a complete theory of exploitation*, causing us to neglect the conditions of labour and of reproduction. Marx does however talk about these conditions — but in other chapters in this work, the so-called 'concrete' or 'historical' chapters, which in fact stand *outside* of the order of exposition (the chapters on the working day, on manufacture and modern industry, on primitive accumulation, etc.). This naturally poses the question of the presuppositions and concepts bound up with this 'order of exposition', which have produced certain practical consequences. You can in fact seriously wonder whether this misunderstanding, concerning the arithmetical presentation of surplus value being taken for a complete theory of exploitation, has not in the end constituted a theoretical and political obstacle in the history of the Marxist labour movement to a correct understanding of the conditions and forms of exploitation, and whether this restrictive conception of exploitation (as a purely calculable quantity) and of labour power (as a simple commodity) has not contributed in part to a classical division of tasks in the class struggle between the economic struggle and the political struggle, and hence to a restrictive conception of each form of struggle, which began to hinder, and is today still hindering the broadening of the forms of the whole working class and struggle of the masses.

There are other difficulties in Marx, and also many enigmas. For example, the enigma of philosophy, and in particular of the dialectic, on which Marx said nothing except to propose a few formulae too schematic to be taken literally and too equivocal to be thought through. There is the question of the relation between the dialectic in Marx and in Hegel. There is a lot at stake in this question, in spite of its apparently very abstract and philosophical character: it concerns the conception of necessity and of history, and of the forms of history (does it have a meaning and an end? Is the collapse of capitalism inevitable? etc.), i.e. the conception of the class struggle and of revolutionary action. Marx's silence, and the difficulty of reconstituting his philosophical positions on the basis of his writings, did in fact — with some exceptions (Lenin, Gramsci) — open the road to positivism and evolutionism, whose forms were fixed and frozen for thirty years by Stalin's chapter on 'Dialectical and Historical Materialism' in the *Short History of the CPSU(B)*.

Another example. There exist in Marx and Lenin two theoretical gaps of great importance: on the one hand on the state, on the other hand on the organizations for prosecuting the class struggle.

We have to be frank about it: there does not *really* exist any 'Marxist theory of the State'. Not that Marx and Lenin tried to dodge the question — it lies at the heart of their political thought. But what you find in the classical authors beneath a discussion of the forms of relation between the state on the one hand and the class struggle and class domination on the other (decisive indications but left unanalyzed) is only a repeated warning to avoid all bourgeois conceptions of the state — a rather negative demarcation line and definition. Marx and Lenin do say that there exist 'types of state'. But how does the state ensure class rule, how does the state apparatus function? Neither Marx nor Lenin begin to analyze these questions. In this light, something pathetic strikes you when you re-read the lecture given by Lenin on July 11, 1919 at the Sverdlov University *On the State*. He insists: this is a difficult, and very complicated question.... Over and over again, Lenin repeats: the state is a special machine, a special apparatus, continually making use of the term 'special' in order to point out very clearly that the State is not a machine like other machines — but without ever succeeding in telling us what 'special' might mean here (nor 'machine', nor 'apparatus'). Something pathetic strikes you when you re-read in the same light Gramsci's little equations written in prison (the State = coercion + hegemony, dictatorship + hegemony, force + consensus, etc.) which are the expression less of a theory of the state than of a search, in terms borrowed from 'political science' as much as from Lenin, for a political line aiming at the conquest of state power by the working class. The pathos of Lenin and of Gramsci comes from the fact that they attempt to transcend the classical negative definition — but gropingly, and without success.

But this question of the state is today vital for the labour and popular movement: vital for the comprehension of the countries of eastern Europe where the state, far from 'withering away', is drawing increased strength from its fusion with the Party; vital when the question is posed of how the forces of the people are to obtain power and to work in the direction of a revolutionary democratic transformation of the state, with a view to its withering away.

Analogously, you will not find in the Marxist heritage any real theory of class struggle organizations, especially of political parties and trades unions. There do of course exist political, therefore practical arguments concerning parties and trade unions, but nothing which really allows us to grasp their *functioning*, including the forms of their malfunctioning. Well before Marx, the labour movement began to equip itself with trade unionist and political organizations of struggle, on the basis of its own traditions but also on the basis of existing bourgeois organizations (including, where necessary, the military model). These forms have been conserved and modified: they have a whole history, which they have survived. In the East as in the West we are confronted with the grave problem of the relation existing between these organizations and the state: the problem, in the East, is of the fusion of these organizations with the state, an open fusion; the problem in the West is of the *risk* of fusion, because the bourgeois state never stops trying to integrate the class struggle organizations of the working class into its own operations, often with success.

Mass initiatives

But these two 'gaps' in Marxist theory are bound up with questions which are decisive for us. What is the nature of the state, and in particular of the type of state found in present-day imperialist societies? What is the nature, what is the mode of functioning of the parties and trade unions? How can we escape the risk of an eventual fusion of the State and Party? How can we grasp now, in order to spur on the process, the need for the 'destruction' of the bourgeois State, and prepare the 'withering away' of the revolutionary state? How can we review and modify the nature and functioning of the organizations of class struggle? How can we transform the traditional Communist image of the Party, whether as 'the party of the working class' or as 'the leading party'? How can we transform its ideology in order to allow it to recognize in practice the existence of other parties and of other movements? And above all — the most important of questions for past and future — how can relations be established with the mass movement which, transcending the traditional distinction between trade union and party, will permit the development of initiatives among the people, which usually fail to fit into the division between the economic and political spheres (even 'added together')? Because we are witnessing more and more mass movements of the people arising by themselves, outside of the trade unions and parties, bringing — or capable of bringing — something indispensable to the struggle. In short, how can we properly respond to the demands and expectations of the masses of the people? In different, negative or positive forms, in a hidden or open manner, objectively or subjectively, the same key questions face us: concerning the state, the trade unions, and those mass movements and initiatives. But as far as answers to these questions are concerned, we have essentially no-one to rely on but ourselves.

They are certainly not new questions. Marxists and revolutionaries have tried in the past to find a way to pose them in critical periods, but they have been forgotten or swept under the carpet. Yet today they are posed on an unprecedented scale, and — what is all-important — they are posed on the scale of the masses, *in practice*, as we are seeing in Italy, Spain and elsewhere. Today we can say: without the mass movement, without the initiatives of the masses, we should not be able to pose these questions openly — questions which because of such mass initiatives have become *burning* political questions. Just as we should be unable to pose them as clearly if the crisis of Marxism had not *exploded*.

A new transformation

Nothing, admittedly, is won in advance and nothing comes into being from one day to the next. The 'blockage' of the crisis of Marxism may — beneath more or less 'reassuring' appearances — last for a long time yet in this or that party, or in this or that trade union. The important point is not that a few intellectuals, from East or West, should raise a cry of alarm: it might get no response. The important point is that the labour movement and the movement of the people, even if it is divided, even if it seems here or there to have reached an impasse, has in fact never been so powerful, so rich in resources and initiatives. The important point is that this movement is beginning to become conscious of the meaning of the crisis of the International Communist Movement and of the crisis of Marxism: I am referring here as much to the seriousness of the risks involved and the depth of the crisis as to the historical opportunity of liberation which it represents. Marxism has in its history passed through a long series of crises and transformations. You only have to think back to the transformation of Marxism following the collapse of the Second International after it had rallied to the 'National Cause'. We are now, in the present crisis, faced with a similar transformation which is already finding its roots in the struggles of the masses. It can bring about the renewal of Marxism, give new force to its theory, modify its ideology, its organizations and its practices, opening up a real future of social, political and cultural revolution for the working class and for all working people.

No-one will claim that the task is not extremely difficult: but the essential point is that, in spite of all the difficulties which it involves, *it is possible*.

Translated by Grahame Lock

Greetings and Solidarity from the Trade Unions of Venice

Luigi Covolo

Luigi Covolo, born in Venice in 1944, joined the metalworkers' union in Milan in 1965. He worked for three years as a lathe operator at Magnetti Marelli and in 1970 entered the secretariat of the labour federation of Venice. He has been in the leadership of many struggles in the Marghera industrial zone. Since 1976 he has been general secretary of the Venice federation of trade unions.

I bring the greetings of the Venice federations of the CGIL, CISL, and UIL.

The great interest in the problems under discussion here is indicated by the attention with which this initiative is being followed. The reason for this is simple: these questions have been posed by the struggles of the Italian workers over the past ten years. These struggles have taken on new forms and acquired a new content oriented as they were towards the search for new ways to renovate society.

Our discussion of what is happening in the East European countries is therefore not a concession to bourgeois propaganda, but a process of reflection about what kind of society the workers' movement wants to build.

Comrade Rossanda's report raised some important points for discussion.

The crux of the problem must be confronted critically, examining the organization of these societies, the relations of production (which remain at the root of any analysis), the degree of popular participation (that is, the decentralization of power) and the right to information and dissent. Formal democracy, guaranteed by particular constitutional rights, and substantial democracy (understood as freedom from need) can in no event be separated.

The testimony that has been presented here demonstrates that human and civil rights are too often violated in these societies. We want to reaffirm that the state of law is also a state of formal guarantees under which the citizen is accorded the broadest freedom of dissent, expression, and the right of diffusion of opinion, not only individually, but also in groups.

Even though many of the problems of the workers have been solved in the USSR and the other East European countries, we refuse to identify state capitalism with substantive democracy. For us, substantive democracy must be based on the decentralization of power, on a lively dialectic both among the various power centres and articulations of the state and society and within these bodies as well. The experience of the Italian trade-union movement, of its struggles and cultural and political elaboration, is leading it to strive for the complete emancipation of humanity, rejecting both western capitalism and 'real socialism'. The Italian workers' movement fights for the self-management of the economy and the state, for the development of all the instruments of participation, and for the conquest of real elements of power and forms of workers' control and industrial democracy.

The socialism for which we are struggling can be built not through a 'seizure of power' and subsequent distribution from above, for this would only provoke conformism and a new authoritarianism, but through the interdependent construction of new power centres from below, new instruments of organization and popular participation.

The opposition to the existing post-revolutionary societies cannot be left to Carter and the bourgeoisie, who are simply engaged in a hypocritical operation designed to strength their own rule. This struggle must be taken up by the workers' movement, by the left, as its own fundamental problem, the protagonists of which are the workers, both East and West. We should, however, bring pressure to bear on the existing governments, not because they are particularly credible, but because the conquest of some liberty will be achieved, at least in an initial phase, through the present governments. The struggle for freedom of information, for the freedom to circulate dissenting points of view, is a precondition for the flowering of the creativity of the masses. In this sense, initiatives like this one and the Biennale assume great value.

In any case, the European left must go beyond mere lip-service solidarity and must build on this unity of objectives in day to day struggle. As the workers' movement, as the left, we must once again pose the universal value of socialism, as a moment of liberation from exploitation, as the liberation of humanity, as individual and collective self-government. This alone can be our response to the crisis of both the capitalist and post-revolutionary societies.

The Elimination of Private Property and the Emancipation of Man

Detlev Claussen

Detlev Claussen is an assistant lecturer at Hanover University. He edits Links *the review of the Sozialistisches Büro. During the movement before and around 1968 he was one of the leaders of the SDS in West Germany.*

If there is one place which can be regarded as the touchstone for judging whether a reciprocal understanding is possible between the left in the West and the opposition in the countries of the East, then that place is undoubtedly Germany. The newly-formed GDR took on an anti-fascist legitimacy for the German left, both in the East and the West. Thus, after the war, numerous comrades went to the GDR to help in the construction of socialism. The fact that German imperialism had lost a third of its territory stirred within us a hope that, in spite of all the defects, a new orientation could be stamped on German history. For a long time, it escaped us on the western left that the social formation taking shape in the East was rather different from the one we might imagine with the aid of our traditional categories.

What the new exegetists call 'real socialism' or 'existing socialism' is a society which is neither capitalist nor socialist. One cannot deny that private ownership of the means of production has been abolished; but during the same period, the emancipatory tendencies within socialism have been gradually repressed to the point of complete annihilation.

The military occupation of Czechoslovakia, in which the GDR played a key role, was the main starting-point for deeper reflection on the nature of the East European societies and on the new attitude to be adopted towards the SED (Socialist Unity Party — the ruling party in the GDR).

After the construction of the Berlin wall, which was designed to halt the mass flight to the capitalist West, the GDR socio-economic system was consolidated for a number of years. But after the invasion of Czechoslovakia, it became more and more unstable. The Party and state bureaucracy is obsessed by the fear of a new mass movement with emancipatory aims, for it is perfectly aware that it is above all its own apparatus which stands in the way of mass emancipation.

We can see that, so far, these emancipatory needs have been expressed in the artistic field. However, such artistic expression points to an emancipatory potential which the societies of 'existing socialism' have themselves produced, but whose fulfilment is prevented by the state and party apparatus.

Comrade Rudolf Bahro has attempted to explain the various elements of this contradictory structure. But having made a public communist critique of 'existing socialism' in two television interviews, he is now threatened with the far from slight charge of spying.

Bahro's theoretical essay *The Alternative* is now circulating clandestinely, and it has been discussed in secret by quite broad circles. He has thus undoubtedly encouraged the present upsurge in oppositon to come right into the open. As members of the western left, we now have a concrete duty to denounce repression in the GDR, so that Bahro's life shall not be liquidated in prison.

For us, Bahro's book is an important sign that human emancipation and the abolition of private property cannot be kept separate for much longer. Such was not the case even during the sixties in the West: owing to its traditionalism, the workers movement was not then capable of expressing the social needs of emancipation. For were not the women's, the ecological and other such protest movements of the sixties a clear indication that the socialist movement must overcome its traditionalism if it is to remain a living force; that it must put an end to those bureaucratic ideas which are so deeply rooted in a form of organization based on the separation of economic and political struggle, and on the postponement of individual emancipation until the coming millenium?

Theoretical analysis itself, at least as far as Eastern Europe is concerned, is quite often obscured by traditionalism. 'The' working class *no longer exists* as an immutable class. Since the publication of Serge Mallet's work, we in the West have analyzed with greater clarity the disappearance of the traditional class and the birth of a new world labour. So why are we unable to rid ourselves of the old schematism and grasp that in the East the proletariat has ceased to exist in its old form together with the bourgeoisie? The pursuit of alienated labour, combined with the very limited possibility of political expression and material compensation, has made it possible for the new domination characteristic of 'existing socialism' to be often still more oppressive than old-style capitalist domination.

It is surprising that, in spite of these features, no component of the GDR opposition seeks a return to capitalism. In this sense, East German society is politically more mature than our own. It is important for us, not only from the point of view of solidarity but also from that of our own interests, that the forces pushing towards emancipation in the East should be able to express themselves to the full, and that the terrible equation of communism and mass oppression should thereby give place to the concrete utopia of communism, understood as the liberty, equality and universal, multi-dimensional emancipation of individuals.

To Conclude and Continue

Rossana Rossanda

Just a very few words about these three days, comrades, but not to conclude the discussion, for I do not want to draw conclusions here. This discussion has been so rich that I could not sum it all up, nor do I think it necessary that this be done. Indeed, the comrades who responded to our invitation have given us more than we could have hoped for. And what Althusser said this morning is true: we are now experiencing a liberating crisis which is triggering a process of reflection that must impel us to go much further.

This process has barely begun. We knew that the beginning would not be easy; all of us in the various left groupings bear the heritage of the past sixty great and terrible years, years that have destroyed not only hopes and illusions, but also political and theoretical categories. Years that have built and divided, have provided the very reasons for our existence, have unified our destinies, but also divided our choices and even our language. We wanted to overcome this division, which often rests on silence, by beginning to do common research again. This we have done. We have had three days of real discussion, not always painless.

I have but one thing to say to the comrades of Eastern Europe, who have brought us not only testimony but also a bill of indictment. They fear — and they have said so — that we somehow underestimate their tragedy, that we feel the need to avoid it, whether through an excess of historicization or through other political and theoretical evasions. This has been true of the left in the past, and to some extent it is still true today. But not because of indifference. If there has been an attempt at flight, it has not been because we were not involved, but because we were too much so. There have been no negative regressions of revolutions for which we also have not paid a price in one way or another. This was true in the thirties and it was also true after the war, in 1956 and in 1968. Claudin has said that the general staffs of the left have acted in complicity with the East European countries. It is true that there has been complicity by the leaderships, but it is also true that all of us, even the simplest rank-and-file comrades who knew little but hoped for much, have been identified by the class enemy with your choices and your fate. And so long as the class enemy looks upon your countries as its enemies — even today, when this is much less the case than in the past — we have to bear the weight of that burden. Your defeats are also our defeats, and we have been made to pay for them.

Comrades of Eastern Europe, these western societies which seem so free to you because they are so intelligently flexible — as Mészáros recalled yesterday, one can say anything but virtually nothing can be changed — have thrown into the balance of the class struggle everything that has been said and done in the name of socialism, in order to destroy the bargaining position and political strength of the working class and to extinguish the hopes of those in the West who speak of revolution and fight for it. This is not a justification of our behaviour, but it does explain the reasons for our attitude. All your testimony of the past three days — Comrades Plyushch, Weil, Franqui, Baluka, Kavin — is not something we can listen to idly; it grips us. We already knew it all, but you have seen in the faces and words of our comrades of Fiat Mirafiori that this history of yours is also our history; our defeats are common, and so are the wounds to be healed. Is this possible? No one thinks it will be easy. But maybe it is possible, if we get to the bottom of the crisis and turn it around.

None of us will leave this gathering exactly as he came into it. Not only because it has not been an academic debate (and of this we never had the slightest doubt), but also because it has been more than just a good political meeting. It has been three tough days. Those who are not part of the left, who have never believed in the 'red flag of freedom', or who now deride this history, content to make brilliant intellectual cracks, who ignore the past greatness and the blood that has been shed and who fail to realize the dimensions of the dangers and choices history has now placed before us, will not understand this. But that does not matter. We have begun and we will continue. We and the comrades of Eastern Europe. We will not lose touch with one another again. And to make sure that this desire does not remain purely formal, the organizers of this meeting have decided to ensure that there will be a follow-up. We have drafted the following motion, as individuals but with the commitment which the political affiliation of each of us entails:

'The participants at the gathering on "power and opposition in post-revolutionary society", held in Venice 11-13 November 1977, propose that the dialogue and research begun during these first three days continue in the spirit of liberty, open confrontation, and political and moral commitment that have characterized the gathering.

'They hold that the European left has been sluggish in analyzing the revolutions that have occurred and the real structural and political conditions that prevail in these societies. To overcome this sluggishness is not simply a matter of solidarity but a political task for all the class forces struggling in the West for the objective of socialist transformation.

'They hold that the conquest and defence of liberty in the post-revolutionary societies is essential; they explicitly support the struggle for democracy and commit themselves to denouncing violations of it. They likewise hold that the lack of freedom in these societies is grounded in deep-going processes during the revolutionary and transitional phases. These processes are of concern to us; they form part of the patrimony of the class struggle and must be confronted and resolved on that terrain.

'The undersigned pledge to continue this initial work of confrontation and active solidarity, broadening participation in it and organizing a second meeting, in Barcelona, during the first half of 1978. This second gathering, ten years after the Prague spring, will examine its origins and results.'

The signers of this motion are as follows: USSR: Leonid Plyushch, Boris Weil; Poland: Edmund Baluka; Hungary: István Mészáros; Czechoslovakia: Ludvik Kavin, Jiri Pelikan; Cuba: Carlos Franqui; Spain: Alfonso Comin, Fernando Claudin; France: Louis Althusser, Charles Bettelheim, K.S. Karol, Robert Linhart; Austria: Franz Marek; Italy: Giorgio Girardet, Lucio Magri, Edoarda Masi, Vittorio Rieser, Carlo Ripa de Meana, Rossana Rossanda, Bruno Trentin, Rosario Villari; United Kingdom: Daniel Singer.

In coming weeks we will broaden the participation and define the content of the Barcelona meeting.

Other motions have also been presented in the course of this conference. Those which deal with Italian questions — workers' struggles or struggles for democracy and freedom, among them a motion protesting the shutdown of Radio Città Futura yesterday — are available for signing in the lobby of the hall. Here we will read the two motions that relate directly to the themes of the gathering. We are not asking for votes on these motions; those who agree with them can simply add their names. One concerns the liberation of Rudolf Bahro. It reads as follows:

'The participants at the gathering on "power and opposition in post-revolutionary society", which united democrats, socialists, and communists of Western and Eastern Europe in Venice 11-13 November 1977, call upon international public opinion to intervene before the government of the German Democratic Republic to free comrade Rudolf Bahro, imprisoned under the false charge of espionage because he produced a Marxist critique of the political and class order that prevails in the GDR and the other countries of Eastern Europe.' This motion has been presented by Elio Giovannini, Alfonso Comin, Lucio Lombardo Radice, Leonid Plyushch, Boris Weil, Bruno Trentin, and Rossana Rossanda.

The second concerns the *Berufsverbot* in West Germany; it has been presented by Rossana Rossanda, Fernando Claudin, Alfonso Comin, Franz Marek, Jiri Pelikan, Louis Althusser, Edmund Baluka, and Lucio Lombardo Radice. Here is the text:

'The participants at the gathering on "power and opposition in post-revolutionary society", held in Venice 11-13 November 1977, uniting socialists, communists, and democrats of Western and Eastern Europe, ask the government and political and trade-union forces of the Federal Republic of Germany to act to put an end to any violation of civil and democratic rights in West Germany and in particular to abolish the discriminatory practice of the *Berufsverbot*.'

Leonid Plyushch and Boris Weil have also signed this motion, while expressing a reservation, namely that the responsibility for the violations of democracy in the Federal Republic must also be ascribed to the forces which have permitted the division of Germany, erected the Berlin wall, and practiced political discrimination in the German Democratic Republic. This reservation was not expressed by the other signers.

Comrade Franz Marek has also presented a proposal, without formalizing it in a motion: that pressure be exerted so that passports be granted the East European comrades who requested them for this gathering and for the Biennale. I think it is obvious that the entire conference agrees with this.

With that, comrades, *il manifesto* thanks all the participants and closes the work of this conference.

APPENDICES

Three Written Contributions

Most of the written contributions have been omitted for reasons of space. They can be found in the original Italian edition [Ed.].

Western 'dissidence' ideology and the protection of bourgeois order

Robert Linhart

Robert Linhart teaches at the University of Paris VIII specializing in the history and economy of the countries of Eastern Europe. Once a militant with La Gauche Prolétarienne, *he is the author of* Lenin, the Peasants and Taylor. *In 1977 he had published an account of his experiences as an unskilled worker at Citroën's from 1968 to 1969 in a book called* L'Etabli (*The Work-bench*) *which had an outstanding success.*

It is important to distinguish clearly between two realities or sets of movements and thoughts which have only their appearance in common.

On the one hand, there are the class and revolutionary struggles, the popular resistance to the old and new bourgeoisie in the USSR and the other countries of the East. In one form or another, the popular masses of these countries have never stopped resisting oppression and exploitation since 1917. The Red Army's heroic resistance to the coalition of fourteen imperialist nations, the 1971 Polish insurrection on the Baltic coast, the Czechoslovak people's resistance to the Russian invasion of 1968, the Kirghiz, Uzbek, Tatar, Lithuanian and other national movements within the new Russian empire, the various strikes and peasant movements — all these mark out the vast history of hundreds of millions who snatched the first great victories against the imperialist system, implanted new forms of social organization, shattered the Nazi onslaught, and took up the struggle against the new bourgeoisie and the new forms of exploitation, injustice and inequality produced by their own irruption on to the arena of history.

On the other hand, there is the western ideology of 'dissidence': a recent innovation, yet one that is already promoted with the energy and advertising sense typical of capitalism. I propose to speak here about this second reality, whose distinctness and efficacity as a capitalist product can hardly be denied.

This ideology of 'dissidence' and 'human rights' — which has been fabricated in the imperialist countries, *our* countries, with instruments befitting the importance of political objectives laid down — is but one element in the structure designed to protect bourgeois order and spread imperialist power throughout the world. It is nothing more than that. The ideology is constructed and utilized as a weapon *against* the popular masses — as a means of opposing the emancipation of the oppressed and maintaining the privileges of the oppressors. It has to be analzyed in its real, concrete mode of functioning. People who organize its promotion, whether they are called Carter, Giscard, Glucksmann, the Archbishop of Braga or the Royal College of Psychiatrists, have to be judged by their actions and by the manifold effects of their public activity.

When all is said and done, what is the spectacle we are witnessing?

A barely-spruced up variant of the capitalist 'freedom struggle' that has massacred whole nations (American-Indians, Australasian peoples, African tribes); deported millions of black slaves and pillaged three continents; condemned billions of men to famine, illiteracy and the horrors of colonial war; bled the peoples of Indo-China through the most sophisticated means of mass destruction that technology has ever invented; and made of industrial labour a brutalizing activity and a method of slow torture. All this in the name of human rights, Religion, Love of One's Neighbour, and Freedom. All in the name of Civilization.

More concretely, let us look at some of the new actors in this age-old farce. In Portugal, we saw at work centuries of Catholic obscurantism (was the 1917 Fatima vision not an 'answer' to the Satanic Revolution that had just broken out in Russia?), the most reactionary forces of the clergy, and the whole network of fascist chieftains. In summer 1975, these were all mobilized by the bourgeoisie and its 'social-democratic' vanguard of the hour in order to break a process of social transformation, terrorize the masses, and isolate or lynch communist and far-left militants in the north of the country.[1] In the name of anti-Marxism and defence against the *gulag*. In the name of freedom.

In the United States, we can see a wily politician whose 'naive' character has been carefully built up by the cream of the techno-cracy, banking circles and assorted experts of American and world capitalism (Brzezinski, Rockefeller, the staff of Chase Manhattan, the men from the Trilateral and Bilderberg). This man holds up the defence of human rights in order to deepen the penetration of the multinationals, intervene in the dominated countries, tighten exter-nal debt blackmail, and increase the powers of US high finance through the medium of the IMF. But such talk does not prevent him from triumphally greeting the Shah of Iran and having Iranian student oppositionists well and truly beaten up. In the name of freedom.

In England, criminal psychiatrists, who practise lobotomy and the worst mutilations of the human person, being attacked for this by the anti-psychiatrists and opposed by democrats in their own country, nevertheless place themselves at the head of a campaign that condemns political psychiatry in the USSR with great pomp and circumstance. In the name of freedom.

In France, a handful of upstart intellectuals, barely over their drawing-room Maoism, are now negotiating a career out of their recantation, the fine points of which fetch quite a good price. The bourgeoisie pays up and asks for more. The moulders of public opinion — Springer's French rivals and Giscard's propagandists — must be really pleased to have this little band of mandarins and young people pronouncing 'the bankruptcy of Marxism' on the front pages. Any real popular revolt, they prophesy, leads to the Gulag. And yet they feel quite free to talk endlessly about 'revolt', so long as it does not pose the question of power. What they are at home with is anything that can be dissolved into individual situations and specific problems with no overall solution; as with mild illnesses, these are supposed to make the organism stronger, better immunized, better adapted. Capitalism digests millions of such 'revolts' every day and is still in good enough shape. The important thing is to stave off its terminal illness. And here the 'new' philosophers are in agreement: nothing is more despicable than revolutionary politics, nothing more reprehensible than the dreams of power that might seize the oppressed masses. Their favours are reserved for a shapeless 'plebs' driven back into some vague spiritualism. As for 'dissidence', it is the preserve of isolated and well-known individuals: intellectuals, scien-tists (or, to keep up the pretence, 'outsiders', 'madmen', and so on). And since no transformation of society is to be feared from that quarter, we may as well go on eating with gusto and see what happens. Michael Foucault expresses this in quite a nice way: 'Today, it is the very desirability of Revolution that is in question ...' Indeed, it could not have been put any better.

The details vary, then, according to national specificities, modes of producing culture, tactical differences in propaganda, and the social composition of executive circles.

To be sure, junctions, intersections and alliances may take place across national boundaries. Thus, in August 1975, Glucksmann published an article in the paper *Libération*, supporting the anti-communist pogroms in the north of Portugal and greeting the Archbishop of Braga as a defender of freedom against Marxist terror. [The article was called 'From Prague to Braga', Glucksmann being particularly fond of the jingle-titles made fashionable by such detective novels as *Danger à Tanger* and *Banco à Bangkok*. They excite the crowds. Other offerings by Glucksmann include: 'Les ballots du ballotage' (*Le Monde*) and 'Le terrorisme des terrorisés' (*Le Monde*).*] Within the same movement of international solidarity, the French 'new philosophers' boost Carter's merits and proclaim that, in terms of barbarity, capitalism is, all things considered, preferable to socialism. (See *Time Magazine*, 5 September 1977, whose front-cover splashes a triumphant: 'Marx is Dead!')

That each bourgeois propaganda apparatus should adapt its strategy in the ideological struggle to 'national requirements' is, if I may say so, perfectly normal. The centralizing and bluff-like system of the French intelligentsia is not the same as either the powerful clerical pressure of the north of Portugal, or the US academic neo-techncracy, so pragmatic, scientistic and divorced from social and political technology. But in the last analysis, there is something constant through all these peculiarities, something which goes even further than the specific points of convergence I have mentioned.

The political strategists of the imperialist bourgeoisies have drawn the lessons of the thirty-odd years since the last war: the collapse of capitalism's system of values; the humanitarian protest against the colonial wars; the sixties explosion among the youth and intelligentsia; the Watergate crisis; the symbol of Vietnam. Ideology, of course, is also a focus of struggle. But by dint of relying on machine-guns and truncheons, they had grown rather slack on this front. After all, the colonial wars were also lost in the metropolises; and the initial

---

*ballots = 'bundles' or 'fat-heads'; ballotage = 'ballot'; 'The terrorism of the terrorized'.

conquest of the colonies had made as much use of 'the missionary ideal' and 'the civilizing mission of the West' as of gunboat diplomacy. What the Lyauteys conquered, the Massus did not let go. Every system of exploitation and every venture in oppression has need of a spiritual supplement. The struggle is no simple matter: there are never simply two classes or forces facing each other; the intermediate elements are often decisive; and it is never pointless to try to maintain the harness of consent within the very thinking of the oppressed.

We are today witnessing the 'moral rearmament' of capitalism. And it will be necessary to face up to it. Whether we like it or not, the bourgeoisie marches relentlessly forward wherever resistance weakens. At this very moment, the Baader-Croissant[2] affair and the brutal offensive of the German and French States reminds us of this truth. What a cold light it casts on those 'new philosophers' who have taken the head of the anti-Marxist crusade in France! With the blood of the Stammheim[3] carnage reeking in our nostrils, we can very well say with John Donne: 'No man is an island entire unto himself ... So do not ask for whom the bell tolls, it tolls for thee.'

However, before talking about this precise event and answering those who may think exaggerated the comparison between the new anti-Marxists and the ideologists of colonial conquest or 'the yellow peril', I would like to quote the following lines by Maurice Clavel (one of the inventors of French 'New Philosophy') which appeared in *Le Nouvel Observateur* on 22 November 1976: 'Let's be quite frank. Is the West bent on suicide? If it is, then the end is not far off. Just look at our little promontory and think that, with the elimination of the Cultural Revolution figures and the ongoing Sino-Soviet reconciliation, a billion robots are already resting their weight on the Elbe. Those two billion eyes blinking, or rather not blinking — we talk much less about them than about the municipal elections. But they are what is key.'

If only some miraculous bomb or special genocide weapon could rid us of those two billion robots in the twinkling of an eye ...

But at Stammheim they deal in small orders: it is just the beginning. And yet, what a terrifying sign of the forces preparing in the shadows while the public entertainers chatter on!

A terrifying sign, too, was the miscarried campaign that accompanied it: all those intellectuals slipping away; the jumble of attacks against terrorism and hazy verbal protests against repression; the sudden silence of professional talkers; the terrible indifference amid which the lawyer Croissant was handed over to the Stammheim butchers. Who would have imagined such abdication a couple of years ago — when the very intellectuals who today keep quiet or slip away were *really* mobilizing against racist crimes (Djellali), police brutality (Jaubert), judicial frame-ups, fascism in the factories (Overney), and terror in the prisons.

The reaction to the Stammheim murders, and then to the handing over of Croissant, allows us to gauge the distance already travelled and the full extent of the debacle.

The majority of 'new philosophers' and their like simply keep their mouth shut. Those who deign to speak do so in order to condemn the German revolutionaries and calmly take part in the campaign of encirclement and liquidation directed against them. Those who speak do not even bother to show how state terrorism has systematically led such revolutionaries into the most desperate actions (Le Bris). Others, when asked to join the campaign to save Croissant, say no right from the start: the issue is not congenial to them; the whole thing is just a 'diversion' (sic) from the real problem of dissidence in Eastern Europe; anyway, one cannot talk of an authoritarian state in the case of West Germany, which is a liberal country! Crushed in the egg, pulled in every direction, the solidarity campaign immediately got bogged down, despite the efforts of the French lawyers' organization, MAJ. Knowing from experience how much cases of this kind depend on the first few hours and on the level of determined support, we can say that Croissant's fate was largely sealed at this stage. The authorities could see that there would be no resolute opposition.

Of those who believed that the 'new philosophers' and their like were sincere in their pronouncements about 'dissidence', 'human rights', 'resistance to the state' and 'struggle against the powers-that-be', many are now discovering to their horror that this one-way discourse has the sole function of masking, and even justifying a real *consent* to the barbarity of capitalism and the state — barbarity which occurs *here*, in the only place where our fight can be effective and demands more than chatter with no bearing, no risk and no subversive effect.

Glucksmann may have demurely announced, after Croissant had already been handed over, that 'tampering with a lawyer does harm to the free circulation of ideas'. (And what harm is done when an immigrant worker is shot, as happened a few days ago at Marseilles railway station? None at all. That is no doubt why the Foucaults, Glucksmanns and other fine souls no longer speak out on such unimportant occasions.) But it was just dust in the eyes: a rearguard manoeuvre to keep up appearances. People are judged by what they do. And the French 'dissidence' ideologists, those 'master-speakers' coddled by the regime and laden with honours of every kind, have clearly demonstrated their abdication since the Baader-Croissant affair.

That was the most spectacular example. But it is merely a drop in the ocean of cowardice.

For many years, and with an intensity now going beyond anything seen since the Algerian War, the Arab immigrant community in France has been living under a regime of racist terror. Scarcely a month passes any more without a North African worker being shot down in cold blood: by street-hooligans (in the rue Montorgueil in Paris), by policemen (Brigadier Marchaudon in Nanterre, four policemen at Saint-Charles Station in Marseilles), by café-owners (Flers), and so on. *With complete impunity.* When a trial happens by chance, it ends with an acquittal (in Flers, the café-owner who paralyzed an Algerian worker *for life* with a rifle-shot was acquitted by the Assize Court), or with a completely token sentence (the concierge who murdered the young Algerian Djellali in 1971 has just been condemned to ... two years in jail! The jury may just as well have congratulated him.)

After Stoléru's anti-immigrant measures, racism and segregation are now becoming institutionalized and, in effect, receiving government backing.

Thus millions of workers and their families live in our land under a regime of emergency and terror, subjected to nefarious disciminatory legislation, superexploited, housed in appalling conditions, and at the mercy of racist guttersnipes and murderers. What do the 'new philosophers' and their like have to say? What is the opinion of these valiant defenders of 'human rights', these 'dissidents', these indomitable adversaries of all power?

Television and the press are always open for them to lecture us about the horrors of Marxism and the Gulag. So what do they say and do when people are killed, expelled or mutilated, when families are broken up, when murderers are acquitted in the name of the French people — in their name?

Nothing.

Let us not go into the details of personal responsibility: the painful record of manoeuvres and counter-manoeuvres, hesitation-waltzes, and sudden absences. The important thing is the crushing fact itself. During the sixties and early seventies, the various popular upsurges, the wars of national liberation and a whole range of factors involving the social crisis and the spread of revolutionary ideas in the West determined a real democratic mobilization of intellectuals. In France, during the fifteen years or so after the climax of the Algerian War (1958), we saw intellectuals resist colonial brutality and the authoritarian state; take up the defence of immigrants, prisoners and victims of arbitrary power; support strikes and mobilize alongside the workers to counter repression. This democratic movement, which sometimes grouped together broad sections of youth and the *mass* of intellectuals, played an important role in the rebirth of revolutionary political forces, the upsurge of the workers movement, and resistance to oppression.

However, led astray by small-group fever, fragmented by the multiple recuperation devices set up by the bourgeoisie after 1968, enervated by the ideology of 'desire' and all manner of justifications for petty-bourgeois egotism, this democratic mobilization began to collapse five or six years ago.

Much more recently, the 'new philosophy' operation, with its chatter about Gulag and 'dissidence', marked a new stage of liquidation and laid the ground for a strengthening of the state and repressive system right here in Western Europe.

It is an open secret that the thundering of the 'new philosophers' is amplified by the Elysée Palace on the one side, and by right social democracy on the other. It is beginning to make an impact on the very recomposition of the 'French political landscape'.

Their message is simple: revolt (i.e., a real revolt of the popular masses, struggle by the working class and all the oppressed to destroy bourgeois power) leads to the world of the Gulag. *It is wrong to rebel.*

A paradoxical conclusion? Hardly. One thing is clear for anyone really seeking to look things in the face, discard the verbiage of the 'master-speakers', and discover where their blows are aimed. The discourse of 'dissidence', such as it is fabricated and promoted by western capitalism, is a discourse suited to maintaining the established order. It is a discourse for consolidating the established order *both East and West.*

Which regime would not be delighted to see its intellectuals denouncing the horrors of the powers-that-be ... over there?

Let us indulge in a little dream — or rather, let us imagine the dream in which Giscard and Brezhnev might indulge.

The 'great' French intellectuals denounce the Gulag, the violations of human rights in the USSR, the psychiatric internment of political opponents, and so on. At the same time, they get along very well with the racist terror that has descended upon three million immigrants in France; the Algerians who are shot down with impunity; the one-and-a-half million unemployed (those who recently set fire to themselves having been swiftly forgotten); the two million psychiatric patients and 200,000 inmates; the muck-heaps of prisons; the pillage of Mauritania, Senegal, the Sahel region, Zaire, the Mato Grosso and Amazonia by French-led multinationals, French 'technicians' and French soldiers. The Soviet intervention in Czechoslovakia horrifies these people, but not the French intervention in Africa and the Sahara … In short, hell is always the others. In return for which the 'great' French intellectuals are entitled to Academie Française awards, the most spectacular publicity, the honours of the regime and society, and the discrete favours of the authorities.

The 'great' Russian intellectuals (for they do exist, whatever some may think) denounce the wretchedness of life in the capitalist countries, the neo-colonial expeditions and the oppression of the Third World. At the same time, they get along very well with social segregation in their own country, the *nomenklatura*, privileges and corruption, the national inequalities and Great-Russian chauvinism, military domination of Eastern Europe, exploitation of the working class, isolation of the peasantry, kolkhoz poverty, and so on. After all, hell is always the others. In return for which the 'great' Russian intellectuals are entitled to Lenin prizes, membership of the Academy of Sciences, *dachas* and all the honours reserved for the most eminent representatives of culture. What touching symmetry! An ideological Yalta, as it were.

Let us go further. The ideology of intellectual dissidence, which focusses on the spectacular resistance of a tiny elite of writers, scientists and other people either already well-known or becoming so through energetic and careful attention, is a significant factor in consolidating the existing order both in the East and the West. For the whole ideology is constructed in order to make unbridgeable the gulf between 'dissident intellectuals' and the masses. The 'drain' of dissident intellectuals from East to West, together with the permanent offer of dubious cultural promotion in the USSR and Eastern Europe, is a way of beheading on-the-spot resistance to oppression as and when it arises. It is a way of diverting oppositional intellectuals from the only forces really able to change these societies: the working class, the peasantry, the urban and rural population, the various nationalities of the Soviet Union and Eastern Europe. It is also a way of keeping silent about the struggle of the Soviet and European popular masses. What is known about life in the factories and kolkhozes? What is known about the struggle of the Kirghiz, Latvian, Uzbek, Tatar, Jewish and Ukrainian nationalities — as *mass phenomena* rooted in the daily life, production, and ordinary relations among people and classes or between governments and the governed? What is known about resistance to productivity norms, the struggle for food, the conflicts that are the very stuff of any society and the site of the really deep changes? So many people want to talk only about the camps (and those *in France* who discovered them so recently have the incredible nerve to make money for jam out of them!) or to build up individual heroes. But at the same time, they slip in the image of a vast herd of resigned, passive and contemptible people — an image supposed to cover these hundreds of millions of men and women who work, think, struggle, change and resist. It is a piece of deceit and, at bottom, a discourse full of reassurance for all the state powers, whether in the East or the West. It is a voluntarily pessimistic vision with no way-out other than circular repetition of a hollow discourse: a few shout amid the resigned silence of the many. And the many are those billions of robots to whom Maurice Clavel referred, with unheard-of contempt and the most mindless racism. We can be sure that this view of things is far more congenial to Brezhnev than the admirable report on East European factories written by the Hungarian Marxist Haraszti,[4] or the materialist critique of the GDR by the East German Marxist Bahro, or the revolutionary-proletarian practice of the Polish workers' leader Baluka. However, these barely find an echo in the western manufacturers of dissidence. For they talk to us about the class struggle, the workers' fight, the struggle against the bourgeoisie, the subversive implication of Marxism — here today, in 1977, in the USSR and the other eastern countries; and not about the cosmic struggle of good against evil, the Satanic character of Marxism, and the elect role of a handful of intellectuals, scientists or technocrats.

How would these Marxists be understood by our 'new philosophers' and the new supporters of 'human rights'? Would they be thought to deserve even the title of 'dissidents', given that they look to the masses instead of drawing away from them? For after all, what would be the meaning of 'dissident masses'? Once the masses are involved, we are no longer in the realm of 'dissidence', but in that of revolution! And is it not being discovered that revolution is no longer desirable? Who is to say that the 'great' intellectuals would find their heads again in the upheaval of a great revolution?

In essence, all these 'great intellectuals' now mobilized against Marxism have only one real wish: *that nothing should change*, either here in the West, or there in the East. They are deaf to class struggles in the USSR and Eastern Europe, just as they are deaf to class struggles anywhere else in the world. We have nothing to learn from them about post-revolutionary societies. They boast about opening our eyes, but in reality they make us drunk with empty words, and seek only to strike a new attitude. The sincerity of their 'resistance to the state' can be gauged by their abdication when faced with racist terror attacks; the terror of the West German State and the handing over of Croissant; the sufferings of a French people ground down by unemployment; and the colonial expeditions in Black Africa and the Sahara. They talk endlessly about their courage, but all we can see is their cowardice.

Why should we be surprised that their hatred is focussed on Marxism to such a degree? Not, to be sure, on the falsified variants of Marxism which serve as a state ideology in the East, and as the food of sectarian stereotyping or academic chatter in the West. No, the Marxism they attack and insult is the Marxism of Marx, Lenin and Mao, of the storming of the Winter Palace and the Long March; the Marxism of proletarian uprisings, peasant revolutions and the armed struggles of the Third World; the Marxism of revolutionary workers, peasants and intellectuals throughout the world; the Marxism which raised whole peoples out of the colonial night of famine, illiteracy and poverty, which broke the centuries-old domination of feudal and capitalist exploiters, which since 1917 has opened, against all opposition, and through currents and cross-currents of victory and defeat, a whole new epoch of history.

Why is their hatred focussed on this living Marxism of revolt and revolution? Because in that Marxism, it is the masses who make history — the countless multitudes of the exploited and oppressed all over the world. Because in that Marxism, intellectuals can change the societies in which they live only if they try to find a road to the workers and peasants, only if they invent new forms of action, thought and language by joining themselves to the broad masses of the people and to the struggles of the exploited. But this also means that intellectuals can change the world only by agreeing to change themselves: to give up part of their privileges, as well as the lofty position gained through their mastery of a certain kind of language and an assumed knowledge.

Whatever the ideological fashion-setters might like to think, history is not made in the columns of Paris newspapers, nor in publishing-houses, television broadcasts, literary groups or conferences. It is made in the plains of the Alentejo and the mines of Silesia; in the shipyards of Lisnave and Gdansk; around the rolling-mills of Annaba and smelting-works of Nowa Huta; in the mines of the Asturias and the cotton-fields of Kazakhstan; in the Brazilian *favelas* and the refugee-camps of Mozambique; in the suburbs of Ferrand and those of Kiev; on the assembly-lines of Renault, Fiat and Volkswagen. The masses make history, and every day that passes shows that they are right to rebel.

NOTES

1. See Gunther Walraff, 'The Coup Merchants' in *The Undesirable Journalist*, Pluto Press, London 1978 for sensationally self-incriminating interviews with the Archbishop of Braga and General Spinola [Ed.].
2. Klaus Croissant, lawyer to the Red Army Faction was extradited from France to Germany, accused of being an accomplice of the 'terrorists' whom he acted for [Ed.].
3. Stammheim, the supposedly ultra-safe, specially constructed prison in which three leaders of the RAF were found hanged or shot supposedly by their own hand in the Autumn of 1977 [Ed.].
4. Haraszti's original title was *Piece Work* but due to some curious editorial whim, it appeared in English under the title *A Worker in a Worker's State* (sic), Penguin 1977 [Ed.].

Socialism in History, History in Socialism

Lucio Lombardo Radice

Lucio Lombardo Radice, mathematician, philosopher, and professor at the University of Rome, has been a member of the PCI since 1938. He is now a member of the Central Committee and is co-editor of the review Riforma della scuola. *During the sixties he was one of the participants in the dialogue between Catholics and Marxists. He is the author of the preface to the Italian edition of Engels's* Dialectics of Nature (*1967*), *as well as of* Socialismo e libertà (*1968*) *and* Gli accusati (*1972*).

It is now clear to the great popular masses who aspire to it that socialism is not the end of history. Indeed, it remains to be seen to what extent the myth of socialism as the 'last judgment' or 'advent of the reign' was actually a feature of modern, proletarian socialism during its first few decades in the nineteenth century and to what extent it was, on the contrary, an argument 'invented' by the enemies of socialism.

This argument — that the socialist perspective was anti-historical — was, for example, of central and decisive importance in Benedetto Croce's attempt at the beginning of the twentieth century to 'liquidate' theoretical Marxism in Italy. Socialism, he said, is presented as the conclusion of human history; but since the latter can never end, socialism must be an impossible myth, since it is unthinkable in reality.

In theoretical Marxism, on the other hand, even in its most elementary and fideistic traditions, socialism does not stand *above* history, as did the eschatologies of the liberation of the oppressed in the political-heretical movements of the Middle Ages and the Renaissance. The transition from utopian to scientific socialism may perhaps be summarized precisely in this: socialism no longer stands above history, but enters into it and is born of it; it evolves and progresses and continues to be history, even after its establishment.

A characteristic element of this disposition of socialism within history is the distinction between socialist and communist society. Communism is constructed in history through an intermediary phase, socialism. But even completed communism will have its own history, will move forward and develop, although in forms and ways that cannot be foreseen.

There is, however, one myth that persists even in the modern conception of socialism as articulated by the sons, grandsons, and great grandsons of Karl Marx; it is found, I would say, in all, or nearly all, the branches, tendencies, and shadings of the school of Marx. That myth is as follows. History does indeed continue after the socialist revolution, but it becomes essentially one-dimensional, a unilinear, ascending process which can undergo oscillations, swings of the pendulum back and forth, but no genuine descending phases.

This myth of socialism as uninterrupted progress is particularly evident today, sixty years after the October Revolution, in the picture of post-revolutionary history presented by official Soviet publications. What is most striking in the commemorative speeches and articles is a singular incongruity.

On the one hand, all the leaders of the Union of Soviet Socialist Republics except its founder, Lenin, are expunged from historic memory: Stalin, Malenkov, and Khrushchev. On the other hand, the country advances constantly and without interruption under the 'wise leadership' of an anonymous Central Committee of the Communist Party. This organ, as such, never makes a mistake. It leads the country and the people ever forward, even though it is headed by men who are condemned, through silence, in the harshest and most definitive manner.

What lies behind this incongruity is precisely the postulate of the unilinear, ascending advance of history after socialism and with socialism. Thus, along with degeneration, distortion and ossification, any phenomenon of conservatism, any period of decadence in the history of socialism are all excluded *a priori* as incompatible with this postulate. The postulate of unilinear ascending progress is not formulated explicitly because it is unconscious. It has been accepted and applied without being formulated because it lies in the deepest stratum of a structure of thought founded on progressive evolutionism, on historic optimism. This postulate expresses faith (of a

dogmatic type) in an immanent providence some of whose consequences (absolute optimism, certainty in constant progress, *a priori*
exclusion of crises and catastrophes) are in truth indistinguishable
from traditional faith in a transcendent Providence. One could even
say that the only real difference lies in whether 'providence' is written
with a lower- or upper-case 'p'.

I have the impression, however, that the 'postulate of unlinear
progress' is also implicit in the arguments of the leftist critics of the
Soviet Union and the countries of 'existing socialism' (or, as it is
usually put, 'real socialism'), when they deny that these countries are
socialist. Indeed, it seems to me that the assertion that the USSR and
the other countries that have gone beyond capitalism are not socialist
rests not on a sober economic and social analysis, but on the
preconceived idea (the axiom!) that there can be no socialism in
countries which have conservative political systems upholding authoritarian and ossified structures, where dogmatism prevails in the
ideological domain and profound crises erupt and periods of decadence take root.

In truth, there are no serious arguments to support the thesis that
the USSR has returned to capitalism, or even state capitalism (which,
if it is to be called 'capitalism' also implies the existence of a private
capitalism interlaced with the public sector into a 'single mechanism'). Such an assertion can be made purely as propaganda, and
rather shoddy propaganda at that. When accusations that the USSR
had restored capitalism poured out of China during the cultural
revolution, one could not help but recall the slanders the USSR (and
the Cominform) had hurled at Yugoslavia after the break in 1948,
namely that the return of capitalism had been initiated under the
leadership of the 'renegade' Tito.

It seems to me that recognition that the USSR went beyond
capitalism in 1917 and has not returned to it, that post-capitalist
economic and social structures exist in this great country, is now
gaining ground among left critics of the USSR. Because of this
underlying postulate, however, there is hesitation, even refusal, to
speak of socialism, even qualified by some adjective: authoritarian
socialism, conservative socialism, state socialism, or even, 'as a limit'
(as non-mathematicians say these days), 'Asiatic' socialism. It should
be noted that I am using the term Asiatic not in the geographic sense
or with any pejorative connotation, but rather to indicate affinity
with the ancient 'Asiatic mode of production' (political concentration of all property in the hands of a prince) cited but not studied by

Marx and Engels. The 'modern price', or, if we want to maintain the analogy, the 'modern king of kings' under Soviet socialism would then be the party-state apparatus. Such a structure, in any event, has nothing in common with state capitalism, which cannot exist in the absence of monopoly and private profit.

I would like to call for reflection on this point. Why in the world should it be maintained that there can be no conservative socialism and therefore no decay or even catastrophe within structures that nevertheless remain socialist? Why should history continue under socialism, but only in the form of constant progress? Why, when we can see that this is not how things are, when stagnation and decadence are quite visible, must we exclaim: 'but if it is not advancing, it cannot be socialism'?

I hold that the dialectic of conservation and innovation continues well beyond the history, or rather the pre-history, that has unfolded thus far, which has been the history of the struggle of antagonistic classes. I believe this because I see a conservative socialism and stagnation, or even regression, in structures that nevertheless remain socialist. On the other hand, I also see that the idea of a 'communist alternative' — an alternative of liberty, innovation, development, and break with hierarchy and the dogmas of 'existing socialism', which yet remains for socialism and not against it — is now emerging from the history of the socialist countries.

'Providence', whether written with a capital letter or not, neither directs the history of the human species nor guarantees its progress. 'All that attempts to remain immobile in being must perish into nothingness'. This phrase of Goethe's is a warning we should all heed, all of us who see a dynamic and open socialist democracy as the way out of the present great crisis, which otherwise could lead to the 'common ruin of the contending classes', could result in a 'modern barbarism'.

The capitalist system was broken sixty years ago. Since then, nearly half of humanity has entered a new historic phase, living and acting under post-capitalism. Great progress, to be sure. But not a guarantee of constant evolution, securely sheltered from any danger of crisis or decadence.

I therefore think it is important for us to shed this last providential myth, the myth of a post-capitalist history conceived as the unilinear ascension towards the 'best of all possible worlds'.

The Party: Truth and Falsehood

Krzysztof Pomian

The Polish historian and philosopher Krzysztof Pomian was one of the main inspirers of the Warsaw student movement in 1956. He was deprived of his post as lecturer at Warsaw University in 1968. Since 1973 he has been engaged in research at the CNRS in Paris. Together with Pierre Kende he has published a collection of articles by different authors called 1956 Warsaw-Budapest. The Second October Revolution.

The Polish United Workers Party (PUWP) was born in December 1948 as the result of a fusion (or rather swallowing-up) congress of the Polish Socialist Party, which had existed since 1892, and the Polish Workers Party. The PWP had been created during the War as a reincarnation of the Polish Communist Party, which was dissolved by the Third International on Stalin's orders at a time, 1938, when its leaders were dying in NKVD prisons and its militants were inhabiting the nooks and crannies of the Gulag Archipelago. While less bloody than either its own past or the parallel evolution of its sister-parties in Eastern Europe, the post-1948 history of the PUWP has nevertheless been marked by purges and violent conflicts. The first to be eliminated, in 1949 and 1950, were supporters of the 'right-wing nationalist deviation': that is to say, all those suspected, rightly or wrongly, of sharing the views of ex-First Secretary Wladyslaw Gomulka, who had been dismissed prior to the 'unification' congress because he refused to slavishly follow the USSR and, in particular, to support forced agricultural collectivization. After returning to the controls in October 1956, Gomulka and his friends led the Party for fourteen years, struggling in their turn against the new deviation of 'revisionism'. Between 1966 and 1968, those holding 'revisionist' positions were expelled from the Party, or else resigned in order to show their disagreement with its policy: from 1967 onwards, they were amalgamated with so-called Zionists (i.e., anyone with Jews among his ancestors) in the context of a mass purge affecting not only the Party itself, but also the state administration, the universities and cultural bodies, the economic organizations, and so on. Qualitatively more dangerous than these internal crises, however, were the workers' revolts that the Party had to confront in June 1956, December 1970 and, just a short time ago, in June 1976. On the first two of these occasions, the danger that popular demonstrations might turn into a general explosion compelled the Party to change its top leadership. But although apparent calm has reigned since summer 1976, a behind-the-scenes struggle is under way whose echoes can sometimes be heard on the outside.

Let us follow this piece of history with an organizational map. At the head of the Party stands its First Secretary — since December 1970, Edward Gierek — who is flanked by a 17-member Political Bureau (including three candidates) and an 11-member Secretariat (five of whom are also part of the Political Bureau). These bodies are elected by the Central Committee (CC), which is in turn elected by a five-yearly congress; the CC is composed of 140 full members and 110 candidates.[1] To be sure, there is a secret ballot, but the area of choice is extremely limited. Once the single list is presented, delegates are able only to cross out certain names and, if they so decide, propose additional candidates. Given the scattering of votes, however, these have only a minute chance of being elected.

Since 1 June 1975, Poland has been divided into 49 voivodships (like the French *départements*), which are themselves subdivided into towns and rural communes. Each voivodship committee controls those of lower echelons, and through them the various base organizations; army organizational structures are placed under the direct tutelage of the Central Committee. Each Party member has to belong to a base organization, which elects its committee or bureau in the way that congress elects the CC. The committees of larger organizations, towns, urban districts (in the large towns), communes and voivodships are elected by indirect vote. At least five separate votes are required in order to elect the top leadership: the base organizations send delegates to the town, district or commune conference; these then elect delegates to a voivodship conference, the voivodship conference to the congress, the congress to the CC, and the CC to the Political Bureau and Secretariat. It is not hard to see that the outgoing leadership, which controls the way this process functions from the bottom to the top, can easily intervene to put its own men on lists of delegates and thus secure a thoroughly docile congress. In short, it can be virtually assured of being re-elected. Invariably, changes at this level take place not at congress, but in closed CC meetings prepared by the Political Bureau and Secretariat. Democratic centralism, as this system is officially known, therefore gives the leadership a completely free hand in relation to a Party membership whose only right is to express support for its actions. No doubt members can openly voice their disagreement with leadership policy, but they then have every chance of being expelled. If an entire local unit acts in this way, the voivodship committee does not fail to dissolve it according to the requirements of the situation.

'The political force guiding society in the construction of socialism is the Polish United Workers Party', we can read in the Constitution of the Polish People's Republic.[2] However, the English word 'guiding' does not quite adequately render the connotation of command which the Polish term carries together with its stress on guidance. In preparatory documents, the Party had been clearly designated as the leading force;[3] but because of the very high number of protest letters and petitions, the term 'lead' was replaced with another, more ambiguous formulation. Thus, despite the risks involved in their action, an important sector of public opinion came out against the privileged place attributed to the Party in the country's political life. And yet the PUWP holds an absolute majority in the Diet or parliament (255 deputies out of 460 before, and 261 since the 1976 elections); and no one can be elected unless his or her candidacy is approved by the Party leadership. Similarly, candidates in voivodship, town, district or commune elections have to be previously endorsed by the respective Party committees. In effect, with regard to both the Diet and sub-national councils, only organizations belonging to the National Unity Front are entitled to put forward candidates for election. This front regroups, under the mantle of the PUWP, the other two parties which exist in Poland (without having the slightest autonomy), as well as the trade unions and various other associations.[4] In the case of both Diet and council elections, the Front presents a single list for each constituency — with the result that the act of voting most often consists in placing the NUF slip, nothing added and nothing crossed out, into the appropriate ballot-box. It is hardly surprising, then, that the Party can count not only on its own parliamentary deputies but also on all the others: the beautiful unanimity is occasionally broken only by some Catholic kamikaze's abstention, effected in the knowledge that it will cost him his seat. The Party can also rely on local delegates and, much more important, on the government itself. The Council of Ministers comprises 38 members, of whom 34 belong to the PUWP and among whom are to be found six members and two candidates of the Political Bureau, as well as fifteen members and eight candidates of the CC.[5] In short, the government emanates from the top Party leadership, just as the praesidia of local councils emanate from corresponding Party committees.

From here, it is only a short step to say that the Party really is a leading force. But before taking that step, we should be certain that we are not thereby falling into a trap. In fact, the very insistence with which appointed leadership spokesmen try to make people believe that the Party runs society cannot but appear suspicious. Those who really hold power generally prefer to remain in the shadows. But could this be an exception, in which the existing power reveals and designates itself as such? Is Polish society perhaps transparent — like every other society built according to the same (Soviet) model? And does the Party itself constitute a homogenous whole that may legitimately be regarded as a collective subject exercising power? That is certainly what the leadership says. But do we have the right to believe it? If we do, then it logically follows that Poland is one of the most democratic countries in the world.

Now, in June 1975, the PUWP had a membership of 2,360,000 — that is to say, one in ten Poles aged 18 or over.[6] Where, indeed, can the claim that ten per cent of the adult population really participate in the exercise of power be bettered? However, just as in the case of the organizational map, our knowledge of the Party statutes arouses certain doubts about the democratic character of this institution. And they are not likely to be dispelled by reading the documents of its various bodies.

Although it has been constantly in the foreground of Polish political life for nearly thirty years, although it fills both newspaper columns and radio and TV broadcasts with its leaders' speeches and reports of its meetings, and although it celebrates with great pomp its self-glorifying festivals, the Party nevertheless acts in the manner of a semi-clandestine organization. Political Bureau meetings are reported in brief communiqués that never mention anything but the agenda — and an imcomplete one at that. For example, is it conceivable that, since such communiqués began to appear six years ago, the highest Party authority should not even once have turned its attention to problems of national defence or public security? As regards meetings of the CC Secretariat, absolutely nothing is known; only sessions of the CC itself are reported in the press at reasonable length, sometimes affording us a glimpse of existing positions and of the debate that has taken place. But even then, as in the case of Party congresses, the most important things remain carefully hidden, and the pre-censored reports offer only the image which the leadership seeks to impose. We are therefore left in the dark about how decisions are taken in the highest Party bodies: what criteria determine choices between different solutions; what views confront one another, if indeed they come into the open at all; what arguments are used in support of the various opinions; what role is played by the pressure-groups bustling about in the corridors; who votes in which way. Nor is it any clearer why these, and not other persons are elected to the various bodies; how many votes each one has received; or why a particular high official is suddenly stripped of his positions. Of course, it would be too much to say that nothing at all is known about such matters. Through comparing the decisions taken over a long period of time, one can throw light on the mechanism that produced them. Through closely observing shifts in personnel, one can draw out the criteria for promotion and demotion. Moreover, periods of open crisis do allow us to identify the different tendencies facing one another. And then, each major decision is preceded or followed by a wave of rumours and indiscreet (calculated or unintentional?) remarks, which, while difficult or even impossible to verify, offer a chance to understand something of what is going on — or at least to have the impression that one understands. In short, people form an idea of the way in which the Party, and above all leadership bodies function, not through information that is made available to them but, on the contrary, through a considerable labour of interpretation.

There are certain other questions about which no clear-cut answer can be given. Thus, the Party budget and finances are among the most closely-guarded secrets — as are the number of full-timers, their level of pay and the various privileges they enjoy. These subjects are not only taboo for people outside the Party: its own members are no better informed, not even low-grade full-timers shut up in their appointed fields and accustomed to not expressing curiosity when it might harm their career. Both on the outside and the inside, the Party is an opaque institution.

However, it is not equally so in every respect. Its social composition, for example, can be studied by examining official statistics.

Truncated though they are, and probably embellished in order to serve as an instrument of propaganda, they still permit those with the necessary knowledge to reach a number of interesting conclusions — in particular, to assess the Party's implantation in various social layers, and to clarify its recruitment policy as practised by the leadership. They also allow us — albeit with certain reservations — to gauge the number of people who really exercise power, and on that basis to answer the fundamental question: is the Party really the leading force, or does it merely conceal a group which alone has the right to tackle problems of vital importance for the country?

The PUWP is primarily composed of town-dwellers: 72.1 per cent as against 27.9 per cent country-dwellers. It is dominated by men; women, who are in any case under-represented in the Party (23.2 per cent) considering their weight in the population over the age of 18 (52.6 per cent), have a still weaker position in leadership bodies. There is not a single woman on the Political Bureau or Secretariat, and only twenty on the CC (8 per cent). No one can join the Party before the age of 18; but the dominant age-group (57 per cent) is of members between 30 and 49. One out of every ten

TABLE 1   SOCIAL COMPOSITION OF THE PUWP

	Number of members	Percentage of the total
Total	2,322,531	100
of which:		
workers	912,798	39.4
engineers, technicians, supervisors	255,693	11.0
peasants	237,876	10.2
retired and pensioned people	144,334	6.2
primary and secondary teachers	144,062	6.2
economists, planners, accountants	115,689	5.0
agronomists and other agricultural and forestry specialists	35,433	1.5
lecturers and scientific research staff	15,889	0.7
doctors	13,740	0.6

Source: *Rocznik statystyczny 1975*, Warsaw 1975, table 40, p. 21

members has a higher education diploma; one out of four has completed his or her secondary education; and one out of three has only been to primary school.[7] So far, so good. But as soon as we begin to examine more closely the representation of various socio-occupational groups in the Party, the enigmas start to mount up.

Let us leave until later everything omitted from table 1 and see what can be deduced from the existing figures. First of all, however, a preliminary remark is necessary. The recruitment of new members is not left to chance, the leadership apparently taking great care to avoid two dangers:[8] if the Party were too small, there would be unrepresented sectors over which it had no direct hold; but if it were too big, nearly everyone would be in it and membership would cease to have any significance. Furthermore, the leadership carefully controls the proportion of various socio-occupational groups in the Party, and thereby the degree of Party implantation in these groups.

Now, what do the available figures suggest? The leadership is very proud of the percentage of workers in its ranks: 39.4 per cent in 1973 (36.7 per cent without agricultural workers). Only leadership reports forget to mention what everyone can easily discover from the highly official statistical yearbook: namely, that in 1973 the workers (about 6.7 million[9]) made up 28.8 per cent of the total population over 18, and 41.1 per cent of the total active population.[10] The percentage of workers in the Party is therefore not at all out of the ordinary. It is worth noting that after the December 1970 events, the number of industrial workers in the Party fell by 40,000; that there were still fewer in 1973 than in 1970; and that the 1970 figures were surpassed only in 1975.[11] As for the peasants, the second great category of manual workers accounting for 26.3 per cent of the active population, they are distinctly under-represented in the Party and the number of members has continually declined since 1970.[12] By contrast, the socio-occupational groups sometimes designated by the term 'intellectual workers' or 'intelligentsia' are clearly over-represented in the membership. It is not enough to point out that people with secondary-school and higher diplomas, who constitute only 25 per cent of the population over 18, provide 45 per cent of PUWP forces (see below, table 3). And this is due not to chance, but to the strategy followed by the leadership in recruitment policy.

In the light of table 2, we can see the character of recruitment policy. The first task is to ensure that the Party's implantation is especially strong in those socio-occupational groups which participate, to a greater or lesser degree, in the exercise of power. The

TABLE 2 DEGREE OF PUWP IMPLANTATION IN VARIOUS SOCIO-
OCCUPATIONAL GROUPS IN 1973

Group	1 number of group members (in thousands)	2 number belonging to PUWP (in thousands)	3 col. 2 as a percentage of col. 1)
Officers	–	–	85
Primary and secondary secondary teachers	370	144	38.9
Lecturers and research staff	51	16	31.4
Engineers and technicians	900	256	28.4
Economists, planners and accountants	469	116	24.7
Doctors	70	14	20.0
Industrial workers	6,400	849	13.3
Peasants	4,291	229	5.3

Source: *Zycie Warszawy,* 24 November 1975 (for officers) and *Rocznik
Statystyczny 1975*, tables 40, p. 21; 657, p. 439; 631, p. 425; 90, p. 58;
738, p. 479; 403, p. 278 (for other categories). See also Note 9 below.

greater the power held by a particular group, the higher its
representation among Party members. In this respect, the fact that
85 per cent of officers belong to the Party is quite illuminating. The
same is probably true in the police force; and although it is
impossible to prove, we can be sure that the percentage is not much
lower in the case of headmasters and among engineers or economists
holding positions of responsibility in industry or management.
However, this is only one aspect of recruitment policy: no less
important is the need to ensure that the Party is well-implanted
among the workers. Thus, two out of fifteen industrial workers
belong to the PUWP. Such attention to the working class stems from
ideological motives: the Party's very name refers to its 'worker'
character; and all the speeches of legitimation and celebration, in
which the Party is at once subject and object, invoke as the ultimate
argument its role in representing the working class. But there are also
other motives, rather more difficult to recognize. Marxist doctrine
shows in the case of capitalism, and history in the case of the USSR

TABLE 3 PUWP IMPLANTATION ACCORDING TO LEVEL OF EDUCATION (1973)

Level of education	1 no. over 18 yrs. who reached this level (in '000s)	2 no. who reached this level as % of population over 18 yrs.	3 total PUWP members having reached this level	4 total having reached this level as % of PUWP members	5 col. 3 as % of col. 1
Higher	803	3	222	10	28
Unfinished higher	525	2	99	4	19
Secondary	3,481	15	585	25	17
Unfinished secondary	1,062	5	140	6	13
Basic occupational	3,127	14	292	13	9
Primary	9,630	42	807	35	8
Unfinished primary	4,484	19	178	7	6
Total	23,112	100	2,233	100	100

Calculated from: *Rocznik Statystyczny 1975*, tables 40, p. 21 and 56, p. 35

and Poland (especially the June 1956 and December 1970 events), that the working class represents a potential counter-power which has to be kept under close and constant watch.

We do not have sufficient data to calculate directly the level of Party implantation in social groups defined according to income or prestige. But the obstacle is not insurmountable, given the very high correlation in Poland between income and prestige, on the one hand, and level of education on the other. In fact, higher education is virtually the only door to positions of responsibility, a high income, and any real prestige confirmed by the marks of official recognition. This is not to say that a higher diploma is enough to climb the social ladder: it is only one necessary condition of success. However, once we know the degree of Party implantation in various categories defined by education, we shall have a first approximation to its level of penetration of social groups defined according to income and prestige.

The meaning of table 3 is clear. A comparison of columns 2 and 4 shows that the top four categories are over-represented in the Party, whereas the bottom three are under-represented. Even more interestingly, the table shows that the degree of Party implantation increases with the level of education. Thus, taking into account what has just been said, we can see that the Party prefers to root itself in the privileged layers of Polish society (not including the private sectors). Tables 2 and 3 together answer the question whether the Party can be treated as a homogeneous whole. A political organization is not and cannot be homogeneous if it groups together people with a different relationship to power, a different level of education and income, and consequently a different life-style. Let us admit that the Party is shot through with social contradictions — and we could mention a number of facts which prove that this is so. But we still have to ask which force allows it to maintain its cohesion and, despite all the conflicts and crises, not to blow apart.

Returning to table 2, we have merely to add up the percentages to discover a full-blown enigma. In fact, all the socio-occupational groups appearing therein only provide 80.8 per cent of the total. Who lies hidden in the other 19.2 per cent about which we are told nothing? What is the social identity of the 447,000 members who fail to answer the roll-call? At the moment, we can say only that they belong to the top four categories of table 3 — categories which account for 1,046,000 of the total PUWP membership. If we subtract all those Party members belonging to groups with an entry requirement of at least partial secondary education [i.e. table 2, column 2, all the categories between officers and doctors, Ed.], then we are left with a total of 465,000. Of these, it is very likely that 16,000 are pensioners and retired people.[13] Which leaves 449,000 — a number only insignificantly different from those missing in table 1. So who are these 447,000 PUWP members with at least incomplete secondary education?

The socio-occupational groups absent from table 1 certainly include: medical personnel (other than doctors); personnel working in the cultural apparatus, state and judicial administration, the army and the police; students and members of the liberal professions (journalists, writers, composers, painters, and so on); and also the apparatus of Party full-timers. A fine amalgam indeed; one knowingly created by the calculator of the table (that is, by the organization department of the CC) in order to conceal the dimensions of the repressive and Party apparatuses. Fortunately, we know the size of all these groups, apart from the last two — although we do not know the percentage of Party members, except in the case of lower medical personnel (11 per cent).[14] Thus, basing ourselves on experience and on the figures quoted above, we can suppose that the total Party membership includes roughly 10 per cent of students and cultural personnel, 20 per cent of those in the liberal professions, and 60 per cent of the state administration and judicial personnel.[15] If we add all these together, we arrive at about 174,000 people. In all likelihood, the 273,000 still left in the shadows work for the military, police or Party apparatus. Of course, this is only a rough estimate which, if anything, under-estimates the size of this group.[16] But it shows well enough that the group provides about 12 per cent of Party forces — second only to the place occupied by the workers.

We can now see the reality which certain people seek to hide by presenting the Party as a leading force, by glorifying its almost mystical unity, and by making it into the subject of various actions, resolutions and speeches: the Party has done this, the Party has decided that; the Party is of the view that ... This reality is the presence within the Party of two broad categories, comprising on the one hand the ordinary membership, and on the other the three-branch apparatus. To this apparatus should be added a part of the state administration and judicial personnel, as well as the propaganda specialists working in the media and the cultural field. The true meaning of the Party statutes — of the mode of election which they prescribe, and the disciplinary powers which they give to various bodies — lies precisely in the fact that they accord sovereign decision-making rights to the apparatus, while creating the illusion that it does not take the decisions. In reality, it is the apparatus, understood in the broad sense of the term, which collectively owns the instruments of violence and the means of production; it too controls the entire system of disseminating ideas. We cannot argue the point in the framework of the present article — and in any case, this has already been done on a number of occasions. What concerns us here is to bring out the fact that the apparatus needs the Party members in order to create the appearance both of mass participation in power and of a non-antagonistic relationship between itself and those whom it has expropriated to its own advantage; in other words, in order to obscure the cleavage between those who collectively monopolize power and those who undergo it. Put in this way, what we have just said may suggest that the apparatus quite lucidly engages in a cover-up operation. But that is not at all how things happen. One can, it is true, find in the apparatus cynics who think clearly in terms of power: indeed, their number tends to increase as the system grows old and its wheels become easier to see. In general, however, members of the apparatus are themselves victims of the illusion they produce. The indoctrination to which they are subjected during their long training-period predisposes them to internalize an image of the Party as representative of the toilers — and, above all, of the working class. This provides them with a ready-made explanation for any fact that might cast doubt on the image. What about the intellectuals who are moving into opposition? They either come from a bourgeois background or are giving in to considerations of vanity, or else are allowing themselves to be influenced by western propaganda. And the workers who come out in revolt? They are not workers at all, but hooligans, drunkards or common criminals. Reference is also made to the vestiges of old habits, the crafty doings of class enemies (or, more recently, of enemies of the nation), and people's inability to see the wood for the trees. There may be passing difficulties and even mistakes. But the Party is capable of surmounting and correcting them, provided that it maintains its vanguard role — that is to say, provided that it has a high percentage of workers in its ranks, welcomes the best elements from other social milieux, applies discipline without bending, strengthens its vigilance, and conducts its policy according to the principles of the scientific theory of society.[16]

Such is the essence of the apparatus view of the world: it cannot conceive of itself without the Party, for it would not then be able to live. But why do the other, ordinary members join the Party? The reasons involved, although as diverse as the individuals themselves, may nevertheless be ranged under a few broad headings. First, a considerable number join simply because they are urged to do so; either they do not have the courage to refuse, or they say to themselves that membership may prove to be useful. All too often, it is overlooked that when the percentage of Party members in an enterprise does not satisfy the apparatus, more people are simply asked to join. In order to avoid the impression that the Party is open to all and sundry, discreet approaches are made to those most likely to accept. But such an invitation from people in a position of authority always constitutes a kind of blackmail. Anyway, the apparatus thereby improves the statistics and extends its influence. For although new members may feel that they are buying peace at a low price, they eventually become aware — during a political crisis, for example — that they are obliged to follow the leadership, take part in rallies and meetings, and vote for or against the various resolutions on pain of being expelled from the Party and perhaps exposed to certain repercussions in their work situation. It then turns out that Party membership, which is not cumbersome in normal times, has nevertheless built up a certain dependence.

The second category is made up of members who come to the Party of their own volition. Here again, we have to distinguish between two cases. For workers and, more generally, for all those at the bottom of the social hierarchy, an important factor impelling them to join the Party is the desire to escape their condition of anonymity and achieve some recognition within, or even beyond the enterprise in which they work. Clearly, a Party member belongs to a special minority at his workplace — one which is sometimes directly addressed by local or national figures, and which does enjoy a right to speak of a kind. The member who knows how to use this right with prudence, choosing his words and speaking against people who can or should be criticized, will gradually become a well-known personality: he may be elected, or rather appointed by the Party, to the local leadership of the trade-union or other mass organization, or even to the Party committee. In this way, he will attain a certain weight proportional to the power which he helps to exercise. In macro-political terms, such power is minute and unable to change anything whatsoever. But it is real enough at workplace level, where a trade-union leader or Party militant can have his say when it comes to sharing out bonuses or allocating accommodation and holiday-home places; and where he is asked his opinion about giving someone a special mention at work, or about a suggested promotion or sacking. However small it may be, the power obtained by becoming a Party militant is not at all negligible and is, in itself, a reward for membership. More tangible benefits may also be gained, although their link with Party membership is less direct, if not altogether obscure. In short, then, someone joining the Party receives a certain number of possibilities together with his membership card. In the exchange-process between apparatus and new recruit, the former gives the latter the right to acquire a small share of power with its associated prestige, and obtains in return recognition of its own total power. A bond of complicity thus grows up between the one and the other — a bond which, on the one hand, allows ordinary members to satisfy their legitimate aspirations to social recognition, and on the other hand, allows the apparatus to base its own power on such channelled aspirations by using them to subject the entire society to a form of surveillance otherwise unattainable.

The situation of people who have completed their secondary, and above all higher, education is somewhat different. For the apparatus draws its future members from this group; and it serves as the recruiting-ground for those who will later be invested with a degree of power corresponding to their real or supposed ability. In this milieu, it is rarer for someone to be directly asked to join the Party. Quite simply, everybody knows that membership is essential to his career — to rising above a certain level in the hierarchy. Should a young person imagine that he can escape from a junior post while preserving an independent mind, life itself soon introduces him to the ways of the world. Once his studies are over, and once he has spent a few months observing the institution in which he works, he realizes that he will be condemned to minor roles unless he joins the Party. Certainly there exist exceptions to this rule in certain areas — for example, in the field of scientific research, where one can make a career without necessarily joining the Party. (It should be added that this applies especially to the natural sciences, and that only a statistically insignificant minority is involved). Thus, a young man starting out in life is very quickly faced with a difficult choice: either to join the Party or to be content with lower positions. The greater his ambition, the greater the chance that he will join. From a subjective point of view, this choice is experienced in a thousand different ways, ranging from easy-going cynicism to sincere and unconditional acceptance of the apparatus image of the Party, the latter case now becoming quite rare. The fact remains, however, that it is possession of a diploma and Party card that allows such a young person to envisage a bright future; and as we have seen, among the intelligentsia, the percentage of Party members is high, the competition fierce indeed. It is not enough to attend meetings and raise your hand at the right moment: you have to show proof of staunch loyalty and devotion; you have to watch what you say and choose your friends with care; you have to subordinate your personality so fully to the role that the mask becomes one with your face. In a word, you have to model yourself on members of the apparatus. That is the condition for a real career, whose high-point arrives with a position of responsibility in the apparatus. By turning people's legitimate aspirations to its own advantage, the apparatus manages not only to forge bonds of complicity with the intelligentsia similar to those mentioned above, but also to ensure its own reproduction as an apparatus.

All these points allow us to understand the membership statistics a little better — in particular, those which indicate the degree of Party implantation in various groups defined according to occupation and educational level. But they also enable us to answer our earlier question: is the Party really the leading force, or does it merely conceal the group which alone has the right to tackle problems of vital importance to the country? In fact, we have just seen that the Party is a very heterogeneous entity, traversed by inter-group boundaries and shot through with contradictions. The principal line of divide, which is systematically obscured by official discourse, runs between the apparatus and the ordinary members. The former, comprising some 270,000 individuals, holds all powers at every level; while the latter, creating through their very presence the illusion that power is exercised by ten per cent of the population, bestows upon the apparatus a certain legitimacy which, perhaps more apparent than real, is yet absolutely essential. But the role of ordinary members is not reducible to this. Some are granted a fragment of power by the apparatus; others are future members of the apparatus itself. All are indispensable helpers without which it would not be able to control society in an effective way.

The apparatus could not exist without the Party. But nor could the Party exist as it is without such an apparatus to maintain its cohesion and ensure its renewal. The apparatus maintains Party cohesion by eliminating all those who, in word or in deed, do some harm to its own authority; and it ensures renewal by operating the mechanism we have just described. Yet it can only achieve these results because it monopolizes the instruments of violence, economic constraint and censorship (in the broadest sense of the term); because it can deprive people of a job as well as expel them from the Party; because it can reduce them to silence; because it can have them put in jail; and because it can bring onto the streets policemen armed with machine-guns and even tanks. Everyone knows this, and it is just as well for the apparatus that they do. Of course, such instruments are not enough for the daily exercise of power: they are useful only in exceptionally grave circumstances. Although a social consensus is out of reach, it is necessary to obtain the complicity of at least an important section of society. And this is done by means of the Party. It is the most effective instrument of constraint, control and mystification, functioning on a daily basis where people spend a great part of their time and earn their living — at their place of work.

The Party is not a leading force. It is merely an instrument of domination in the service of the apparatus.

NOTES

1. See *VII Zjazd Polskiej Ziednoczonej Partii Robotniczej. 8-12 grudnia 1975. Podstawowe dokumenty i materialy*, Warsaw 1975.
2. *Konstytucja Polskiej Rzeczpospolitej Ludowej*, Warsaw 1976, article 3, paragraph 1.
3. See *O dynamiczny rozwoj budownictwa socjalisycznego — o wysza jakosc pracy i warunkow zycia narodu. Wytyczne Komitetu Centralnego na VII Zjazd PZPR*, Warsaw 1975, chapter III, article 4.
4. See *Ordynacja wyborcza do Sejmu PRN i rad narodowych*, Warsaw 1976, articles 1.1, 39 and 40.
5. Z. Szeliga, 'Nowy Sejm i Rzad', *Polityka*, 3 April 1976.
6. *VII Zjazd*, *op. cit.*, p.49.
7. *Rocnzik Statystyczny 1975*, Warsaw 1975, table 40, p.21 (the figures refer to the date 31 December 1973) and table 56, p.35.
8. See *VII Zjazd*, *op. cit.*, p.49.
9. The number of workers, which is nowhere to be found, is calculated from *Rocznik Statystyczny 1975*, *op. cit.*, tables: 230, p.170; 310, p.223; 364, p.262; 587, p.387; 628, p.422; 632, p.426 and, in the case of transport and commercial workers, table 89, p.57.
10. For the active population see *Rocznik Statystyczny 1975*, table 80, p.51.
11. This can be seen from a comparison of *Rocznik Statystyczny 1975*, table 40, p.21 with *VII Zjazd*, *op. cit.*, p.49.
12. This can be seen from a comparison of *Rocznik Statystyczny 1975*, table 40, p.21 with *VII Zjazd*, *op. cit.*, p.49.
13. The percentage of retired and pensioned people with incomplete secondary, completed secondary, incomplete higher and completed higher

education has been calculated from *Rocznik Statystyczny 1975*, table 56, p.35.

14. Calculated from *Rocznik Statystyczny 1975*, table 733, p.479, and *VII Zjazd, op. cit.*, p.49.
15. Calculated from *Rocznik Staystyczny 1975*, tables 733, p.479; 688, p.454; 734, p.477; 84, p.53; 39, p.20.
16. These arguments are developed to the full in the pamphlet: *Aktualne zagadnienia walki klasowej* (*Material pomocniczy na zebrania POP, zajecia szkoleniowe i lektorskie*), published by the section for ideological and educational work attached to the CC of the PUWP, Warsaw 1977. The pamphlet is intended solely for active Party members.

Further Titles from Ink Links

Sport - A Prison of Measured Time. Essays by Jean-Marie Brohm; 195 pages; Cloth: £6.50; US$ 15.00 0906133 017; Paper: £2.95, US$ 6.45 0906133
  '. . . *it represents a very scholarly, Marxist view of sport and society. I recommend it.*' **Tribune.**

Law and Marxism: A General Theory by Evgeni B Pashukanis; 195 pages with an introduction by Chris Arthur; Cloth:£5.95; US$ 13.00 0906133 041
  '*The analysis is powerful and sustained*'; '*A major contribution*'.
                                                        Tribune.

One Hundred Years of Labor in the USA by Daniel Guerin with an introduction by John Amsden. Approx. 220 pages; Cloth:£5.95; US$ 13.50 0906133 106; Paper: £2.95; US$ 4.95 0906133 Spring 1979.
  A first rate and much needed introduction to the subject by the author of **Fascism and Big Business** and **Bourgeois et Bras Nus.**

Theses, Resolutions and Manifestos of the First Four Congresses of the Third International; introduction by Bertil Hessel. Newly translated and never before complete in English, this is an indispensable reference work. Approx. 430 pages; Cloth: £11.50;US$ 25.00 0906133 122

A History of Economic Thought by Isaac I Rubin, author of **Essays on Marx's Theory of Value.** Introduction and theoretically extremely innovative and daring postscript by Catherine Colliot-Thelene. Approx. 420 pages; Cloth: £11.00; US$ 24.00 0906133 165.
  A masterful exposition which spans the period from the Mercantilists to the decline of the Classical school.

Russian Formalism and Futurism Face to Face with Marxism; introduced by Chris Pike. Approx. 200 pages. Cloth: £7.00; US$ 15.00. ISBN 0906133 149. Autumn 1979.
Literary criticism can only gain from having this debate between the Bolsheviks and Formalists available at last.

Ten Years in the Land of the Disconcerting Lie by Anton Ciliga; approx. 550 pages. Cloth: approx. £10 ISBN 0906133 22X; Paper: approx. £5.00 0906133 238; Autumn 1979.
  Ciliga's taut, often lyrical prose seems to encompass the whole awesome experience of the revolution's degeneration and a new society in construction. Infinitely more than a personal account.